Aspects of Teaching Secondary Science

The Open University *Flexible*
Postgraduate Certificate of Education

The readers and the companion volumes in the *flexible* PGCE series are:

All of these subjects are part of the Open University's initial teacher education course, the *flexible* PGCE, and constitute part of an integrated course designed to develop critical understanding. The set books, reflecting a wide range of perspectives, and discussing the complex issues that surround teaching and learning in the twenty-first century, will appeal to both beginning and experienced teachers, to mentors, tutors, advisers and other teacher educators.

If you would like to receive a *flexible* PGCE prospectus please write to the Course Reservations Centre at The Call Centre, The Open University, Milton Keynes MK7 6ZS. Other information about programmes of professional development in education is available from the same address.

Aspects of Teaching Secondary Science

Perspectives on practice

Edited by Sandra Amos and Richard Boohan

London and New York

First published 2002
by RoutledgeFalmer
11 New Fetter Lane, London EC4P 4EE

Simultaneously published in the USA and Canada by
RoutledgeFalmer
29 West 35th Street, New York, NY 10001

RoutledgeFalmer is an imprint of the Taylor & Francis Group

© 2002 Compilation, original and editorial material,
The Open University

Typeset in Bembo by Bookcraft Ltd, Stroud, Gloucestershire
Printed and bound in Great Britain by Bell & Bain Ltd, Glasgow

British Library Cataloguing in Publication Data
A catalogue record for this book is available from the British Library

Library of Congress Cataloging in Publication Data
A catalog record has been requested

ISBN 0–415–26082–5

Contents

SECTION 3   Imagined worlds

SECTION 4   Communicating science

SECTION 5   Science in a broader context

SECTION 6   Putting it all together

Figures

Tables

Abbreviations

ACCAC	Qualifications Curriculum and Assessment Authority for Wales
ACOP	Approved Code of Practice
AKSIS	ASE–King's College London Science Investigations in Schools
APU	Assessment of Performance Unit
AQA	Assessment and Qualifications Alliance
ASE	Association for Science Education
AVCE	Advanced Vocational Certificate in Education
BECTa	British Educational Communications and Technology Agency
BTEC	Business and Technology Education Council
CGLI	City of Guilds of London Institute
CHIP	Chemical (Hazard Information and Packaging) Regulations 2000
CLEAPSS	Consortium of Local Education Authorities for the Provision of Science Services
CLIS	Children's Learning in Science
COSHH	Control of Substances Hazardous to Health Regulations 1988
CREST	Creativity in Science and Technology
DARTs	Directed Activities Related to Text
DENI	Department of Education Northern Ireland
DfE	Department for Education
DfEE	Department for Education and Employment
DISS	Discussion of Issues in School Science
EU	European Union
GCE	General Certificate of Education
GCSE	General Certificate of Secondary Education
GNVQ	General National Vocational Qualification
HSE	Health and Safety Executive
HSW Act	Health and Safety at Work etc Act 1974
ICT	Information and Communications Technology
NACCCE	National Advisory Committee on Creative and Cultural Education
NCC	National Curriculum Council

NCVQ	National Council for Vocational Qualifications
NGfL	National Grid for Learning
NVQ	National Vocational Qualification
OCR	Oxford, Cambridge and RSA Examinations
OES	Occupational Exposure Standard
PPE	Personal Protective Equipment Regulations 1992
QBL	Question Based Learning
QCA	Qualifications and Curriculum Authority
QUESTCUP	Questions for Conceptual Understanding Project
RSA	Royal Society of Arts
SCAA	School Curriculum and Assessment Authority
SSERC	Scottish Schools (Science) Equipment Research Centre
STEM	Students' and Teachers' Educational Materials (A Science Museum project)
STS	Science, Technology and Society
TIMSS	Third International Mathematics and Science Study
VET	Vocational Education and Training
VTC	Virtual Teacher Centre

Sources

Where a chapter in this book is based on or is a reprint or revision of material previously published elsewhere, details are given below, with grateful acknowledgements to the original publishers. In some cases chapter titles are different to the original title of publication; in such cases the original title is given below.

Chapter 2 This is an edited version of an article originally published in *School Science Review* 79(289), Association for Science Education, Hatfield (1998).

Chapter 3 This is an edited version of an article originally published in *School Science Review* 72(261), Association for Science Education, Hatfield (1991).

Chapter 4 This is based on two chapters originally published as 'Classrooms, explaining and science' and 'Opening up differences' in Ogborn, J., Kress, G., Martins, I. and McGillicuddy, K. (1996) *Explaining Science in the Classroom,* Open University Press, Buckingham.

Chapter 5 This is based on two articles originally published as 'Questioning and conceptual understanding: the quality of pupils' questions in science' in *School Science Review* 76(277), Association for Science Education, Hatfield (1995) and 'Questions of understanding: categorising pupils' questions in science' in *School Science Review* 79(286), Association for Science Education, Hatfield (1997).

Chapter 6 This is an edited version of a chapter originally published as 'Rhetoric and reality: what practical work in science is really for' in Wellington, J. (ed.) (1998) *Practical Work in School Science,* Routledge, London, with additional material.

Chapter 7 This is an edited version of an article originally published in *School Science Review* 80(292), Association for Science Education, Hatfield (1999), with additional material.

Chapter 8 This is based on two articles originally published as 'The computer as an aid for exploring graphs' in *School Science Review* 76(276), Association for Science Education, Hatfield (1995) and 'New data-logging tools – new investigations' in *School Science Review* 79(287), Association for Science Education, Hatfield (1997).

Chapter 10 This is based on a booklet originally published as 'Critical incidents in science', PGCE course materials, The Open University, Milton Keynes (1995) and an article originally published as 'Critical incidents in the science classroom and the nature of science' in *School Science Review* 76(276), Association for Science Education, Hatfield (1995).

Chapter 11 This is an edited version of an article originally published in *School Science Review* 75(271), Association for Science Education, Hatfield (1993).

Chapter 13 This is based on two chapters originally published as 'Classrooms, explaining and science' and 'The construction of entities' in Ogborn, J., Kress, G., Martins, I. and McGillicuddy, K. (1996) *Explaining Science in the Classroom,* Open University Press, Buckingham.

Chapter 14 This is an edited version of an article originally published in *School Science Review* 80(293), Association for Science Education, Hatfield (1999).

Chapter 16 This is an edited version of an article originally published in *School Science Review* 81(297), Association for Science Education, Hatfield (2000).

Chapter 17 This is based on two articles originally published as 'Alternatives to practical work' in *School Science Review* 75(271), Association for Science Education, Hatfield (1993) and 'Practical alternatives' in *School Science Review* 78(285), Association for Science Education, Hatfield (1997).

Chapter 19 This is an edited version of an article originally published in *School Science Review* 74(269), Association for Science Education, Hatfield (1993).

Chapter 21 This is an edited version of a chapter originally published in Ratcliffe, M. (ed.) (1998) *ASE Guide to Secondary Science Education*, Stanley Thornes Publishers Ltd, Cheltenham.

Chapter 22 This is an edited version of an article originally published as 'Discussing socio-scientific issues in science lessons - pupils' actions and the teacher's role' in *School Science Review* 79(288), Association for Science Education, Hatfield (1998).

Chapter 23 This is an edited version of an article originally published in *School Science Review* 71(257), Association for Science Education, Hatfield (1990).

Chapter 24 This is based on three chapters originally published as 'Life and living processes', 'Materials and their properties' and 'Physical processes' in Reiss, M. (1993) *Science Education for a Pluralist Society,* Open University Press, Buckingham.

Chapter 25 This is based on an article originally published as 'Making differentiation manage-able' in *School Science Review* 77(279), Association for Science Education, Hatfield (1995) and a chapter originally published as 'Differentiation' in Ratcliffe, M. (ed.) (1998) *ASE Guide to Secondary Science Education,* Stanley Thornes Publishers Ltd, Cheltenham.

Chapter 26 This is based on two articles originally published as 'Formative assessment strate-gies in secondary science' in *School Science Review* 80(293), Association for Science Education, Hatfield (1999) and as 'Formative assessment' in *School Science Review* 77(281), Association for Science Education, Hatfield (1996).

Chapter 27 This is an edited version of a chapter originally published in Ratcliffe, M. (ed.) (1998) *ASE Guide to Secondary Science Education,* Stanley Thornes Publishers Ltd, Cheltenham.

The Editors and Publishers would like to thank the following copyright holders for permission to reproduce these figures.

Figure 9.2 From *Nuffield Co-ordinated Sciences Teachers' Guide* (1992), Harlow: Longman. Copyright © The Nuffield–Chelsea Curriculum Trust.

Figure 12.3(c) From Atkins, P.W. (1987) *Molecules*, New York: Scientific American Library. Illustration by Chip Clark.

Figure 12.3(d) From Holman, J. (1991) *The Natural World*, Walton-on-Thames: Thomas Nelson and Sons Ltd.

Figure 24.1 Taken from Reiss, M.J. (1993) *Science Education for a Pluralist Society*, Buckingham: Open University Press. Originally published in Manjo, G. (1975) *The Healing Hand: Man and Wound in the Ancient World*, Cambridge, Mass.: Harvard University Press.

Figure 24.2 Taken from Reiss, M.J. (1993) *Science Education for a Pluralist Society*, Buckingham: Open University Press. Originally published in Perry, G.A. and Hirons, M.J.D. (1970) *Progressive Biology Book 3*, London: Blandford Press.

Figure 24.3 Taken from Reiss, M.J. (1993) *Science Education for a Pluralist Society*, Buckingham: Open University Press. Reproduced by permission of Peter Schmidt.

Figure 24.4 Taken from Reiss, M.J. (1993) *Science Education for a Pluralist Society*, Buckingham: Open University Press. Reproduced by permission of Marie Curie Cancer Care.

Foreword

The nature and form of initial teacher education and training are issues that lie at the heart of the teaching profession. They are inextricably linked to the standing and identity that society attributes to teachers and are seen as being one of the main planks in the push to raise standards in schools and to improve the quality of education in them. The initial teacher education curriculum therefore requires careful definition. How can it best contribute to the development of the range of skills, knowledge and understanding that makes up the complex, multi-faceted, multi-skilled and people-centred process of teaching?

There are, of course, external, government-defined requirements for initial teacher training courses. These specify, amongst other things, the length of time a student spends in school, the subject knowledge requirements beginning teachers are expected to demonstrate or the ICT skills that are needed. These requirements, however, do not in themselves constitute the initial training curriculum. They are only one of the many, if sometimes competing, components that make up the broad spectrum of a teacher's professional knowledge that underpin initial teacher education courses.

Certainly today's teachers need to be highly skilled in literacy, numeracy and ICT, in classroom methods and management. In addition, however, they also need to be well grounded in the critical dialogue of teaching. They need to be encouraged to be creative and innovative and to appreciate that teaching is a complex and problematic activity. This is a view of teaching that is shared with partner schools within the Open University Training Schools Network. As such it has informed the planning and development of the Open University's initial teacher training programme and the *flexible* PGCE.

All of the *flexible* PGCE courses have a series of connected and complementary readers. The *Teaching in Secondary Schools* series pulls together a range of new thinking about teaching and learning in particular subjects. Key debates and differing perspectives are presented, and evidence from research and practice is explored, inviting the reader to question the accepted orthodoxy, suggesting ways of enriching the present curriculum and offering new thoughts on classroom learning. These readers are accompanied by the series *Perspectives on practice*. Here, the focus is on the application of these developments to educational/subject policy and the classroom, and on the illustration of teaching skills, knowledge and understanding in a variety of school contexts. Both series include newly commissioned work.

This series from RoutledgeFalmer, in supporting the Open University's *flexible* PGCE, also includes two key texts that explore the wider educational background. These companion publications, *Teaching and Learning and the Curriculum in Secondary Schools: A reader* and *Aspects of Teaching and Learning in Secondary Schools: Perspectives on practice,* explore a contemporary view of developments in secondary education with the aim of providing analysis and insights for those participating in initial teacher training education courses.

Hilary Bourdillon – Director ITT Strategy
Steven Hutchinson – Director ITT Secondary
The Open University
September 2001

Introduction

It may be tempting to think that *science* teaching is a special kind of activity. It is, after all, done in *laboratories* whereas most subjects are taught in *classrooms*. While it is true that practical work is an important and characteristic element of learning science, much of what pupils do in science lessons is no different from what they do in other lessons. They discuss things, they are asked questions, they listen to explanations and try to make sense of them, they ask questions, they read and write, they work in groups – the list goes on. We prefer, therefore, to think about science as being taught in *science classrooms*; for certain kinds of activities these rooms may also serve as laboratories. In this book, we explore the wide range of different kinds of activities that take place in science classrooms.

The chapters in this book have been written by people who are making contributions to science education in a variety of ways. These include involvement in initial teacher education, undertaking research as part of funded projects, researching into their own classroom practice, and supporting the work of science departments and the continuing professional development of science teachers. A significant proportion of the chapters in this book is based on work that originally appeared in *School Science Review*, the main journal of the Association of Science Education. Many different kinds of people are contributing to the shaping of science education - teachers in primary and secondary schools, university lecturers, local authority advisers and many others. This book represents some of the conversations taking place within this professional community.

The structure of the book reflects our view that a useful way of thinking about learning science is through three inter-related aspects.

- Science is a practical subject. It is concerned with understanding phenomena in the physical world. Through practical work, pupils gain experience of these phenomena, are able to test out ideas and can attempt to explain what is happening.
- Science is a theoretical subject. Scientific explanations go beyond what is directly observable, and invoke not just entities in the physical world, but conceptual entities in what we have called 'imagined worlds'. Pupils need to understand what these scientific concepts are like, how they behave and how they can be used to make sense of the physical world.
- Science is a human construction. It is done by people working, not as individuals, but as part of communities. Scientific knowledge is created by the

sharing of ideas, and by developing, refining or rejecting them. Pupils need to be able to make sense of the various ways in which scientific knowledge is communicated and they need to be able to communicate to others.

In Section 1 of this book, we begin with what is perhaps the most obvious feature of the science classroom. It is a place where there is a lot of talk. Practical work is also a very obvious characteristic of science lessons and this is discussed in Section 2. If scientific understanding could be constructed by an individual solely on the basis of their experience of the physical world, then that would be the end of the story! But understanding science is about understanding the way that scientists see the world. Section 3 is concerned with the 'imagined worlds' of theoretical entities created by scientists. Talking is not the only way in which science is communicated, and in Section 4 we turn our attention to reading, writing and other forms of communication. In Section 5, the emphasis moves from the learning *of* science to learning *about* science. It is concerned with the place of science in a broader context, and looks at the nature of science, its moral and ethical dimensions, and its place in a cultural context. Finally, Section 6 considers the complexity of teaching as a whole and how science teachers can create an environment in which each individual pupil is able to learn and is motivated to learn.

This book complements the companion volume *Teaching Science in Secondary Schools: A reader*, which the focuses on key debates and issues in science education. In this book, the focus is more directly on teaching science in the classroom. As such, we hope that it will be useful as a source of ideas that can inform day-to-day practice. But it is not a book of 'recipes' that prescribes procedures to be followed in the classroom. What it does aim to do is to provide some ways of thinking that can inform the understanding of classroom practice and to offer sources of possibilities for future action.

We should like to thank the authors for their permission to use their work, and for all their efforts in adapting and abridging existing text and in writing new material.

Sandra Amos
Richard Boohan
The Open University
February 2001

1 Talking about science

Introduction

You turn the handle and open the door to a classroom where a science lesson is under way. What do you expect to see? Pupils engaged in practical work, perhaps? The teacher demonstrating a procedure? Pupils writing up notes while the teacher checks they are on task? What you are almost certain to see when you enter the room is people talking. It is almost too obvious to be seen. Talk is such an integral part of our lives that its value and significance are easily overlooked. Not so long ago, a 'good' teacher may have been regarded as one that kept their classes quiet. Pupils were to be seen and not heard. Yet talking is central to the teaching and learning of science. It is through talk that we communicate and explore our ideas about the world and how it works. Talk can shape those ideas, and create new ways of thinking.

Within the classroom, talk is highly organized even if it does sound like a noise. Different sorts of talk, involving different people, are used for different purposes. Teachers explain, give instructions, use talk to manage the lesson and the pupils, promote discussion and learning. Pupils talk to each other as well as the teacher. Talking, particularly discussing, debating and sharing ideas, helps to make science more human and interesting to pupils, and widens its appeal to those who might otherwise see science as being too impersonal. Teachers are under pressure to 'get through the curriculum' and talking takes time. But for effective learning to take place, pupils need to be given a chance to really talk about their ideas.

Questions are an important part of classroom talk, and pupils' questions play an extremely important role in developing their understanding of science. But there is tension between the management of thirty or so learners in the classroom, and encouraging them to ask lots of questions. Let's be honest. It is easier for teachers if pupils are seen as mere receivers of teaching, rather than as active questioners and explorers of scientific ideas. If so, pupils' questions may not be capitalized upon or may even be discouraged. Science education is impoverished if this happens.

We construct, as well as communicate ideas using language. Words carry meanings that can present problems to those learning science. The reason that scientific language can be difficult is not necessarily because the terms are strange, long or difficult. Some terms are complicated words for simple things, for example haemorrhage or Eustachian tube. Some terms, such as ion or gene, are simple, but behind them lie difficult concepts. And many simple, everyday words have a particular meaning in science that is different from the everyday meaning, for example, food, energy or force. The challenge for science teachers is not only to help pupils develop their scientific vocabulary, but also to ensure they gain the scientific understanding necessary to use the language appropriately.

- Questions, and the search for answers, are fundamental to science itself. Sandra Amos begins this section by exploring the questions used in the science classroom, and how they can be used to support teaching and learning science. She provides a framework for analysing questions and drawing together the different ways of categorizing questions found in the literature.

- Teachers can, and do, carry out research into what happens in their classrooms. Derek Carr provides an account of a small-scale research project carried out by the members of the science department he leads. He examines the usefulness of questioning in science teaching, the framework they used to analyse their practice, and ends with a critical discussion about the practice they uncovered. Their findings are not unusual or unique to them, and as such, the key points are well documented in the research.

- In her chapter, Joan Solomon considers how discussion in science classrooms can serve a variety of purposes, and in particular, those relating to activities specific to science classrooms - carrying out practical work, interpreting results and understanding social issues. What is important for effective learning from discussion is that activities are structured in ways that will require real participation.

- Explaining things to pupils is an essential part of science teaching, but it involves much more than simply talking at them. Jon Ogborn, Gunther Kress, Isabel Martins and Kieran McGillicuddy consider what is involved in making a scientific explanation, and what drives explanations in the classroom. Creating interest, expectations and surprises is what makes pupils want explanations; it is this that they refer to when they argue the importance of 'opening up differences'.

- The principal focus of the first two chapters is *teachers'* use of questions. Steve Alsop, Gillian Gould and Mike Watts examine the importance of encouraging *pupils'* questions, drawing on the research carried out as part of the Questions for Conceptual Understanding Project (QUESTCUP). Their chapter provides an analysis of the questions pupils ask, and they discuss the implications of these findings for science teachers and ways of fostering a climate of questioning.

1 Teachers' questions in the science classroom

Sandra Amos

Introduction

There can be no doubt that questions play an important part in the teaching and learning of science. Indeed, questions and the search for answers are central to science itself. It is, therefore, important that science teachers ask questions and encourage pupils themselves to ask questions. The focus of this chapter is the questions used by science teachers, why they are used, and how they can be used effectively. It is not intended to be read and then simply put it into practice; rather, it aims to provide a framework for looking at and thinking about teachers' questions in the science classroom. Teaching, and learning to teach, are complex activities, so how do teachers learn to use questions effectively? We use questions in our everyday lives, and children quickly learn how to use questions to achieve their desired goals. We develop some questioning skills as a result of our experiences, but for teachers, will this be sufficient to ensure effective practice in the classroom? Some of the ideas in this chapter may be used to inform planning, or help in the analysis of questioning practice. When teachers are learning to use questions effectively, the frameworks provided can be used to analyse what they do and plan action for improvement. Using such frameworks may be useful not only in the early stages of learning, but also in continuing to develop greater professional expertise.

Up to one-fifth of what a teacher says in a classroom is likely to be in the form of questions; it is one of the skills that teachers use most in the classroom. It is, therefore, not surprising that a great deal of research has been carried out into teachers' use of questions, and many ways of analysing teachers' questions are to be found in the literature. But, it would be naive to think that the analysis of teacher questioning is straightforward. Such a view would fail to recognize the complexity of the social situations in which questioning takes place, and the less obvious aspects of teacher-pupil interactions, such as the accompanying facial expressions and body language. Nevertheless, there are some useful ways of looking at questions and questioning that provide valuable insights into their use in teaching and learning.

Categorizing questions

The usual approach to analysing questions is to categorize them and examine how teachers use them in practice. The different ways of categorizing questions described in this chapter are simply put forward as ways of looking at and thinking about questions. There are no clear-cut divisions between the categories and there are inevitable overlaps. Each way of categorizing has its own particular strengths and weaknesses, and its usefulness will depend on the focus of the enquiry being undertaken.

The categories of questions that follow have been divided into two groups: those that focus on the *characteristics* of a question, such as how it is expressed and what it demands of the respondent, and those that focus on the *purpose* of the questions in relation to teaching and learning.

Question characteristics

An important effect of teacher questions is that they, intentionally or not, disrupt the flow of what is going on in the learner's mind. This is likely to be a calculated action on the teacher's part and done to move the learner's attention and thinking to their agenda. The sort of question asked, and how it is asked, will have a considerable influence on the learner's cognitive and emotional state. Effective questioning does not threaten the learner's self-esteem or close down their thinking. Used well, questions promote learning, enable a dialogue between the teacher and learner, and encourage the learner to think. The characteristics of the questions used will have an effect on the extent to which this happens.

Open and closed questions

This is perhaps one of the most well-known and widely used ways of classifying questions. Closed questions have a single, correct answer, and are mainly used to test for the recall of facts (e.g. what is the green pigment in plants?). In contrast, open questions have no right answer, or several possible answers (e.g. how are cacti adapted to their environment?). The degree of openness also depends on the teacher. If a teacher asks an open question but plays the 'guess the answer in my head' game, ignoring all other responses, the question is effectively closed. Asking truly open questions involves being open to all possible answers.

More important than the definitions of open and closed questions is the role each has in learning. Teachers use a mixture of open and closed questions although, as Ofsted (1998) and many other studies report, far more closed than open questions are asked. Is this a problem? To answer that question, we have to examine what open and closed questions achieve. Consider the questions below.

Q1   In which circuit are the bulbs brightest?
Q2   In which circuit would the bulbs be the brightest?
Q3   What are the differences between the two circuits?

It is important to note that the cognitive demand of a question is not related to whether it is open or closed. The first closed question draws the pupil's attention to an observable phenomenon and is not cognitively challenging. The second question is also closed, but is considerably more difficult as the learner has to apply their knowledge in order to make a prediction. The third, open question gives the teacher access to the pupil's ideas and can be used to help the learner develop their own understanding. Several responses are likely to come to the learner's mind when asked an open question. Closed questions, on the other hand, bring one answer to mind, or failing that, the desperate search for it. Closed questions are about the teacher's agenda, and reliance on them results in reduced opportunities for finding out about the learner's ideas. The 'guessing game' approach has the added disadvantage of encouraging thoughtless responses from the pupils as they desperately attempt to hit the target. Closed questions with a 'yes' or 'no' answer are even less useful because pupils are prone to guessing without thinking. The report from the National Advisory Committee on Creative and Cultural Education (NACCCE) highlights the role of open questions in providing greater opportunity for creative activity on the part of the learner (NACCCE 1999). Closed questions rely on linear processes and logical reasoning, providing no opportunity to stray from the teacher's path.

Closed questions are also potentially more threatening to pupils' self-esteem. Unless reasonably sure, a pupil may not venture an answer in case they suffer the humiliation of getting it wrong. Open questions provide greater opportunity for pupils to contribute an appropriate answer and, therefore, are not as threatening. How a teacher responds to pupils' answers also has a profound impact on their willingness to contribute, and this is explored in more detail later.

So, the conclusion is that closed questions are bad and open questions are good? Not at all. It would be nonsense to suggest that closed questions do not have a place in the classroom. Closed questions can be used to reassure, find out what pupils know and can recall, lead them from one idea to another, and help them to make connections between phenomena, ideas and events. The criticism levelled by Ofsted and others is that there is too great an emphasis on the use of closed questions.

> The quality of teachers' questioning is very variable to the degree to which it extends pupils' thinking, draws out their ideas, and encourages them to volunteer points and explore further, thus providing evidence for achievement. Too often teachers engage in closed questioning, limiting pupils' responses or even neglecting to take up issues that pupils raise, and ultimately failing to register how far they have understood the objectives of the work.
>
> (Ofsted 1998: 92–3)

Person and subject-centred questions

As well as being open or closed, questions vary in the extent to which they are *person-centred* or *subject-centred* (Harlen 1996). Person-centred questions ask something about the individual and are identifiable by use of the words 'you' or 'your'. Examples are: What do *you* think goes into a plant?, What do *you* notice about the rock?, What are *your* opinions about genetic engineering? In subject-centred questions, the person is omitted. For example, What goes into a plant?, What is known about energy? Like open questions, person-centred questions are less threatening and more learner-friendly because they ask for their ideas, not for the 'right' answer.

Lower and higher order questions

Another characteristic of questions is their level of cognitive demand, and this is the basis of Bloom's (1956) taxonomy of educational objectives and questions. According to Bloom, questions can be put into two broad groups – *lower order* questions and *higher order* questions. Lower order questions are concerned with testing the recall of knowledge, while higher order questions require analytical thinking. Each of these broad categories is further divided into three, resulting in a hierarchy of questions. Details of each of the six categories and the uses to which they can be put are found in Table 1.1.

Bloom's taxonomy can be criticized for being too simplistic and mechanical, thereby under-representing the richness and complexity of the interactions between teachers and pupils. What it does do, however, is to highlight that there are different levels of thinking required of learners, and it can be used to examine which types of question teachers use in practice. Harlen (1999) reviews a range of research that shows that lower order, recall questions dominate classrooms. This is a matter for concern, as emphasis on lower order questions, focusing on the recall of facts, reduces opportunities for the more creative and enriching aspects of thinking and results in learning without understanding.

Purposes of questions

The purpose behind using questions is perhaps a more useful way of thinking about them when planning. There are, inevitably, links between the characteristics of a question and its purpose. For example, closed, lower order questions are mainly used to test for the recall of knowledge. The purpose behind using particular questions or sequences of questions is usually known only to the teacher. This can lead to resentment on the learners' part as they try to answer questions to which they know the teacher already has the answer. By letting learners know the purpose of questioning, such resentment may be avoided.

For an experienced teacher, asking questions is almost a reflex action. Their expertise is an embedded skill that is used routinely. However, reflexes are used without thinking, and it is important to stop and think about what is to be achieved, and how it is to be achieved. For inexperienced teachers, this is an important aspect of their planning which is explored later.

Teachers use questions for a variety of purposes. Cohen *et al.* (1996) present the findings of some research carried out as part of the Leverhulme Primary Project and use this to categorize teachers' reasons for questioning as *cognitive/intellectual*, *emotional/social* and *managerial*.

The purpose of managerial questions is to manage and control pupils. This can be achieved in variety of ways. It is unacceptable to use questions to humiliate a pupil in order to change their behaviour, but directing a question to an individual who is not paying attention can be an effective way of re-focusing them on the task in hand.

Questions that are used for emotional and social reasons are part of the pastoral side of teaching. The use of such questions may be aimed at developing the social cohesion of the group, showing concern for pupils, or reassuring them and increasing their confidence.

Table 1.1 Bloom's taxonomy of questions

	Purpose	Example
Lower order questions		
Recall	To test what has been remembered.	Who is ...? What is ...? Where are ...? When did ...?
Comprehension	To check the understanding of what is recalled.	Can you describe ...? What are the differences between ...? Explain why ...? Explain what is meant by ...?
Application	To see if a pupil can directly apply the rules or knowledge recalled.	How would you classify these invertebrates? In which circuit would the bulb light? How does this apply to plants?
Higher order questions		
Analysis	To see if a pupil can identify causes or reasons, make inferences, deduce and conclude. Requires pupils to think critically.	Why ...? What would happen if ...? What would be the effect on ...? What can you infer from ...? What do your results show?
Synthesis	To encourage the creation of new ideas from existing information. (There is a creative element to this process).	How would your life change if you got your food in the same ways as plants get theirs? What do you think would happen if there was suddenly no friction? What features might a new marsh animal have?
Evaluation	To encourage judgement, reasoned argument and opinions.	In what ways are ...? Which is the best? How effective is ...? Do you believe that ... is good or bad? What do you think of ...? What are the advantages and disadvantages of ...? Which of these is the most important?

Source: Bloom 1956

It is the cognitive and intellectual questions that are central to the learning of science. These questions themselves have different purposes, and a discussion of some specific purposes follows.

Promotion of thought and understanding

In a survey of teachers' reasons for asking questions, carried out as part of the Leverhulme project, one third said that they use them to encourage pupil thought and understanding. Using questions to guide learning is a common teaching technique, and one that Bruner (1985) describes as 'scaffolding'. Questions are used to structure the learner's thinking and take them from their existing ideas to a more complex state of understanding. A word of warning is needed, however. Learning is not that simple, and the extent to which the learner has actually developed their ideas as a result of this interaction with the teacher may be limited, even though they may have answered the questions correctly.

Encouraging enquiry and investigation

As we have already seen, questions have a special place in the teaching of science. A particularly important role for science teachers is to encourage learners to ask their own questions and help them test their ideas. Elstgeest (1985) suggests the following sequence of questions to encourage investigation and develop process skills:

- *Attention-focusing questions* – these draw pupils' attention to the salient features of a situation. For example: What do you notice about plants growing near the path?
- *Comparison questions* – these draw pupils' attention to similarities, differences and patterns. For example: What have these organisms got in common? How are they different?
- *Measurement questions* take qualitative observation into the quantitative. For example: How much salt will dissolve? What mass will extend the spring by 10 centimetres?
- *Action questions* encourage the next steps in testing ideas. For example: What happens if you add a resistor to the circuit?
- *Problem-posing questions* provide pupils with a challenge to work on. For example: How could you make a coloured shadow?

Questions also play an important role in supporting pupils as they hypothesize, predict, plan, interpret and draw conclusions. The most useful questions for this purpose are open, person-centred questions that require pupils to think, and provide a basis for discussion with the teacher.

Assessment

The last purpose of questions to be examined in this section is that of assessment. Assessment is not simply concerned with testing the recall of knowledge, or what pupils can remember from the previous lesson. More importantly, questions can be used to find out what ideas and understanding pupils have in relation to the science topic being taught. Indeed, Garnett and Tobin (1988) argue that effective teaching includes using questions to check on the development of pupils' understanding. In the Leverhulme survey, almost one-third of the teachers said that they use questions to check understanding, knowledge and skills. Assessment that does more than test factual recall is more demanding and requires more thought on the part of the teacher. The informed use of open, higher order questions is essential in the process of eliciting pupils' ideas. Consider these two questions:

A   What gas is needed for photosynthesis?
B   Where do you think a plant gets its food?

The first, closed, question does not probe the pupil's understanding; the second, open question invites the pupil to reveal his ideas about food and plant nutrition. This provides the teacher with valuable information about the pupil that can be used to inform future planning. For example, if he responds that plants get their food from the soil, subsequent teaching will have to be planned to help him change his ideas.

Developing the skill of questioning

Through exploration of the different categories of questions, several issues have arisen about the effective use of questioning to achieve various purposes. As well as the questions themselves, there are other factors that need to be considered when using questioning with a whole class. One of these is how questions are directed and distributed to those in the class. Are questions fairly distributed? Who is answering? To what extent are pupils able to 'hide' from answering, either by sitting in a part of the room that the teacher unconsciously ignores, or by choosing not to put up their hand? If a teacher takes answers only from those with their hand up, it gives pupils a choice as to whether they actively participate or passively wait for the next part of the lesson. Some pupils are more likely to be passive than others in the competitive environment of the whole-class question-and-answer session. For example, this is a particular issue with girls in mixed-sex groups. In order to ensure equitable distribution of questions, the teacher has to be aware of who is chosen to answer and who is not participating. They are then in a position to target appropriate questions to different groups of pupils and ensure greater involvement.

Part of encouraging this greater involvement by learners is ensuring that they are not deterred from answering questions. The teacher has to create an environment in which the pupils feel encouraged and supported, and one of the most important factors in this is how the teacher responds to their answers. Brown and Wragg (1993) offer a range of possible responses to pupils:

- ignore
- acknowledge and build on the pupils' response
- repeat it verbatim to reinforce and ensure all heard
- paraphrase to check you have understood correctly
- praise

- correct
- prompt for further information by asking more questions
- probe to develop relevant points.

Some responses will have negative effects on pupils. Not surprisingly, ignoring an answer, being critical, sarcastic or dismissive will deter pupils from answering. When a pupil puts up their hand to answer, they are taking a risk. The risk is low if they are very confident of their answer. The risk is much higher if they are offering tentative ideas and opinions. However, being aware of the importance of the teacher's response to pupils, and having a desire not to deter pupils from participating, can result in inexperienced teachers finding it difficult to deal with incorrect answers. It is important that the teacher does not ignore or play down incorrect answers as this has the effect of sanctioning them, and sending confusing messages to the pupils.

The following examples of teacher response make it clear that the answer is not correct, but are less likely to deter pupils than a simple dismissal or correction of their answer. 'Are you sure you mean chlorophyll?' is a suitable response if you are reasonably sure they are simply confused. 'Why do you think it's chlorophyll?' enables the teacher and the pupil to explore the ideas behind the answer more thoroughly. 'No, I think you are getting confused' is a kinder response than a simple 'No, that's not right' followed by swiftly moving to somebody else. Responses such as 'Close, but not quite right', along with a little more time given for thinking, can be used to encourage and support the learner. Coming back to a pupil with another question (that you are confident they will be able to answer) shortly after they have given a wrong answer can help to restore their confidence and check that they have understood.

Thinking time is another important aspect of questioning. The time between the teacher asking a question and getting an answer from a volunteer is often as little as 2 seconds. All this does is to provide the teacher with an indication of who in the class has the answer readily to mind. From the pupil's perspective, if the answer doesn't immediately spring to mind, there is little reason to continue thinking. Someone else will be chosen to answer from the several hands that have shot up, and the teacher will choose one of them, as usual. Strategies that allow pupils more time to think and increase the number of those participating are more useful for formative and diagnostic assessment purposes than the traditional, whole-class, quick-fire question-and-answer teacher activity. An example of such a strategy is to give questions to small groups of pupils, allowing them time to discuss their responses. This gives the teacher an opportunity to listen to them as they talk. Taking answers from a representative of each group is also less threatening than directing specific questions to individuals.

Planning for questioning

It is clear from the preceding discussion that questioning is a complex and important activity. Yet, it is often not thought through carefully before the lesson or considered as something to be improved and developed. Planning is vital, especially for the novice who will not have internalized this skill. Planning involves identifying what the learners need to pay attention to, and then selecting key questions, thinking about the purpose and sequencing of the questions, and strategies for distribution.

Questions can also be used to differentiate the work. Planning questions that target individuals according to their attainment ensures all are able to contribute and participate. Using the number of hands that go up as an indicator of whether questions are at the right level for the group, leads to teaching that addresses the needs of only some of the pupils. If all the questions are too difficult for the lower-attaining pupils in the group, they are likely to become de-motivated. So, too, will the higher-attaining pupils who find all the questions too simple.

A key factor in the effectiveness of teachers' questioning is their own knowledge and understanding of science. Carlsen (1987) found that teachers with good subject knowledge ask fewer questions and encourage more questions from their pupils. Those with insecure subject knowledge use more lower order, closed questions, and avoid whole-class discussion and questioning. This is understandable, as this strategy protects the teacher's own self-esteem by reducing the risk of not being able to deal with pupils' questions and ideas.

Summary

Questioning is not as simple as it first seems. When used expertly, it can help to develop positive relationships within the class, can be supportive of learners' attempts to make sense of what they are seeing and doing, and can provide valuable insights into their thinking. When used insensitively and without thought, it can de-motivate pupils, lower their self-esteem and provide very little information about their understanding. Questioning is a powerful way of communicating with learners and plays a key role in the development of questioning minds in pupils, which is something teachers of science must surely value highly. The questions you ask say a great deal about you as a science teacher. Your view of science and teaching, and the extent of your concern for and interest in learners, will have a profound influence on the questions you ask and how you ask them. It is personally challenging to critically examine and develop practice, but by doing so, pupil achievement and their attitudes to science can be greatly improved.

References

Bloom, B.S. (ed.) (1956) *Taxonomy of Educational Objectives: Handbook 1 (Cognitive Domain),* London: Longman.

Brown, G. and Wragg, E. C. (1993) *Questioning,* London: Routledge.

Bruner, J. (1985) 'Vygotsky: a historical and conceptual perspective', in J. Wertsch (ed.) *Culture, Communication and Cognition: Vygotskian Perspectives,* Cambridge: Cambridge University Press.

Carlsen, W. S. (1987) 'Questioning in classrooms – a sociological perspective', *Review of Educational Research* 61: 157–78.

Cohen, L., Manion, L. and Morrison, K. (1996) *A Guide to Teaching Practice,* fourth edition, London: Routledge.

Elstgeest, J. (1985) 'The right question at the right time', in W. Harlen (ed.) *Primary Science: Taking the Plunge,* London: Heinemann Educational Books.

Garnett, P. J. and Tobin, K. (1988) 'Teaching for understanding: exemplary practice in high school chemistry', *Journal of Research in Science Teaching* 26(1): 1–14.

Harlen, W. (1996) *The Teaching of Science in Primary Schools*, second edition, London: David Fulton.
Harlen, W. (1999) *Effective Teaching of Science*, Edinburgh: The Scottish Council for Research in Education.
NACCCE (1999) *All our Futures: Creativity, Culture & Education*, London: DfEE.
Ofsted (1998) *Secondary Education 1993–7: A Review of Secondary Schools in England*, London: HMSO.

2 The art of asking questions in the teaching of science

Derek Carr

Knowledge isn't just there in a book, waiting for someone to come along and 'learn it'.

Knowledge is produced in response to questions ... once you have learned to ask questions ... you have learned how to learn. ... The art and science of asking questions are not taught in schools.

(Postman and Weitgartner, *Teaching as a subversive activity,* quoted in Aicken 1984: 112)

Recent comment has focused attention on questioning skills in the classroom and laboratory. Ofsted raised the issue of questioning skills in the report *Subjects and Standards,* which reported the main findings from the inspections in 1994–5. The section devoted to effective teaching highlights the use of questions as a key issue for schools:

> In order to provide effective teaching for pupils of all abilities, teachers should consider whether enough questions, oral or written, are open, so that pupils can respond at length and in depth, according to their abilities.
>
> (Ofsted 1995: 35)

Our school's Ofsted report highlighted the fact that in science, 'Few questions are asked of individuals ...' (Ofsted 1995). It was apparent from discussion with our Ofsted Inspector for Science that, while questions were asked to the whole class and to those with their hands raised, many, more passive, students were being ignored. Staff in the department were not asking questions of named individuals nor were they ensuring that all boys and girls were involved.

Brown and Wragg (1993: 5) discuss teachers' justifications for asking questions. They surveyed a sample of forty primary school teachers to find out why they asked specific questions of specific pupils (Table 2.1).

These are good reasons for the use of questions. But, of course, wouldn't it be expected that science teachers and science teaching would be full of questions? Isn't that how science has developed and develops today'? Isn't science with us because of that one unanswerable question, 'What is truth?'. As Niels Bohr once said:

> Every sentence that I utter should be regarded by you not as an assertion but as a question.
>
> (Aicken 1984: 5)

Table 2.1 Teachers' reasons for asking questions

Reason	% of sample
Encouraging thought, understanding of ideas, phenomena, procedures and values	33
Checking understanding, knowledge and skills	30
Gaining attention to task. To enable teacher to move towards a teaching point in the hope of eliciting a specific and obscure point, and as a warm-up activity for pupils	28
Review, revision, recall, reinforcement of a recently learned point, reminder	23
Management, settling down, to stop calling out by pupils, to direct attention to teacher or text, to warn of precautions	20
To specifically teach the whole class through pupil answers	10
To give everyone a chance to answer	10

Focus of the study

To address the issue raised by Ofsted as part of the department's Ofsted action plan, I, as Head of Science, prepared a briefing paper giving the context for the exercise. The department agreed that the issue was relevant and needed to be addressed. The proposal to organize a paired observation exercise was discussed at a departmental meeting and accepted as a way forward, to take place in the October half term of 1996. Science staff would pair up across their subject disciplines and would arrange to observe each other's lessons and compare notes.

The focus would be class questioning, either orally or by use of written questions. The following issues were noted in discussion: the importance of directed questioning, the issue of gender when questioning students, the position and movement of the teacher in the laboratory in discussion sessions with a class, the best length of these sessions.

Some possible types of question (see box opposite) were noted.

Staff would provide me with a record and summary of the essential features of the practice that had been observed.

Observations

Two strategies were used to collect information in the paired observation exercise. Staff completed grids like those in Table 2.2, during their observation of each other's lessons. The grids contain the summary of the numbers of questions asked from all observations. There were six paired observations of lessons across the age range of this 11–18 secondary grammar school. All the lessons observed were one hour long.

Department briefing paper on questioning skills

Effective questioning using different types of question encourages pupils to talk about and articulate science ideas, concepts and practices.

Open questions allow a pupil to answer freely, encouraging natural conversation. They tend to be simple, unbiased and straightforward questions that enable the pupil to give factual information as well as explaining ideas and understandings without constraint. They are ideal questions to start a discussion.

Examples of open questions are:

- Tell the class about …
- How do you think that happened … ?
- What do you think might happen … ?
- What do you think might happen … ? Why?

Probing questions focus on a particular point, question or issue to obtain more detailed and specific information.

Examples of probing questions are:

- Can you give an example of … ?
- Which of these do you think … ?
- Could you explain how that happens?

Reflective questions pick up on the vocabulary used in discussion between teacher and pupil or between two pupils, often repeating a word or phrase. They are very useful in crystallizing a particular point.

Examples of a reflective question might be:

- But what if this happened?
- Are you sure of that?

Closed questions usually have a straight one- or two-word answer. We often use them to check a pupil's understanding.

Examples of closed questions in science might be:

- What is the formula of sulphuric acid?
- How many moles of water in 36 g?
- Did you say that … ?
- So you mean that … ?

Hypothetical questions are very useful, especially in teaching investigative skills. These questions pose a situation for the student to investigate or ask the student to compare a new situation with one they have already learned.

An example of a hypothetical question is:

- If magnesium is oxidized when burned in air what might happen if … ?

Table 2.2 Number and types of questions asked

A Total number and types of questions that teachers asked pupils

Question type	Boys	Girls
Closed	57	53
Open	13	11

B Total number and types of questions that pupils asked teachers

Question type	Boys	Girls
Procedural	5	5
Science content	10	11

We agreed as a department to collect data on open and closed questions because that was the Ofsted focus. Each pair of teachers was also asked to collect data on the questions pupils were asking. The more detailed analysis of probing, hypothetical and reflective questions would form the basis of a follow-up exercise.

Procedural questions refer to questions such as: 'What do I do next?' and 'Where is the work in the book you want me to do?' Science questions refer to questions like 'Why is fluorine more electronegative than chlorine?'

Discussion

In my analysis of these responses, I would like to focus first on the art of teachers asking questions. As Ofsted commented in their report (Ofsted 1995), open-ended questions were not being asked as frequently as closed questions. In this study, this was because specific closed questions tended to follow an introductory open-ended question as the teacher sought to converge the pupils' thinking on the topic under consideration. In such a period of discussion, periodic reassurance was used to support a pupil and, at an impasse in answers, the bringing of another pupil into the discussion was often used to resolve the situation and support their peer. Staff also used closed questions in a period of review after a short discussion in order to consolidate the description or explanation and to keep straying pupils on track. It was felt by all staff that it was best to keep such teacher–whole class discussion sessions to about 10 minutes for maximum attention to task and interest from pupils. The balance and frequency of questions asked of boys and girls reflected the gender balance in the classes. It is important to involve all pupils in the lesson, irrespective of gender, because this provides the teacher with an opportunity to gauge the learning needs and level of understanding of the pupils. In addition to these quantitative observations, there were other insights gained from the study. These qualitative conclusions are summarized below.

- It was observed that questions coupled with ad hoc diagrams and illustrations were a richer learning experience and likely to be more effective at prompting pupil involvement, questions and answers.
- We considered that close groups of pupils gathered together in the laboratory for discussion improved teacher–pupil control through closer eye contact and helped to keep pupils focused on the argument developing in the discussion.
- We were concerned when a pupil was asked multiple questions on the same theme, questions coming in pairs or threes before the pupil had a chance to respond. It was confusing and unhelpful to their thinking and their learning.
- We felt, too, that we needed to focus on asking more open-ended questions both in discussion and *in written work*. We felt our able pupils needed to be given the opportunity and scope to develop extended answers and to learn, by so doing, to structure their thinking.

Finally, it may seem obvious, but this exercise in questioning skills presupposed that the staff involved knew their pupils by name and that the staff had established clear ground rules and routines for answering questions in each class.

I would like now to consider the issue of pupils asking questions. When Brown and Wragg (1993) interviewed primary school teachers they reported that most of the questions primary school pupils asked their teachers were procedural. They asked procedural questions such as: 'What time are we going home?' and 'Should we put the date?', rather than cognitive questions, such as: 'Why is the sky blue?' or 'What happens if…?' (good science questions, incidentally). In this study, albeit with a very much smaller sample, the opposite was observed. This is not surprising as pupils in this school are selected by ability, and are older and more experienced. However, more remarkable was the general paucity of questions asked by these pupils. The staff collecting this data might, if anything, have been biased to increase the number of questions pupils were asking. Yet so few questions came from such a large number of pupils. Clearly, there is scope to ask if this is common across a wider spectrum of pupils, of a wider range of ability, in secondary schools. Furthermore, if it is so prevalent, why is this the case and is it desirable? It is interesting to compare the low frequency of questions asked by pupils in this small study with comments by Susskind:

> Children may ask a lot of questions – but not usually in school. Indeed one researcher estimated that in elementary schools in the United States *most teachers* ask questions at the rate of two per minute and *most classes of pupils* [my italics] at the rate of two per hour.
>
> (Susskind, 1969 and 1970, quoted in Brown and Wragg 1993: 6)

It is worth pointing out that, in this study, pupils asked questions at a rate of five questions per hour on average. On the other hand, pupils were asked questions by science staff at an average of twenty-two per hour and in one session, the observer reported counting at least thirty questions in a 10-minute period. What does this say of our science curriculum and teaching, if pupils are not asking questions? What needs to change if, as Susskind supposes, the asking of questions is desirable for effective learning? How can a more obvious enquiring mind be encouraged among our pupils? Maskill and Pedrosa (1997) report an interesting strategy used in teaching the particle model. They suggested to the teachers in their study that they stop the lesson from time to time when convenient and ask the pupils to write down any questions they would like to ask about the topic. And they noted that pupils do ask good questions: the pupils knew what they didn't know and could express it.

Conclusions

The art of questioning is a complex area of study. As Oakes (1996: 26) comments 'questioning can be used to extend pupils, maintain the pace of the lesson, involve all pupils in the work and provide encouragement.' This article has barely scratched the surface but it does raise further questions, particularly concerning the seeming paucity of questions pupils ask in science lessons about science. It seems self-evident that pupils should be encouraged to question their learning as a step on the road to mature reflection and action. Science is part of the school curriculum because it is a cultural pursuit, an apprenticeship for the training and preparation of future scientists and it offers pupils an opportunity to explore the wonders and curiosities of the natural world. One key to unlocking the success of these purposes is that our pupils ask questions themselves *and of each other* about what they are learning. To that end, science teachers need to think more carefully about the use of questions and developing questioning minds in their pupils. They should also consider the way in which they provide opportunities for pupils to do this. As one science teacher commented recently: 'A science teacher should be seen by his students as a co-inquirer, not as an authority… he should always answer a question with a question…' (Carlton 1996).

We may not be comfortable with all the conclusions of Postman and Weitgartner, but their comment with which we began this chapter has that challenging ring of truth.

References

Aicken, F. (1984) *The Nature of Science*, London: Heinemann.

Brown, G. and Wragg, E. (1993) *Questioning*, London: Routledge.

Carlton, E. (1996) 'Throw the monkey into the sea…', *Times Educational Supplement*, 6 December.

Maskill, R. and Pedrosa, H. (1997) 'Asking model questions', *Education in Chemistry* 34(5): 132–4.

Oakes, M. (1996) 'Curriculum leadership: science secondary', *Managing Schools Today*, September.

Ofsted (1995) *Subjects and Standards: Science*, London: HMSO.

3 Group discussions in the classroom
Joan Solomon

To judge by illustrations of school science laboratories at the turn of the century [1] both practical and paper work used to be strictly solitary and silent activities. Talking between pupils was made as difficult as possible so that the deathly quiet of good discipline could be maintained at all times and at all costs! Few, indeed, even supposed that there were any costs.

Nowadays our science classrooms can be alive with pupil talk. Policy documents of the Association for Science Education (ASE) and the Department for Education and Employment (DfEE) have encouraged teachers to let children discuss together, without making any specific claims for its functions.

> reading and talking are as important to science education as listening, doing and writing. [2]

The aim of this chapter is to review the various purposes that discussion may serve for science education. It is necessary to make this specific to science, since discussion may well have different objectives for different subjects. Penny Ur [3] speaking for language teachers, suggests the following aims:

- Efficient fluency practice
- Achieving an objective
- Learning from content
- Logical skills
- Debating skills.

As part of the movement for 'language across the curriculum' we may hope that these aims are furthered by all talk in the classroom. Within science lessons, however, discussion takes on new tasks which it can carry out in special and valuable ways – for carrying out practical work, for interpreting results, and for understanding social issues.

Discussion for practical work

The commonest claim made for discussion is that it helps in the planning and design stages of practical work. The APU studies of investigation, to which science education owes so much, were too individual and research-based to suggest how discussion might help; their document *Language in Science* [4] was more concerned with written work and the oral skills involved in describing – as it might be, a butterfly – than with the special purposes of group discussion. However, many practising teachers already had a strong feeling for the value of discussion, and in the run up to GCSE, some of these ideas became inscribed in recommendations for preparing students for the assessment of their practical skills.

There is astonishingly little recorded evidence of how pupils profit from talk during practical work. What follows is drawn from a very patient listening and observing study of a second year science class by June Wallace [5]. The pupils worked in pairs and she reported snippets of discussion which had value for different purposes.

1   Negotiating doing (e.g. arranging collection of apparatus and turn-taking in the experiment).
2   Removing tension (e.g. when disappointments or near quarrels have occurred).
3   Giving help and tutoring (e.g. reiterating what the teacher meant, or explaining the task).
4   Non-task talk (e.g. for greeting and 'stroking' as they settle into their pairs).
5   Negotiating knowledge (e.g. agreeing or disagreeing about what colours, measurements or tastes they perceive).
6   Constructing meaning – which will be explored separately.

It would be misleading to divide these six categories into those which seem more or less valuable. The point that Wallace makes in her commentary is that all this talk is essential. Without (1) the children would collect the wrong materials or bump into each other, and without (2) individual quarrels might break out. It is almost impossible for any two individuals to enter into such close and active proximity without a word or two of salutation (4).

The fifth category on Wallace's list is puzzling at first sight. Surely the pupils know whether it is hot, or red, or dissolving, without speaking to each other about it? The evidence from both this classroom study and from teachers' own experience insists that pupils do need to talk it over. Seeing is not quite the same as believing. Our certainty about observations is greatly increased by receiving confirmation of them from others.

Pupil 1   Purple is it?
Pupil 2   Yes, sort of.
Pupil 1   Would you say purple?
Pupil 2   Yes, purple, (Pause) … I think purple.
             (Satisfied at last they write it down.)

(Wallace [5]: p. 38)

Being sure, it seems, means being sure that others would agree with our judgement. So, our pupils need to speak to each other about what they notice.

Discussion for the interpretation of results

In Attainment Target Sc1 of the KS3 National Curriculum for England, it is stated that: 'Pupils should be taught about the interplay between empirical questions, evidence and scientific explanations…'.

Since different interpretations of evidence are possible, this can set an agenda for discussion. Pupils should, at least at first, be unconstrained by the need to get to the 'right' way of thinking. The discussion of the interpretation of evidence may follow hard on the heels of the discussion of their perceptions of the evidence. Indeed, when a pupil comments: 'I can see (or feel) the vacuum sucking' or 'The salt is disappearing into the water', it would be hard to know whether to place this as an interpretation or a perception! Obviously, we interpret what we observe in line with our private ideas and expectations.

Documenting discussion of the children's ideas has been a prominent feature of the Children's Learning in Science (CLIS) project [6] and other research projects (e.g. [7, 8]). In some cases, the general questioning area is still set by the teacher: 'What happens to food when it is cooked?', 'How do plants feed?', 'What does energy mean?' – but after that there may be more general discussion within the class. The single most important criterion for helping this to happen is that the teacher has no hidden agenda of a 'right answer' to be reached. So, the concepts and theories talked about may not be what the teacher expects.

The purpose of this kind of classroom talk cannot be to learn accepted science. I sometimes doubt if it even makes the pupils' own ideas clearer as Driver and Oldham claim [9]. It does, however, fulfil some very important functions:

1   It demonstrates that different interpretations do exist.
2   It encourages children to think about ideas.
3   It provides the teacher with a rapid survey, in broad brush strokes, of the variety of notions that the pupils hold.

Pupil discussion in groups

More hidden kinds of contribution to scientific knowledge take place whenever pupils talk together. As people speak, even when they are not trying to argue about the meaning of a scientific concept, the words they use, and the gestures they make, may suggest new meanings. It happens everyday through phrases like 'taking the goodness out of food' or 'leeks are heavy feeders'. It also happens serendipitously during talk in the classroom.

In a small-scale piece of research by a physics teacher [10], this was illustrated by an unexpected happening while groups of 11-year-olds learnt about electricity. The course consisted almost entirely of worksheeted experiments with circuit boards. The pupils' prior notions of electric current, and their final understanding of it, were tested before and after the work. The results indicated that the overall 'progress' towards the accepted view of current was disappointingly small. But then it became clear that the pupils within each practical group had changed their ideas so as to agree with each other. They had obviously been speaking together about the experiment, what wires to put in and what connection to make, in terms of their own meaning for current. Some pupils had even dropped the 'correct' view, in order to fit in with their friends!

Similar effects can be seen in some of the CLIS transcripts:

> We had to explain why block A weighed more than B. I thought it was something to do with atoms being compressed densely in A and not so densely in B. Pete said something about air trapped in B so it made the weight lighter … (I said) if you get two bins and put boxes in A and compacting it and then putting more in. Then you just put non-compacted boxes in B. I think (Pete) agreed but still pressed on with his idea … I settled to go along with Pete's idea.
>
> (CLIS [11] 1987)

The following snippet of discussion illustrates this ready acceptance of a multiplicity of meanings for a single concept [12].

Pupil 1   You *get* energy from exercise.
Pupil 2   By doing exercise.
Pupil 3   You *lose* it by doing exercise.
Pupil 1   You may *lose* energy.
Pupil 4   It makes your body fit.
Pupil 1   Yes … I think both.

No possible logical contradiction between the two views about energy-and-exercise prevents Pupil 1 from agreeing with both concept meanings, without any trouble at all.

Once the pupils are given real freedom to discuss concepts and theories entirely on their own, there is no guarantee that either the right answer or the right method of argument will be used. This is *not* a strategy for instruction. Such discussion can certainly motivate children to take a more active part in the lessons and to contribute their own ideas and meanings. In both these ways it is valuable.

Social activities like small group discussion depend crucially upon collaboration and friendship. All of us, adult and child alike, need the agreement of others if we are to be comfortable with our own ideas about the world's happenings. We talk, it seems, just as much to get reassurance as to convince others. 'D'you know what I mean?' is one of the commonest phrases used. Sometimes we just hear meanings in the language that is being used. Light bulbs 'use up' electricity, and 'taking exercise builds up your energy'.

Science itself is a social process and there have been times in its history when there were groups of scientists holding different concepts. (The devotees of the One Fluid or Two Fluid theories of electric charge, in the eighteenth century, were like this. Benjamin Franklin's group even held social events, like their famous 'electric picnic' which, no doubt, reinforced concept solidarity!) Through plenary sessions in which children try to pool their group ideas, they can also learn about the uncertain nature of scientific theorizing, in a way which mirrors that of science itself.

Discussion for understanding science-based social issues

For evaluating social problems, where there can be no concealed 'right answer', most objections to free discussion evaporate. If the topic is controversial, there will be different public points of view and a cluster of answers according to personal or group interests. So, it seems sensible to let the pupils' views surface in free and varied contributions. Ever since Science, Technology and Society (STS) first broke in upon the school science curriculum in the late 1970s, there have been calls to develop new and appropriate strategies for teaching it, and several of these have involved discussion.

Discussion within gaming and simulation

According to Ellington *et al.* [13] exercises of this kind can fulfil objectives such as: '*educating through science* – e.g. interpersonal and communication skills, and *teaching about science and technology* – making political, social and economic decisions.' There is little doubt that the first of these objectives can be most valuably met by group discussion. The second objective becomes problematic only if the decisions lie too far beyond the students' experience.

Games such as *Minerals in Buenafortuna* [14] use discussion in rather contrived and restricted situations. Students work with circumscribed sets of information and find that the agenda is already set by the authors. Questions such as whether the country really wants to develop its mineral resources, are taken for granted. Although the authors state that open-ended questions such as 'the consequences in terms of pollution, noise and the disruption of the local community' can be put to the group, the 'only problem of any importance', they say, is predetermined by the game makers.

The students are asked to act out particular roles in order 'to appreciate hard decisions made by others'. This creates two serious problems. The first is that most pupils will be making their own difficult decisions as citizens rather than as technocrats. Varied personal values and culture-dependent aspects that might influence a citizen are largely neglected in these games. The second problem is that acted parts call for artificial opinions. Participants who have already formed ideas on the public issue in question, might be precluded from expressing what they really believe.

Discussion of controversial issues in small groups

David Bridges, in his book *Education, Democracy and Discussion* [15] argues that there are four functions for discussion when it is applied to a controversial issue. All of them begin with a sharing of personal perspectives on the topic. How and where these discussions finish indicate different kinds of achievement.

a   sharing perspectives is a sufficient goal in itself
b   reaching an understanding of the variety of available subjective responses
c   making an existential (arational) choice between different values
d   finding a rational resolution of the controversy.

(Bridges [15]: 44)

Setting up such small group discussions itself presents some problems. In the first place, the expression of personal values requires time and a supportive environment. There is an element of 'weighing up alternatives' [16], private or social, in any evaluation. Students who do not yet know where they stand are likely to go through a process of hesitant thinking and talking.

The second problem is the role of the teacher. They may be determined not to influence students, and yet trying to follow the austere prescription of the Humanities Teaching Project by being a 'neutral chairman', can result in everyone's speech drying up into an atmosphere of embarrassed silence.

The third problem is the stimulus for discussion. The teacher's bidding is certainly not enough to set the ball rolling on just any cold Monday morning. There will be a need for some trigger which presents the issue as a matter for controversy.

In the Discussion of Issues in School Science project [17] we had to take all three problems into account. Through the teachers, we arranged for the students to talk privately in small friendship groups of just three or four pupils, we used selected video excerpts to stimulate talk, and neither we, nor the teachers, set the agenda for discussion. Indeed, on the single occasion when a teacher misunderstood our instructions and set the students a list of specific questions to discuss, it proved to be a constraint. The list of questions encouraged those students who thought they had 'finished' to cut short the others' talk by going on to the next question.

Values, knowledge and understanding

The National Curriculum Programme of Study for KS3 science states that pupils:

- 'use scientific ideas and models to explain phenomena and events, and to understand a range of familiar applications …'
- 'think about the positive and negative effects of scientific and technological developments …'
- 'take account of others' views and understand why opinions differ.'

However, the connection between the knowledge and understanding of scientific concepts, and decisions based on personal values, is not a simple one.

The Discussion of Issues in School Science (DISS) project was a part of a linked research programme on the Public Understanding of Science which looked beyond the normal meaning of 'understanding'. The different projects explored how such emotive reactions as trust or distrust, fear or wishfulness, and even the glamour or status of the 'knower', affects how scientific knowledge is received. Research in this vein examined the exchange of knowledge between Cumbrian farmers, and the MAFF scientists whose task it was to communicate knowledge and regulations about radioactivity. Other projects looked at how people in a self-help group acquire medical knowledge, or at how scientists in environmental groups perceive the contribution of mainstream science. In every case, the group involved 'reconstructs' the scientific knowledge in order to see its relevance to them.

Our project was commissioned to explore how school science knowledge and media presentation of issues influence the kind of discussion that groups of students can carry out in the classroom. This category of discussion is more complex than those considered in the first two sections, and yet it has much in common with them. The category of talk that Wallace called 'removing tension', is present, as is also the search for corroboration of perception. (This was shown by the way the students talked about incidents in the video.) The social solidarity that was noticed in the context of learning science concepts also appears in the DISS transcripts. We found plenty of cases where the groups talked so closely together that they were even completing each other's sentences. They often asked each other questions, such as 'What would you do if it was your Mum?', but these were clearly not designed to find a right answer. They seemed to be posed in order to set the issue in a more familiar context. By careful deliberations and through helping each other to imagine the possible consequences, their scientific knowledge from school and the video was gradually put into a personal perspective.

Other connections between discussion of social issues and scientific knowledge appeared. One was the frequent comment that 'we need more research' which usually signalled their arrival at a point where no one in the group had relevant information.

The second effect was not so happy. Either when the group decided that they were being fed biased or incomplete information, or when they felt powerless in the matter, they could be made angry or disaffected. At this point, the discussion often abruptly changed course. Interestingly, another research group in the Public Understanding of Science programme found a similar effect. They were investigating the views of adults who lived and worked near a chemical plant. In their report the group noted that:

> where social powerlessness is perceived to be high, efforts at information dissemination may achieve low success rates.
>
> (Irwin and Jub [18])

The incentive for discussing social issues constructively is not successful assessment, nor just relevance; it is the feeling that the citizen can achieve some just social objective through the combination of scientific understanding and social evaluation.

Conclusion

This chapter has touched upon at least five different uses for discussion within science education:

- Negotiations before and during practical work.
- Estimation of alternative ideas within the class about a particular topic.
- Demonstration to pupils of different interpretations of experimental evidence.
- Expression of values relating to social issues.
- Exploring the reception of knowledge from television and other informal sources.

Methods of learning which depend on pupil discussion have some common features. They all require real participation. Genuine contributions will include the pupils' own experiences – relevant or not – their doubtfulness about new knowledge, and their trust in the people talking with them. All this makes the work so significant and so memorable that we have found average-ability students who were able to rehearse quite complex opinions worked out during group discussions after a gap of two or more weeks.

Science has a reputation for being exact, which can make it seem remote from everyday thinking and evaluation. Discussions between people colour its topics with human factors, making them more appealing to some of those who are not at all attracted to it at present.

References

1　Jenkins, E.W., *From Armstrong to Nuffield* (John Murray, 1979).
2　ASE, *Education through Science* (Association for Science Education, 1981).
3　Ur, Penny, *Discussions that Work. Task-centred Fluency Practice* (Cambridge University Press, 1988).
4　APU, *Language in Science* (DES, 1988).
5　Wallace, J., *Social Interaction within Second Year groups doing Practical Science,* unpublished MSc thesis (Oxford University, 1986).
6　Wightman, T., P. Green and P. Scott *The Construction of Meaning and Conceptual Change in the Classroom* (University of Leeds, 1986).
7　Solomon, J., 'Classroom discussion: a method of research for teachers?' *Brit J Educ Res,* 1985, 11(2),153–62.
8　Caravita, S. and C. Giuliana, *Discussion in School Classes: Collective Modelling of Schemata,* (Istituto di Psicologia, (Rome, 1988).
9　Driver, R. and V.A. Oldham, 'Constructivist approach to curriculum development in science', *Stud in Sci Educ,* 1987, 13, 105–22.
10　Kennedy, J., *Some Aspects of Children's Ideas in Basic Circuit Electricity,* unpublished MSc thesis (Oxford University, 1984).
11　Children's Learning In Science Project, *Approaches to Teaching the Particulate Theory of Matter* (University of Leeds, 1987).
12　Solomon, J., *Children's Ideas in Science and the Epistemology of Jean Piaget,* paper given at the BERA conference (University of Lancaster, 1985).
13　Ellington, H., E. Addinall and F. Percival, *Games and Simulation in Science Education* (Kogan Page, 1981).
14　ASE, *Minerals in Buenafortuna* (ASE, 1983).
15　Bridges, D., *Education, Democracy and Discussion* (NFER, 1979).
16　Kitwood, T., 'Cognition and emotion in the psychology of human values', *Oxford Review of Education,* 1984, 10(3), 293–302.
17　Solomon, J., 'DISS – discussion of issues in school science', *Educ in Sci,* 1988, (129), 18.
18　Irwin, A. and A. Jub, *Comments on the Manchester Project* (Paper presented at the SPSG conference Leicester University, 1990).

Further reading

Solomon, J., 'The social construction of school science', *Doing Science: Images of Science Education,* Ed Millar R. (Falmer, 1989).

4 Explaining science
Opening up differences
Jon Ogborn, Gunther Kress, Isabel Martins
and Kieran McGillicuddy

Almost every science teacher would agree that explaining things is fundamental to a science teacher's job. It is not, of course, the whole job, but it is a central and crucial part of it. And there is a lot of explaining to do. Why can metal ships float even though metals sink? How do we catch colds? What keeps the Moon going round the Earth? What is the greenhouse effect and does it matter? What are plastics made of?

Many explanations are related to demonstrations or experiments to be carried out. If the teacher arranges for an effect to be clearly seen, will it be clearly understood? We all know that this doesn't happen. We show the atmosphere crushing a tin can as air is removed from it, but the class sees the vacuum pump sucking the sides of the can together.

There are also theoretical things to explain. Teachers have to explain that it is the ceaseless motion of molecules which gives a gas its pressure, and which accounts for the energy we call heat. They have to explain that plants build their tissue using carbon dioxide, water and sunlight.

Finally, and hardest of all, science teachers have to explain things that don't seem to need explaining at all. Why are our bodies warm? Why do hot things cool down? Why is the sky dark at night? Why are solids hard and liquids runny? Such things seem, to common sense, to be so obvious that there is no need to explain them. It is typical of the sciences that they shake the foundations of knowledge in this way.

The act and art of explaining to a class is much less discussed than the scientific ideas to be explained. This chapter discusses some of our research on the nature of science teachers' explanations (Ogborn *et al.* 1996). In particular, we will focus here on what it is that drives explanations, which we have characterized as 'opening up differences'.

An example of explaining

We briefly offer an example of explaining occurring in the science classroom, to illustrate the kinds of things we found in our study. Here is a teacher (David) explaining the digestive system to a Year 10 class:

David   Now, the tube that goes through the middle of the worm, is [ ] The tube that goes through the middle of the worm is actually connected to the outside world. Here's the outside world here, here's the outside world here, and the tube going through the middle is part of the outside, of the outside

Figure 4.1 *An earthworm brutally reduced to essentials*

world. It's not actually part of the worm, it's just a hole going through the middle. Let me put it to you another way. You know packs of Polo mints, yeah? You know if you buy a pack of Polo mints they look like this – and then you unwrap them, and you find that this Polo mint looks like this up to the top here, when you take the top Polo mint off and you eat it. But in the middle of the Polo mint there's a hole, yeah?, and if you've got a packet of Polo mints then that hole goes in and out the other end. Now – is the hole part of the Polo mint or not?

The teacher had a diagram on the blackboard. Figure 4.1 shows more or less what it looked like, in all its stark simplicity.

There are some key features about this episode which characterize scientific explanations in general:

- The words are not enough. The diagram, and gestures involving it, are all part of the explanation. So is the imagined tube of Polo mints. What David says is important, but the way he is making meanings goes well beyond language.
- The earthworm pictured here is like no recognizable earthworm. Indeed, this teacher is not really discussing earthworms at all. He is working towards the fundamental but apparently bizarre idea that our digestive insides are open to the outside. David is making the familiar and comfortable become strange.
- The explanation works by opening up a gap of understanding. By referring to such a picture as an earthworm, a feeling of a *difference* of view is being created which needs to be resolved. There is a tension, deliberately created, between what is said and what is seen.
- The Polo mints serve as an analogy. Science teachers continually transform ideas through metaphor and analogy.
- This explanation is not isolated. It comes from somewhere and it is going somewhere. It will develop into a more detailed account of how digestion works in a variety of organisms. Explanations in science classrooms cannot be understood without seeing how they fit into larger-scale explanations.

Where do we come from?

We are not, of course, the first to express an interest in explanations, or in science classrooms. But previous work has tended to focus either on explanations as such (e.g. Antaki 1988) or on language in the classroom. Much discussion about problems in science teaching has revolved around the role of practical activity; of 'doing and understanding'. Sutton (1992) gives a well articulated argument for a necessary change of focus. He traces the metaphorical origin of scientific terms, wanting teachers to focus on them as active interpretations rather than as passive labels. At the larger scales of clause and of text, Halliday and Martin (1993) analyse the grammar of scientific discourse. They note how the strikingly dense nature of scientific writing is achieved through what they call grammatical metaphor. In this, a whole physical process is condensed into a single entity, for example, 'the bending of light as it enters a transparent material, such as glass or water, is called *refraction*'. We see this, however, as much more than simply a question of writing and grammatical structure. We see it as building new and different views of the world.

A linguistic starting point very naturally leads to seeing learning science as learning scientific terms and how they are related. For example, Lemke (1990) sees the student's job of understanding the teacher's explanations as one of identifying thematic patterns and grasping semantic relationships between words. This may give undue importance to language, especially in the case of science where we see much meaning being made through acting on things and doing things with them. Others, particularly Edwards and Mercer (1987) have been clear that the language in the classroom is by no means everything that matters – 'Overt messages, things actually said, are only a small part of communication' (Edwards and Mercer 1987: 160). We have tried to go further and look at all the activity of the classroom – talk, gesture, pictures, graphs and tables, experimenting, doing demonstrations – as ways of making meanings.

The main outcome of our work has been a language for describing explanations in the science classroom. This language does not tell you what is good or bad, what is effective or ineffective. What it does is to offer a way of thinking about what explanations are, when and why they are felt to be needed, and what constructing an explanation involves.

Opening up differences

In our view, the fundamental motor of communication is that there is something known to one participant and not – or often *assumed* not – known to another. I have something to say to you, which I think – or pretend – you don't know. There is a *difference* between us. It may be a difference of knowledge or information. It may be a difference of interest – perhaps I want to inform you of, or recruit you to, my interest. It may be a difference of status and power, which I want to acknowledge or impress on you. The difference may be in the realm of feeling. Communication ensues in order to bridge these differences. Conversely, where there is no difference, there is no communication.

Conversation may be thought of as that form of communication where the social, the affective and the pleasurable dimensions, are all in the foreground. There *is* a difference, but this difference is not felt by participants to be particularly significant. Participants have roughly equal rights of participation.

Explanations differ from conversations. They have distinct and unequal roles for participants to fill. The difference at issue is related to knowledge; the explainer knows something the explainee wants or needs to know. The other crucial difference is in their relationships of power and responsibility.

Everyday explanations generally start from a request for information; the explainee takes the initiative. In teaching, the roles are very different. The context of school sets up the student as needing knowledge – and knowledge determined not by the student but by the system of schooling. Thus, one essential difference is that between what the student *knows* and what the student *ought* to know. But there is then a second difference: that between what the student *ought* to know and what the student *wants* to know. So the teacher may need to provoke, stimulate, demand or coax students into wanting it.

Creating interest

Let's return to the obvious. Students are naturally interested in some things, and when they are, the number and variety of questions they ask increases notably. Common areas of interest include environmental issues and – even more so – bodily functions, especially sexual, as in the example below from Year 10. The teacher is David.

Student	What's that?
David	It's underneath its tail, this is a male rat, and that's its …
Student	What happens when you're constipated, what causes that?
David	Wait on, wait on, let's have one question at a time. Just sit down and wait. Right, as I was saying …
Student	Is that his willy?
David	That is its penis.
	(Laughter)
David	We might as well use the correct words.
	(Laughter)
David	Here are its testes … its sperm …
Katie	Can you get female rats?
	…
Student	Don't be such an idiot, Katie. How do they do reproduce?

Science teachers face the task of creating interest in many other matters of much less concern to students. Perhaps the movement of continents is not too hard a case, once students have been told the surprising fact that they do in fact move. How to electrolyse copper sulphate or measure the acidity of a solution is less obviously fascinating, though both may be linked to their practical uses in the hope of making them more appealing. The question of what determines the period of oscillation of a pendulum, not to mention how to analyse motion under gravity, might stand as prototypes of the inherently uninteresting, whilst acknowledging their passionate interest for physicists.

What is a matter of interest or concern varies from one culture to another. The problem is that the sciences have their very special interests which are not necessarily shared with others. Understanding the motion of pendulums is one of them, for reasons not to do with pendulums but to do with much larger issues, namely understanding the causes of motion throughout the Universe. The teacher's task is to reproduce some such structure of interests in students, if possible. That is what it would mean to make them more scientific. This is no small matter: to change one's interests is to become a different kind of person who belongs in a different culture.

The rest of the chapter concerns how teachers set about creating new structures of interest – interest in our wider social sense – in scientific explanations. The many ways of opening up differences are grouped here into two main types. One type is when the difference is between what students don't know and what they need to know or 'What we're going to do next'. The other is when the difference is between what students think they know and knowledge which runs counter to that or 'What do you expect?'.

'What we're going to do next'

In this example, the teacher (Elaine) is introducing a topic on organic chemistry to Year 11 students. Elaine is well aware of the lack of meaning of this expression to students, and that difficulty shows in the responses to her next questions.

Elaine	Anyone have? – got any ideas what this topic might include? From the word organic? Yes?
Student	… growing things.
Elaine	Growing things. Okay. Don't write this down. Let's just put up some of the ideas that you've got. Growing things. Can you be a bit more explicit about that?
Student	Health … growing …
Elaine	Sorry. Health. Natural. Okay. Healthy. Put some hands up – the word organic – what does it mean?
Student	*(inaudible)*
Elaine	Sorry? Crops.

On the surface, Elaine is co-opting the students' interest by starting from ideas and associations which they already have. In fact she has a much deeper concern than doing simply that. As this interaction continues, Elaine brings out that the main associations of the word 'organic' are with living things. She does so because she is going to spring a surprise. The surprise is that organic chemistry is not the chemistry of living things, but is just the chemistry of carbon compounds. She will do this through telling the story of the accidental synthesis of urea – an organic substance made from inorganic materials at a time when this was thought impossible.

Elaine	They thought that these special chemicals could only be made inside living things or they were the waste products of living things or the decayed products of living things. In fact, they had a theory called the Vital Force Theory.

This introduction, easily mistaken for a case of eliciting what students know, is going to be used to undermine what they know. To do organic chemistry is to ask a completely new set of questions; no longer questions like, 'Is this substance good for you?', but questions like, 'How many carbon atoms do the molecules of this substance contain?' Elaine's job has been both to expose this difference, and through interaction with the class and some history of chemistry, to try to bridge it.

Utility

A common strategy in introducing a new topic is to stress its usefulness. Indeed Elaine, in her introduction to organic chemistry that has just been discussed, deploys this strategy too:

Elaine   It's an extremely important part of chemistry because it's the chemistry that we use when we're talking about biology, the chemistry of carbohydrates and proteins and things like that. It's also the chemistry for producing the things that we take for granted now like plastics, dyestuffs, the things that one hundred years or so ago, weren't around.

Here Elaine evokes two kinds of usefulness – for understanding biology, and for making new and useful materials. She later goes on to talk about a third kind of usefulness – that of the organization of knowledge to make it easier to learn. Though there are many different organic compounds they can be put into groups:

Elaine   Within a group they have quite a lot in common so you really only have to learn about one member of the group, then you can make some pretty good guesses about all the other members of the group. So we can organize our knowledge about these different carbon compounds into discrete little packages which is going to make it much easier for us to learn.

Thus she appeals not only to students' expected natural interests in living things and in technical novelty, but also to their concerns as learners. Or, to put it differently, she creates three kinds of difference between students as they are now and as they might become: a change in knowledge of things that already interest them, a change in what they are interested in towards the interests proper to chemistry, and a change in the facility of their job as students.

Promises and anticipations

A good many science lessons start by naming the topic to come, and this may include some kind of definition of what it is about. Here is the start of one Year 10 lesson:

Tom   OK, the alkali metals. [ ] So what – would you start off by doing [ ] is copying those first three into your book. Copy the three boxes into your book. It may be bigger.
Student   Sodium.
Tom   Lithium, sodium, potassium.

The teacher is going to do a demonstration to show the similarities and differences between the three elements, the nature of which leads to their being called alkali metals. One might argue that it would be better if the label 'alkali metals' were to come at the end, when some reason for choosing it had been provided. But this argument is to mistake the function of this kind of action taken by a teacher. The title is best understood as making a promise. It names something not yet known and promises that it can, and will be understood. A difference is opened up between where students are now and where they will be, in the shape of a blank but labelled conceptual space.

Here are some further examples of talk near the start of explanatory episodes which are also, in the above sense, not yet strictly comprehensible, but which serve to promise an understanding, and so once again open up a difference between students' present and anticipated knowledge:

Teacher   Electricity and magnetism are two things which are very closely related, OK?

Teacher   I'm going to summarize the Periodic Table for you … we're going to look at drawing particles in relation to the Periodic Table.

The first may be quite mysterious to someone who knows nothing of electromagnetism. The second promises the 'drawing of particles', but what could that be, 'in relation to the Periodic Table'? In no way do we want to suggest that the teacher is making any sort of mistake in producing such statements. It is a quite common strategy, though teachers may not be aware of it as a strategy. And it is not necessarily a problem for students. They learn to understand such utterances as a harbinger of work to come which will make the utterances make sense.

'What do you expect?'

Teachers constantly draw on students' expectations as another main way of creating a difference which can produce a need to explain. We use the term expectations in a broad sense, ranging from letting students see surprising phenomena to getting them to commit themselves to an answer before finding out if it is right.

Counter-expectation

In the extract which follows, the teacher (Leon) provokes a disagreement on purpose. All the students in the Year 9 class are girls.

Leon   Do you think that you can tell if you're having a baby or a, or, if you're having a boy or girl, by, where, the where? *(gestures a rounded belly.)*

Student 1   The shape of it, that's what I heard.

Student 2   I don't believe that.

Student 3   That's what I heard.

Leon   Who from?

Student 1   From you. *(The teacher is stunned.)*

Student 3   My auntie.

Leon	Oh, your auntie, must be true. It must be true.
Student 4	*(to another student)* Don't laugh about it.
Student 5	It's funny. [ ]
Leon	So are you trying to tell me – okay, think of this little, this little fetus, about to be born right, okay, has it gone through secondary sexual development?
Student	No.
Students	No.
Leon	Okay, a little baby brother, a penis about this big, okay. *(Teacher holds fingers close together in front of his eyes.) (Student laughter.)* True? True? You're telling me, that that alters, the swelling? *(Teacher makes a curved shape with his arms around his stomach.)*

This clearly creates a tension to be resolved, or a gap to be bridged with further understanding. Even if the teacher's biological rejection of the idea is accepted, the issue still remains why reasonable people known to and trusted by the students believe it. A large and important difference is created; that between two worlds of knowing and their respective authority and basis.

I wonder if I'm right?

Although science teachers often ask questions and nominate or allow one student to answer – often to the relief of those passed over – they sometimes get a whole class to commit themselves to an answer, so raising the tension at least a little. In another of Leon's lessons, which was about the skeleton, he gave out statements to judge true or false. One of these was 'Bone is not a living tissue'. When students were told that this statement was false, a lively discussion ensued.

The bringing into existence of that issue must owe something to the prior commitment of each student to an answer. The students had formed some expectation of what the answer might be, and were interested in how it would turn out. A difference was created and helped drive explanations of why bone is living material and of why one might think the opposite.

Imagine that!

Meaning-tension can be created by seeing or thinking about surprising or unusual things. A sign that this has happened is that students themselves start posing spontaneous questions. They sense the difference that has been created.

There are two different kinds of 'imagining strange things'. One is seeing something strange and not easily explicable, such as an upside-down image, a ball supported on a jet of air, a big spark from a small battery – and so on. The phenomenon is unexpected and the issue is one of explaining it. The other is hearing one of the stranger explanatory stories of science, such as motion going on forever, light travelling through nothing, or the unfolding of a new organism from a single egg. Now the problem is one of coming to terms with the odd behaviour of the entities in that story, and of believing that the phenomena it suggests actually happen.

What do we think now?

We must avoid giving the impression that creating differences or motivating explanation is something to be done to get things going and to be abandoned afterwards. On the contrary, it happens continually. As bits of explaining are completed, students have to think what each means, and whether there are gaps yet to be bridged or tensions to be resolved. 'Does that mean that if …?' questions from students are one sign of such work going on. Below, a Year 9 student checks with the teacher (Tom) if a newly created way of thinking about measuring volumes makes sense.

Tom	So if I wanted to know what your, what your volume was, you'd get a big dustbin, and you'd get in it, and you'd get under the water for a second and you'd see how much water overflows.
Student 1	You might get killed trying to get out.
Tom	Well, you have to do it very carefully, under strict controls.
Student 2	Sir, erm, say, you've got a massive swimming pool, like say about thirty people, and you've got, say, twenty people going in it, you'd put one by one and then you'd measure …
Tom	Measure how much it grows, that's right, that's it.

Nothing to explain?

We conclude with an example of a very difficult case of creating differences; of making what seems obvious into something which needs explaining. With a Year 8 class, Leon sets himself the problem of making the simple and obvious fact that we see things where they really are, into something to be explained in terms of the way light travels. The following is an extract from a much longer explanation:

Leon	How do I know your hand is in that line from me to you?
Student	'Cos you can see it.
Leon	But how can I see it? What? – there's light in the room, there's light coming in, and where is it shining?
Student	Everywhere.
Leon	Is some of the light shining here? *(points to student's hand.)*
Student	Yes.
Leon	And then what does it do? Shines onto you?
Student	And reflects.
Leon	It reflects. To me? Does it reflect to me in curved lines or in straight lines?
Student	No, straight lines.

Leon has not only to make it seem a problem that he can see a hand where it is, but has to get further involved in making it a problem that he can see the hand at all. It cannot be easy, if only because in everyday thinking, we reason the other way round, that things are where they are because we see them there.

Scientific and everyday knowledge

One more difference that must be taken into account is that between established scientific knowledge and common everyday knowledge. Scientific knowledge is not just common knowledge writ large; it is often totally different in kind. It sees the world differently, filling it with new entities – from photons to pharmaceuticals. Everyday explanations are in terms of familiar entities doing familiar things. Scientific explanations are often in terms of unfamiliar entities doing unfamiliar things, and the student is a stranger in an unknown world. It follows that much explanation in science classrooms is not the explanation of phenomena, but is the explanation of resources the student needs in order to explain phenomena. We discuss the construction of entities in Chapter 20 of this book.

When the teacher explains about sound being a wave or about chemical bonds being electrical in nature, the explanation forms, as it were, the tip of an iceberg. Unseen, underneath and keeping it afloat, is a large hidden mass of scientific explanation. The student experiments with dissolving sugar in water; underneath lies all the science of solids and liquids, molecular theory and thermodynamics. It is this, unknown to the student, which gives point to putting sugar in water at different temperatures.

References

Antaki, C. (ed.) (1988) *Analysing Everyday Explanation,* London: Sage.

Edwards, D. and Mercer, N. (1987) *Common Knowledge: The Development of Understanding in the Classroom,* London: Methuen.

Halliday, M. A. K. and Martin, J. R. (1993) *Writing Science,* London: Falmer Press.

Lemke, J. L. (1990) *Talking Science: Language, Learning and Values*, Norwood, New Jersey: Ablex.

Ogborn, J., Kress, G., Martins, I. and McGillicuddy, K. (1996) *Explaining Science in the Classroom,* Buckingham: Open University Press.

Sutton, C. (1992) *Words, Science and Learning,* Buckingham: Open University Press.

5 The role of pupils' questions in learning science

Steve Alsop, Gillian Gould and Mike Watts

Introduction

If there is energy in cornflakes, why can't they jump around in the bowl?

How would you respond to a question such as this from an inquisitive 8-year-old? What possible reasons could you come up with for not answering it? One reason might be that the answers (and there are several) seem neither direct nor straightforward, especially when they have to be communicated to one so young. Or, perhaps the exact answer to the question lies outside of your immediate knowledge system.

Learners' questions are unpredictable, often not easily answered, and they can make adults (especially new teachers) feel very insecure. An understandable reaction might be to close down opportunities for pupils to ask questions – after all, it's much easier to stick to the script! However, pupils' questions and teachers' answers are of fundamental importance to good classroom practice. This chapter examines pupils' questions and their role in developing conceptual understanding, drawing on the work done as part of the Questions for Conceptual Understanding Project (QUESTCUP) based at the University of Surrey at Roehampton. We focus on encouraging pupils' questions, exploring the understandings that give rise to these and what meaning we can make of them.

Constructivist teaching

The context in which we examine pupils' questions is that of a constructivist approach to teaching. Although this approach has been the source of some debate (Fensham *et al.* 1994; Yager 1995), it is firmly embedded in the science education research literature and new curriculum materials, and is regarded as one means to maximize learning. Constructivism commonly refers to how people learn, how they construct and build up knowledge – something which individuals must do for themselves. It is not something a teacher can do *for* them, teachers cannot *give* learning to pupils: teachers teach and learners learn, and there may (or may not) be correspondence between the two. In general terms, constructivist teaching aims to reach into and change pupils' understanding of science. A broad description (Bliss 1995) involves allowing pupils' thinking to drive lessons. This involves teachers:

- Being flexible about content and teaching strategies used during the lesson;
- Encouraging pupils to ask thoughtful and open-ended questions;
- Allowing lots of 'wait time' for questions and asking pupils to elaborate what they mean by them;
- Asking pupils to talk about their theories and concepts, to connect ideas and phenomena with experiences in their daily lives, to reflect on their ideas and predict future outcomes.

'Pupils' understandings' are particular kinds of entities. They might usefully be pictured as an amalgam of everyday expressions, TV images, personal ideas, chunks of school learning, conversations with friends and family, experiences in daily life and so on. These clusters of ideas are more or less coherent and 'work' for the learner because they satisfy an immediacy of description, explanation and logic; they are usually confirmed by common, taken-for-granted experience and social convention, and possess a greater degree of intuitive common sense. That which is already understood shapes and gives meaning to what is about to be understood, so diagnosing this is important in order to understand the perspectives from which the learner sees the world and thus engage in a meaningful dialogue with him or her. The point of interest here is the extent to which learners' questions are indicative of their understandings:

> A further reason for fostering children's interrogative skills is that, by posing questions, pupils are shaping and exposing their thoughts and hence opportunities will be provided for teachers to have some insight into children's thinking and conceptual understanding. Questions asked by children can lead teachers towards making appropriate assessments of children's understanding or alternatively their misconceptions.
>
> (Woodward 1992)

Potentially, therefore, we suggest, pupils' questions can be used to diagnose conceptual change, between points of relative security of understanding and periods of perplexity and doubt. They may also be indicative of the frame of mind of the learner and the quality of the understandings they have. In order to use pupils' questions in this way, it is helpful to analyse them in more detail.

Pupils' questions

While there has been much scrutiny of teachers' questions (Elstgeest 1985; Brown and Wragg 1993), research that focuses on the broad range of learners' questions is not as plentiful. Where classroom conditions are appropriate, learners will ask a range of questions. These may vary from the merely curious, where any answer is of only passing consequence, to those questions which reveal deep consternation and troubled thinking, where the form and detail of the response is significant. Learners' questions have the capacity to expose both sophisticated and naive thinking, to tackle complex issues and to focus on minutiae and detail.

Fairbrother (1988) suggests that posing a question and formulating a hypothesis are often linked together, leading to the identification of a practical problem.

However, many questions are posed for reasons of conceptualization, for thinking aloud, and are not expressed in a way that will obviously lead to an investigation. As Swatton (1992) points out, not all questions raised by children are necessarily expressed in formal terms amenable to empirical test and, therefore, one part of the teachers' job must be to facilitate the translation of these questions into testable hypotheses. Indeed, many questions are probably more in the way of open 'thought experiments' and are not intended to be formalized or even necessarily answered. Questions such as, 'What would happen if … ?', 'Why is it that … .?', 'Why do spiders have eight legs (and not two like humans)?' and 'Is the sky cold?', are more by way of exploration of a situation than the requiring of a simple answer.

Three categories of learners' questions

The three broad categories of pupil questions that follow draw from two empirical lines of inquiry carried out by QUESTCUP. One was a case study of one teacher as she established an approach to 'Question Based Learning' (QBL) within her own classroom (Gould 1995), and the other was based on a collection of pupils' questions accumulated through collaborative work with teachers.

The empirical work was used to develop a framework for categorizing children's questions based on moments in their learning. The three categories developed, *consolidation, exploration,* and *elaboration,* reflect the process of learning. In the first category are those questions that are indicative of the learner moving towards a *consolidation* of their thinking on a particular set of issues. Questions in the second category of *exploration* are from learners who feel reasonably secure in their under-standing, and who are tentatively testing and expanding their ideas. In the third category, *elaboration,* the questions are indicative of learners trying to reconcile competing ideas; the demands of a new theory against the call of experience. In this way, the researchers claim that children's questions can be used to identify particular moments in cognition.

Category 1   Consolidation questions

During this period, learners are attempting to say what they think, clarify the ratio-nale for classroom tasks, confirm explanations and consolidate understanding of new ideas in science. These questions are attempts to sort out conceptual issues. Learners may feel they have grasped an idea, or the structure of an argument, and are testing for reassurance that this is, in fact, the case.

An illustration of this category uses an extract from a class conducting practical tests to analyse the nutrient content of various foods; tests that depend on being able to distinguish colour changes:

Pupil 1	What colour is 'brick red'?
Teacher	Well, what does the old school look like? What's the colour of the old school building?
Pupil 1	Brick red.
Teacher	That's 'brick red' colour, yes.
Pupil 1	Is blue …?

Teacher	Blue means no sugar at all, but sometimes you get a bit of sugar. Then what happens? I'm not going to tell you the answer. What do you get?
Pupil 1	Green.
Teacher	Green. Yes, if you see green it means that there is a little bit of sugar present. OK?

In some instances, questions like this precede procedural decision making of the 'Should this go here?' kind. The purpose of such exchanges may be simple reassurance, though in a stronger sense they serve to consolidate thinking through verbalizing and testing constructs in the process of formation. For example, an initial question may be straightforward, but this might signal the beginning of a sequence of questions of the type, for example, 'Do you think …?', 'What about …?', 'Is it is because …?" These, in turn, are followed by 'Well, I think it's because …'. Such a sequence continues as the learner asks a range of questions as they search for an answer that makes sense to them.

The following extract is from the lesson on digestion:

Pupil 2	… if there isn't any starch in there [a test tube] does that mean it won't go on changing colour, or will there be different shades of brown?
Teacher	What do you think is going to happen?
Pupil 2	I'd have thought that it would have been different shades of brown because, I mean. … the first drop … it's only been left in there a few minutes, the starch may be concentrated at the top or the bottom of the tube. … Is it turning into something else?
Teacher	Yes, it's turning into something else. So, will all of it turn at once do you think?
Pupil 2	Some of it will turn first …
Teacher	Don't forget that you will be mixing up the enzymes. Do you think the concentration of what you are making will go …?
Pupil 2	… up?
Teacher	… and the starch will go …?
Pupil 2	… will go down.
Teacher	Very good.

Pupils seem to want approval or validation from the teacher for their ideas. They hold a particular view of a scientific idea and want to test it against the authoritative view, although, at times, they are almost interrogating themselves and their constructs rather than taxing the knowledge of an expert. Perhaps to make a statement might be to risk rejection by the teacher, a situation much more difficult to accept than simply putting a question. These question sequences are potentially extremely useful to teachers because they give a very clear indication of the form and status of the learner's understanding.

Category 2 Exploration questions

Questions in this category are indicative of *exploration*. Learners who, having reached a sense of conviction in their understanding, then use the security of this base camp to launch a few excursions into the neighbouring terrain. At this stage, which has been called a position of strength, learners' questions seek to both expand knowledge and test constructs that they have formed.

In this next example, a class of 12-year-olds is beginning a series of lessons designed to explore the concepts of the Periodic Table, reactivity series and chemical reactions. The first lesson begins with demonstrations of reactions of alkali metals in water. On marking the homework, it becomes apparent that the idea of reactions is very poorly understood. The following lesson starts with the reinforcement of the concept. In addition, the teacher writes the word-equation on the board. Very rapidly, the class seems to understand. One pupil asked:

Pupil 3   Miss, water is H_2O, isn't it? If hydrogen gas is produced by the reactions, is it because there is more hydrogen in water? If water was HO_2, would the metal push out oxygen?

This is an unorthodox response and contrary to the scientific notion of reactivity. However, the pattern of the pupil's question indicates that he has a strong appreciation of the ideas of elements, compounds and reactions and used these ideas to generate a novel thought, which he then expressed as a question.

Another example is taken from a genetics class, from a discussion of haemoglobin and the difference between foetal and adult haemoglobin. Haemoglobin's measured affinity for oxygen changes with the oxygen concentration to which it is exposed, producing the mechanism for collecting oxygen in the lungs and releasing it within tissues. In this example, a pupil asked:

Pupil 4   Miss, given that foetal haemoglobin has a greater affinity for oxygen, is it also more reluctant to release it in the embryo?

Commonly, in teaching, it is sufficient to mention only that the foetal haemoglobin has a slightly higher affinity compared to that of the adult at the same partial pressure of oxygen – hence its ability to move oxygen from the mother's blood in the placenta. This example illustrates a learner's ability to use questions to extend his constructs. Where learners already have some firm understanding of the topic, a secure construct, and they want to apply the construct to a novel situation, it sometimes seems easier to pose this as a question to be considered, rather than make an assertive statement that could be rejected.

Category 3   Elaboration questions

In the third category are questions even more indicative of change. Learners lack conviction about either their own frameworks of understanding or those on offer to them. They are examining claims and counterclaims, *elaborating* and challenging both their previous knowledge and experience and that being presented to them, what has been described by QUESTCUP as a 'point of conceptual plasticity'. Questions are of the 'Well … if *that's* the case, then … why not …?', 'But what happens if …?, and 'Why, then, is it not possible to …?' Questions within this category are attempts to reconcile different understandings, resolve cognitive conflicts, test circumstances, force issues and track in and around the ideas and their consequences. Such questions may have some direct relevance to the classroom topic being taught, although questions may be triggered by side issues or stimulated by something from beyond the class entirely.

An example might be:

Pupil 5   Miss, just how fast do cells divide?

Implicit in this question might be the query: 'I know cells divide. However, I cannot see my own cells dividing – so just how fast is cell division?'

Other examples of elaboration questions include:

Pupil 8   Meteorites burn up because of friction as they move through the air. Why, then, is wind cold and why does it feel cold when you stick your hand out of a moving car window?

Pupil 9   If light travels as fast as it does, then how is it possible to *see* it?

Pupil 10   Miss, do you know the boiling point of liquid nitrogen? What makes it so cold?

This type of question can be an indicator of points of plasticity between a learner's own constructs and the formation of a scientifically orthodox construct from the science classroom or elsewhere. Where this is the case, it would be of considerable use as an indication of where teacher intervention may be most successful.

This classification system is not intended to be exhaustive or comprehensive. There will inevitably be examples which do not fall exactly within one category or another, for instance, rhetorical questions, or questions which are riddles or conundrums ('If you were me, would you still like chocolate?'). There can be many reasons for asking questions – to know the right answer, to prompt further discussion, to generate red herrings, to make an overt display of interest, to make a claim for attention (regardless of the answer), and so on. However, this categorization offers a starting point for an analysis of the types of questions that occur during science classes.

Why are these questions so important?

Science itself is based on the asking of questions and the search for answers. Some, like Einstein's Gedanken experiments (Helm *et al.* 1985), led to considerable theoretical advances, while experimental science has developed through endless empirical questions: as science progresses, so the next questions seem to arise almost automatically. Pupils need both to understand the nature of science itself and feel they, too, can ask scientific questions. They need to appreciate what falls within the domain of science, what constitutes an empirical question, what an appropriate answer might be, from where answers might be derived, what serves as good evidence and data gathering, and so on.

It is also important that teachers engage with pupils' questions. We suggest that there are periods in the process of learning school science where learners will form fixed and tight definitions, concepts and frameworks. At other periods, their thinking on the same issues becomes loose, more flexible and open to change. Both periods are important, as it is essential to fix some ideas so that progress can be made with the next. What is possible, though, is for the teacher to appreciate 'where the pupil is at' through the quality of the questions they ask. Questions can indicate areas of understanding and incomprehension. They are diagnostic of the state of the individual's thinking and can indicate the routes through which learners are seeking understanding (where they are looking from and where they are going). This can reveal something about each person and their understanding of neighbouring issues and topics. That is, the questions come from somewhere and portray a direction of thinking.

Fostering a climate of questioning

It is well documented that student questions are very infrequent and unsophisticated and, further, that … they are normally shallow, short-answer questions that address the content and interpretation of explicit material; they are rarely high-level questions that involve inferences, multistep reasoning, the application of an idea to a new domain of knowledge, the synthesis of a new idea from multiple information sources, or the evaluation of a new claim.

(Graesser and Person 1994)

This is not a perspective we accept. It is not uncommon for pupils to find the content and context of lessons confusing and that the things being said by teacher or peers do not make sense. Sometimes, incomprehension or frustration will build to the point where a pupil will ask for clarification, to 'fill a semantic link in the chain needed to make sense of what is being said' (Lemke 1990). When a pupil asks a question of this kind, teachers will commonly check to see if the answer that they have provided is satisfactory. Sometimes, a pupil will find a contradiction between what is being said and their own conceptual understanding. In this case, they may question or challenge what the teacher has said:

It takes a lot of frustration, and not a little self-confidence, for a student to do this. Perhaps it happens more often silently than out loud, but when it does happen publicly we get a rare glimpse of the differences in thematic patterns that lie behind so many odd-sounding student questions and so much of the miscommunication and confusion that occurs in everyday classrooms.

(Lemke 1990)

Furthermore, the opinion has been expressed that:

Children qua students do not ask questions. They may be raising questions in their own mind during the class hour. They may be questioning as they read and study their texts. They may be asking questions of their friends and family and of adults in other roles or contexts. But they do not ask questions aloud in the classroom.

(Dillon 1988)

Clearly, there is need for an atmosphere of trust and acceptance with low risk of censure for questions to proliferate. Pupil confidence in asking questions is an important aspect of effective teaching. We see it as a willingness of pupils to seek understanding, an expression of their curiosity and, therefore, an indication of the quality of the non-threatening and trusting atmosphere extant within the classroom. To ask a question can expose ignorance, render the questioner very vulnerable and require particular kinds of peer and teacher relationships to happen easily. Where classroom conditions are not appropriate, learners will not venture questions except, perhaps, of the most transactional or procedural form. There may be considerable barriers to be overcome before some pupils can bring themselves to ask a question aloud across the room; not least the fear of being thought of as 'stupid' – or the converse, the loss of peer esteem if treated as a 'boffin' by the group.

The teacher is central to the creation of such a supportive, safe, classroom atmosphere, in which questions are encouraged. It is not always easy, however, to create this. A number of factors may work against the teacher, such as the pressure to get through the curriculum, or their own confidence with the subject matter. Teachers who lack confidence in an aspect of their science knowledge tend to compensate by restricting the range of activities and interactions with pupils. This often leads to carefully formulated planning, organization, assessment and materials, and more tightly-managed and controlled learning situations to minimize exposure of their own limited expertise. Consider the teaching of a new topic – a first A level class, or a chemistry lesson for the biologist. A series of unexpected questions from the gathered throng can serve to unseat the supposed specialist and ready expert. It is not surprising, then, that a teacher working outside their subject knowledge comfort zone is unlikely to encourage pupils' questions. The implication is that the teacher must feel secure and confident before progress can be made in promoting pupil questioning.

Strategies to encourage pupils' questions

Pupils' questioning has been promoted by their own investigative problem-posing. Much of the approach to 'open learning' and 'open-ended problem solving' (Watts 1991; 1994) has fostered pupils' own investigations. The OPENS Project (Jones *et al.* 1992), for example, describes how teachers offered secondary pupils the opportunity to develop their own questions relating to a laboratory investigation. Here, the authors indicate that some pupils needed guidance in the asking of questions. Creativity in Science and Technology (CREST), too, is a national project devoted to pupil problem-solving which gives kudos, through its award system, for the quality of the empirical questions pupils pose and solve (CREST 1994).

However, as previously discussed, not all questions can be empirically tested. All types of questions should be encouraged and, if we are to treat pupils' thoughtful (and 'thought full') questions seriously, we also need to use classroom strategies to develop this. Not only must the teacher be sensitive to pupil questions at all points in the lesson, but there might also be specific times for strategies such as:

- a period of 'free question time' within a lesson or block of lessons;
- a question 'brainstorming' session at the start of a topic;
- a 'question box' on a side table where pupils can put their (anonymous?) questions;
- questioning in turn around the class where each pupil or group of pupils must prepare a question to be asked of others;
- 'question-making' homework.

Alsop (1994) reports on strategies used in a primary science classroom (equally valid for secondary pupils) to encourage the asking of questions, and describes three particular occasions:

1   After an initial input from the teacher, groups of children were asked to generate a list of five questions to form the basis of their topic work. They were also asked how they might find the answers to their own questions as a means of emphasizing how different questions require different kinds of solutions.

2   Prompted by some puzzling situation, demonstration or activity, groups of children were encouraged to think of a question that would pinpoint the answer – rather like a 'twenty questions' quiz. The groups took turns to present their questions to the class and subsequent groups therefore had to modify their version in the light of the previous questions (and answers).

3   Following a class discussion, children were expected to ask a question immediately after they had answered one. The teacher began by asking the first question and the respondent then asked someone else the next question so that turns were passed around the class. It was not enough to know the answer; it was important to have a question ready too.

Summary

We have sought here to foster questioning and questioners. We see a need to nurture learners' natural curiosity by developing a spirit of enquiry in the classroom, 'in which questions are respected for themselves, whether or not we know or can even find out the answer' (Fisher 1990). We believe that teachers are better prepared if they have some sense of the nature of pupil questioning and some strategies through which to work in response.

We leave the last word with an astronomer and science educator, who says:

First, my questions are just that, they are my questions. They spring from within me and have been formed by my experience of the world. Further, it is these questions that motivate the research. Much more than answers, I search for meaningful questions. In our attempts to represent science before our students, do we do justice to the nature of question?

(Martin and Brouwer 1993)

References

Alsop, S. (1994) 'Case study 12: questioning', in D. Bentley and D. M. Watts (1994) (eds) *Primary Science and Technology. Practical Alternatives,* Milton Keynes: Open University Press.

Bliss, J. (1995) 'Piaget and after: the case of learning science', *Studies in Science Education* 25: 139–72.

Brown, G. and Wragg, E. C. (1993) *Questioning,* London: Routledge.

Creativity in Science and Technology (CREST) (1994) *CREST Awards Scheme,* Surrey: Surrey Research Park, Guildford.

Dillon, J. T. (1988) 'The remedial status of student questioning', *Journal of Curriculum Studies* 20: 3.

Elstgeest, J. (1985) 'The right question at the right time', in W. Harlen (ed.) *Taking the Plunge,* London: Heinemann.

Fairbrother, R. W. (1988) *Assessment of Practical Work for the GCSE*, London: Nuffield Chelsea Curriculum Trust.

Fensham, P., Gunstone, R. F. and White, R. T. (1994) *The Content of Science: A Constructivist Approach to its Teaching and Learning,* London: The Falmer Press.

Fisher, R. (1990) *Teaching Children to Think,* Oxford: Blackwell.

Gould, G. (1995) 'Questions and the questioner', unpublished MA dissertation, Roehampton Institute, London.

Graesser, A. J. and Person, N. K. (1994) 'Question asking during tutoring', *American Educational Research Journal* 31(1, Spring): 104–37.

Helm, H., Gilbert, J. K. and Watts, D. M. (1985) 'Thought experiments and physics education: part II', *Physics Education* 20: 211–17.

Jones, A. T., Simon, S. A., Black, P. J., Fairbrother, R. W. and Watson, J. R. (1992) *Open work in Science. Development of Investigations in Schools,* London and Hatfield: King's College and Association for Science Education.

Lemke, J. L. (1990) *Talking Science,* New Jersey: Ablex Publishing Corporation (p. 56).

Martin, B. and Brouwer, W. (1993) 'Exploring personal science', *Science Education* 77(4): 441–59.

Swatton, P. (1992) 'Children's language and assessing their skill in formulating testable hypotheses', *British Educational Research Journal* 18(1): 73–85.

Watts, D. M. (1991) *The Science of Problem Solving,* London: Cassell.

Watts, D. M. (1994) *Problem Solving in Science and Technology. Extending Good Classroom Practice,* London: David Fulton Press.

Woodward, C. (1992) 'Raising and answering questions in primary science: some considerations', *Evaluation and Research in Education* 6(2 & 3): 91.

Yager, R. E. (1995) 'Constructivism and the learning of science', in S. M. Glynn and R. Duit (eds) *Learning Science in the Schools. Research Reforming Practice,* New Jersey: Lawrence Erlbaum Associates.

2 Practical work

Introduction

Why undertake practical work in science? To many, the relationship between science and practical works seems so self-evident that the question is hardly worth asking. It is almost like saying 'Why is a circle round?'. A circle is round because roundness is what defines a circle; we do practical work in science because science is a practical subject! But this kind of justification clearly needs examining. There has been a lot of research and debate about what pupils really learn from practical work and how the use of practical work can be made more effective.

There is often a tendency to think that every scientific idea needs to be illustrated through practical work. But doing practical work does not *of necessity* help to develop *conceptual understanding*. It may sometimes make simple ideas seem complicated; the conceptual understanding is lost amongst what has been referred to as the 'clutter of reality'. Certainly, practical work helps to develop *practical skills*, but this only has a purpose if developing these skills is required in order for pupils to undertake practical work! There is no inherent value in developing such skills, since there is little evidence that they are transferable outside the science laboratory. There is little evidence either, that practical work *on its own* helps pupils to understand what *science itself* is like or what scientists do. Finally, the *motivational* aspects of practical work are often overstated. While it is true that younger children may be motivated by manipulating apparatus or observing new phenomena, for older pupils, practical work also needs to engage them intellectually.

There is a strong temptation in the classroom to use practical work as a means of social control. 'If you don't behave better, then I won't let you do any practical work today!' There are problems with this. An immediate problem for the stressed teacher trying to bring a class under control is that the strategy simply may not work. It relies on the myth that all pupils find all practical work interesting and motivating. Some pupils might not care if they don't do practical work; others may be relieved at the prospect. If pupils are bored, anxious or frustrated, then this approach does not begin to address the real difficulty.

A second problem, more fundamental and longer-term, is the impression given by from this approach about what the teacher appears to value and about their view of science. From this perspective, thinking about ideas, or theoretical work, seems to be second-best, and activities that involve, for example, reading and writing, are seen as punishment. Too much emphasis on the importance of practical work in science can lead to a restricted repertoire of teaching strategies and a narrow view of learning.

In arguing that the role of practical work is problematic we are *not* saying that it is unimportant. What we *are* saying is that it is necessary to be clear about how it can be used effectively. Practical work is *essential* in enabling pupils to gain first-hand experience of phenomena. It can stimulate pupils into wanting to find explanations for events that seem surprising, and may challenge their existing beliefs. It can give them an insight into the nature of scientific enquiry, and through their own investigative work they can apply their conceptual understanding in new contexts. Different kinds of practical work are appropriate for different purposes. What is important is that practical work is not just about *hands-on* but *minds-on* too. Ensuring that pupils are active learners and not passive receivers of information has nothing to do with keeping pupils busy with tasks that keep their hands occupied; active learning happens in the head! The following chapters show how practical work can be used to support real learning.

- Practical work can serve a variety of purposes. Robin Millar begins this section by considering how practical work can be used to support pupils in gaining *scientific knowledge*. He considers some examples of practical work undertaken in schools and how, in different ways, they build a bridge between the 'world of objects' and the 'world of ideas'.
- Rod Watson, Anne Goldsworthy and Valerie Wood-Robinson recently completed a major research and development project (the ASE-King's College London Science Investigations in Schools (AKSIS) Project) into *investigative work* in science. Here, they discuss different kinds of investigations that pupils can undertake, extending the range from the restrictive view of 'experimentation as fair testing' that has resulted from earlier versions of the National Curriculum.
- ICT has the potential to make an enormous contribution to practical work. By reducing the time required for the lower-level skills of measuring and processing data, pupils can focus on the higher-level activities of analysis and interpretation. Laurence Rogers reviews some of the difficulties that pupils have in interpreting graphs of experimental data, and shows how data-logging can provide much support for pupils in collecting, representing and analysing data.
- Practical work presents risks, and safety is a key issue for science departments and teachers. Because of this awareness and the strict regulations that control health and safety, evidence shows serious accidents in science laboratories are, thankfully, relatively rare. Peter Borrows, director of CLEAPSS (Consortium of Local Education Authorities for the Provision of Science Services – a key source of information and advice about safety issues in science education), suggests how safety issues may be addressed by schools.
- Finally, Mick Nott and Jerry Wellington discuss how teachers may respond when 'things go wrong' in practical work. They illustrate how teachers' reactions in the classroom to what, at first sight, appear to be fairly mundane day-to-day occurrences in practical work, may draw on and reveal fundamental views about the nature of science.

6 Thinking about practical work
Robin Millar

Practical work in science teaching

Practical work is very widely used in teaching science at all levels. It is more than simply a common practice; many science teachers see it as constitutive of the business of science teaching – being a science teacher *means* working practically with pupils in a laboratory setting (Donnelly 1998). The danger in this is that practical work can come to be done unthinkingly, because it seems the 'natural' and 'right' thing to do, rather than being chosen and designed to achieve a specific learning outcome.

So, thinking about what practical work is for, and how it works, is an important exercise for any aspiring science teacher. 'Practical work in science', however, is a very broad category. It doesn't make much sense to ask what practical work is for. Different pieces of practical work are for different things. Instead, we need to ask what individual examples of practical work are for – so that we can tailor each practical task, and the associated classroom discussion, to maximize our chances of achieving the aims we had in mind.

Perhaps the commonest aim of practical tasks in science lessons is to help pupils learn some science content knowledge – to know something about how the world behaves, or understand a relationship, or receive an explanation of a phenomenon. Some practical tasks, on the other hand, are intended to teach pupils how to use a piece of equipment, or follow a standard procedure. And others aim help them think about how to design and carry out an investigation. In this chapter, I will be looking just at the first type: practical tasks that aim to teach some science knowledge.

Rather than talk in general terms, it may be more useful to look at a few examples of school science practical work, asking the questions: What is the learning purpose of this task? What do we expect pupils to learn by doing this practical task that they could not learn at all, or not so well, if they were merely told what happens?

Examples of practical work

Cooling and insulation

A class of 14- or 15-year-olds is investigating the rate at which hot water in a beaker cools, when different materials are wrapped around it. They take several beakers and wrap each in a different material (such as felt, cotton wool, plastic foam or bubble-wrap); they may also have one beaker which is left unwrapped for comparison

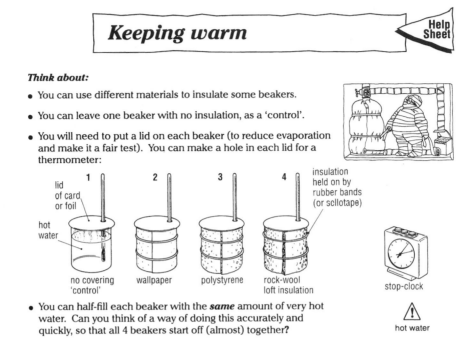

Keeping warm Help Sheet

Think about:

• You can use different materials to insulate some beakers.

• You can leave one beaker with no insulation, as a 'control'.

• You will need to put a lid on each beaker (to reduce evaporation and make it a fair test). You can make a hole in each lid for a thermometer:

• You can half-fill each beaker with the *same* amount of very hot water. Can you think of a way of doing this accurately and quickly, so that all 4 beakers start off (almost) together?

• What else must you do, to make it a *fair test*?

• You can take the temperature of each beaker, every 2 minutes, for 20–30 minutes. You can use a table like this:

	Time (mins):	0	2	4	6	8	10	12	14	16	18	20	22	24	26	28	30
Temperature (°C)	no insulation																
	wallpaper																
	polystyrene																
	loft insulation																

Figure 6.1 The cooling and insulation task

Source: Johnson, K., Adamson, S. and Williams, G. (1995). p. 81

purposes (Figure 6.1). Then they pour hot water into each beaker and measure the water temperature at 1 minute intervals for about 15–20 minutes. They make measurements of this sort on several beakers, either simultaneously or in sequence, and draw graphs to show how the temperature of the water in each varies with time.

What are the students supposed to learn from this practical activity? They are very unlikely to be expected to recall the detailed outcomes of their work – to remember, for instance, which material is better than another for keeping the water hot. Usually, in this activity, no effort is made to ensure that the thickness, even less the mass per unit area, of the materials is kept the same, so any comparison can only be of the available specimens of the various materials used. The students will, however, be expected to recall that all of the materials resulted in the water staying hot for longer than it does with no wrapping around the beaker, and to be able to explain this in terms of a model of energy (heat) moving spontaneously from the hot water in the beaker to the cooler surroundings and of the different materials slowing down this process by differing degrees. The practical activity as a whole is a kind of enactment of the scientific model of the thermal process involved: the actions undertaken, and the interpretation of the results obtained, make sense when viewed from within this particular mental model of thermal processes. The practical activity provides an opportunity for the students to think, and to talk and write, about this phenomenon from within the 'mental landscape', and using the terminology of an imagined model. What they do makes sense within this model. The model also determines how they interpret their observations. The primary purpose of the task is to help students to see thermal processes in this way, by working within a model and by talking the language of the model. This is a powerful means of consolidating ideas, because it involves *acting* and not merely thinking.

Green leaves

In the first example, the actual results are less important than the overall model. Some practical tasks, however, seem to depend more strongly on getting the 'right result'. Consider, for example, another class of 15-year-olds, carrying out some investigations on the green leaves of plants. A few days previously, the students have carefully wrapped some of the leaves of a growing geranium in aluminium foil, to exclude light from them. For the practical task, each group uses one wrapped leaf and one unwrapped leaf from the same plant. They cut discs from each leaf and, taking care to keep the discs from the two leaves separate, they extract the green colour from them by immersing them in boiling ethanol for several minutes. They then wash the leaf discs and place them on a spotting tile, where they can add a few drops of iodine solution to each (Figure 6.2). They should find that the discs from leaves which have been covered in foil are unaffected by the iodine, but those from leaves which were not wrapped turn dark blue – indicating that starch is present in these leaves.

What is the purpose of this practical task? Clearly it is intended to help the students to grasp the idea that green plants produce starch and that light is essential to this process. In other lessons on the same topic, they may carry out other practical tasks, involving plants which have been kept for some time in an atmosphere from which carbon dioxide has been removed, or using variegated leaves. These tasks will help them build up a model of a process (photosynthesis), in which carbon dioxide is converted into starch when light shines on the leaves of green plants.

So, does this practical task provide a reason (or part of the reason) for students to accept the scientific account of photosynthesis? To answer that, we need to ask: What would be the consequence of failing to obtain the expected outcome – of getting positive starch tests from leaves kept in the dark, or negative ones from leaves kept in the light? This, in fact, often happens in practice. However it is handled in the classroom, we *know* that it does not really pose a challenge to the accepted scientific account of events. Accepted scientific knowledge is supported by much more extensive evidence than this, collected by many scientists over a period of years. It has survived the scrutiny of the scientific community before becoming generally accepted. Further work based upon it has demonstrated the usefulness of the know-

Testing a leaf for starch

Most of the sugar made in the leaves of a plant is changed to starch.
You can test for this starch with iodine.
If the leaf turns blue-black with iodine then starch has been made.

- Dip a leaf into boiling water for about 1 minute to soften it.
- Turn off the Bunsen burner.
- Put the leaf into a test-tube of ethanol. Stand the test-tube in the hot water for about 10 minutes.
- Wash the leaf in cold water.
- Spread the leaf out flat on a petri dish and cover it with iodine. What colour does the leaf go?

h   Why was it important that you turn off the Bunsen burner when you were heating the ethanol?
i   What was the leaf like after you heated it in the ethanol?
j   Was there any starch in the leaf that you tested?

Into the light

If starch is present we can say that the leaf has been making food. Plan an investigation to see if a plant can make food without any light.

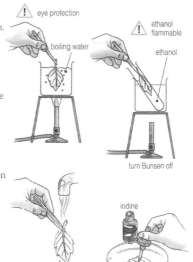

Figure 6.2 Testing leaves for starch

Source: Johnson, K., Adamson, S. and Williams, G. (1994). p.147

ledge in other contexts. Results obtained in a short time by novices, and using rudimentary equipment, cannot challenge this. We are not going to give up the accepted account of photosynthesis, or encourage pupils to hold an alternative view, just because some results in the school laboratory appear to conflict with what we would expect. The sensible response is to look for other ways to account for the deviation from the expected – in the quality of the apparatus and the level of expertise of the investigators.

Again, the function of this task is to help pupils to see the world in a certain way – a way that is known in advance to the teacher and to the expert community of which they are a representative. Newman (1982) makes the point succinctly:

> The young child is often thought of as a little scientist exploring the world and discovering the principles of its operation. We often forget that while the scientist is working on the border of human knowledge and is finding out things that nobody yet knows, the child is finding out precisely what everybody already knows.

> (Newman 1982: 26)

The pupil's real task is to produce the phenomenon as expected. Indeed, our best evidence that a pupil has carried out the task correctly and with sufficient care and skill is that they obtain the expected outcome.

If an unexpected outcome to this practical task does not challenge the accepted account, does obtaining the expected outcome in fact provide support for it? Logically, the answer would seem to be 'no'. If the failure of a practical task to display the expected outcome does not undermine the accepted account, how then can its success provide grounds for accepting it? In fact, obtaining the expected outcome, particularly after a long and complex series of operations, *does* make us more confident in the chain of reasoning that led to the prediction. In a complex world, failure to get the result we predict is endemic; success is noteworthy. The riskier (that is, the less likely) a prediction, the more impressed we are if it is borne out by events. It seems unlikely that it could turn out this way if the ideas on which the prediction is based are wholly wrong. In this way, it acts to persuade us that the prediction is based on sound knowledge.

The key challenge, then – and the real reason for carrying out practical tasks like testing the leaf – is to *produce the phenomenon*. The aim of the task is to get things to work as expected. This, as Hacking (1983) has also noted, is also the aim of much practical activity in the science research laboratory:

> To experiment is to create, produce, refine and stabilise phenomena. If phenomena were plentiful in nature, summer blackberries there just for the picking, it would be remarkable if experiments didn't work. But phenomena are hard to produce in any stable way. That is why I spoke of creating and not merely discovering phenomena. That is a long hard task. ... The pre-apprentice in the school laboratory is mostly acquiring or failing to acquire the ability to know when the experiment is working.
>
> (Hacking 1983: 230)

In a teaching context, producing the phenomenon is a kind of ritualized display of the power of the scientific knowledge involved. The event implicitly proclaims: 'See, we (that is, the scientific community as embodied in the teacher) know so much about this that we can get this event to happen, reliably and regularly, before your very eyes!' The less likely the event, the more powerful this is. Practical tasks carried out by the students are really 'auto-demonstrations', so they carry the even stronger implicit message that 'Our understanding, and consequent control of materials and events, is so good that I (the teacher) don't even have to do it for you – you can do it for yourself.'

Metals and acid

As a final example, consider a group of pupils carrying out a series of observations on the reactions of metals with dilute acids. They have been given samples of magnesium, zinc, iron and copper, and a supply of dilute hydrochloric acid. They are to add samples of each metal in turn to a small sample of acid in a test tube, to observe what happens and to put the metals into order according to the vigour of the reaction.

What is the point in doing this practically, as opposed, for example, to telling pupils the outcome? Clearly, there is a phenomenon to produce, but its production, in contrast to the previous example, requires little expertise. The outcome, especially of the reaction with magnesium, is a memorable event which pupils may remember and recall. This function of practical tasks, of providing a memorable episode, also applies to the cooling water and green leaf tasks discussed above. It is an important element of the justification of such tasks, as there is some evidence that our memories store whole episodes rather than separate ideas or principles (see White 1988: ch. 3). This can, however, be a mixed blessing, as often the important learning point is associated with the *explanation* of the event and not with its surface features, yet these may be what are retained in memory.

Does the task, however, do what it appears to do? That is, does it provide a warrant for accepting the order of reactivity of metals that the pupils will later be expected to recall? In my description, I carefully omitted aluminium from the list of metals provided, as many teachers would in practice. This is because we know its behaviour in this reaction is not consistent with its place in the reactivity series – for other reasons which would be a distraction if mentioned at this point in the teaching sequence. So the task is simplified, to ensure the desired outcome. What if aluminium were provided? Then the observations would not be allowed to dictate the conclusion about order of reactivity, and instead, a form of special pleading would take place, to explain why aluminium should go higher in the series than its behaviour in this reaction would suggest. But surely that also undermines the significance, as evidence, of all the observations actually made? How, logically, could we rule out any other piece of special pleading that would alter the observed order of reactivity? The case of aluminium shows us that these observations, in fact, provide no conclusive evidence about the order of reactivity of these metals.

What this practical does do, however, is to teach learners what a metal–acid reaction is like, and provide some concrete referents for ideas like 'gas evolved', 'vigorous reaction', 'less vigorous reaction', and so on. Imagine trying to explain any of these ideas, using words alone, to a person who had never seen an actual example. Of course it will be easier to communicate the idea by showing the real thing. What is going on here is teaching by ostension (what Wittgenstein (1953) calls 'ostensive definition'). Pupils are learning new ideas by being shown examples of them, rather than by being given formal definitions. All of us, and especially young children, learn much of what we know in this sort of way (see Kuhn (1977) for a discussion with some examples). Many practical tasks have this function – to display the meaning of terms and ideas that could not be grasped from an account using words and pictures alone.[1]

Supporting the learning of scientific knowledge: how practical work works

One point that is implicit in all of the discussion above is that the purpose of much practical work in science is to build a bridge – between the realm of objects and observable properties on the one hand, and the realm of ideas on the other. If we do practical work 'because science is a practical subject', then it is almost equally true that we do it 'because science is a theoretical subject'. The three tasks discussed above aim, in different ways, to help students make links between things they can see and handle, and ideas they may entertain which might account for their observations.

In the first example (hot water cooling), the task invites students to 'see it this way' (Ogborn *et al.* 1996: ch. 7) – by using a particular model to view phenomena. The second also expects them to see reality through the 'spectacles' of a model, but here the model is less directly related to the objects and events observed than in the cooling water task. The priority is to *produce a phenomenon* which the model predicts. The third communicates the meaning of general ideas and concepts by providing several concrete examples, saying in effect 'this is an example of an X' – as only by seeing examples can students come to appreciate what 'an X' is, and begin to use the term in their own description and discussion of phenomena.

Practical work that is intended to support the teaching and learning of scientific knowledge is best understood, and evaluated, as a communication strategy – as a means of augmenting what can be achieved by word, picture and gesture. Parallels with the activity of real scientists in research laboratories are unhelpful and may be misleading. Exploring the unknown is not the same as communicating the known. For this reason, practical work in the school laboratory does not have to be 'authentic', or similar to our idea of what 'real' science is like. This is not an appropriate criterion for judging a practical task. A good practical task is one which communicates effectively the ideas it sets out to communicate.[2]

Notes

1   Even seeing a video recording of an event is often a less-clear communication than seeing the real thing, where the details can be more clearly and directly perceived, and where the range of senses employed can be wider.

2   The ideas in this chapter are discussed at greater length in Millar (1998), from which the three examples of practical activities have been extracted.

References

Donnelly, J. (1998) 'The place of the laboratory in secondary science teaching', *International Journal of Science Education* 20(5): 585–96.

Hacking, I. (1983) *Representing and Intervening,* Cambridge: Cambridge University Press.

Johnson, K., Adamson, S. and Williams, G. (1994) *Spotlight Science 9*, Cheltenham: Stanley Thornes.

Johnson, K., Adamson, S. and Williams, G. (1995) *Spotlight Science, Teachers' Guide 9*, Cheltenham: Stanley Thornes.

Kuhn, T. S. (1977) 'Second thoughts on paradigms', in T. S. Kuhn *The Essential Tension,* Chicago: University of Chicago Press, pp. 293–319.

Millar, R. (1998) 'Rhetoric and reality: what practical work in science education is *really* for', in J. Wellington (ed.) *Practical Work in School Science: Which Way Now?,* London: Routledge.

Newman, D. (1982) 'Perspective-taking versus content in understanding lies', *Quarterly Newsletter of the Laboratory of Comparative Human Cognition* 4: 26–9. (Cited in Rogoff, B. (1991) 'The joint socialisation of development by young children and adults', in P. Light, S. Sheldon and M. Woodhead (eds) *Learning to Think*, London: Routledge, pp. 67–96)

Ogborn, J., Kress, G., Martins, I. and McGillicuddy, K. (1996) *Explaining Science in the Classroom,* Buckingham: Open University Press.

White, R. T. (1988) *Learning Science,* Oxford: Blackwell.

Wittgenstein, L. (1953) *Philosophical Investigations,* Oxford: Oxford University Press.

7 What is not fair with investigations?

Rod Watson, Anne Goldsworthy and Valerie Wood-Robinson

Introduction

A burglar prises open the front door, and steps onto a pressure pad switch that should set off a burglar alarm. Does all hell break loose, alarms flash and buzzers wake up the neighbours? Alas no! The problem is that the burglar was not being 'fair'. The pressure pad switch was made at school and, in order to carry out a fair test, the switch was tested using the *same person* each time. Unfortunately, this person was one of the larger lads in the class, not like the burglar, who was distinctly lightweight. The burglar had failed to realize that, in order to give the occupants a fair chance, he would have to put on a lot of weight!

Although this scenario seems distinctly unlikely, it does illustrate a point: there are different kinds of scientific investigations and not all of them are fair tests. What is important is to know that the switch works reliably with burglars of different sizes. Applying fair testing procedures to this investigation was not appropriate.

Other examples that are difficult to fit into the fair testing model are:

- ecological investigations where controlling variables is often difficult if not impossible;
- explorations where pupils simply observe something changing over time such as a bean growing on blotting paper;
- classifying substances as solid, liquids or gases;
- chemical analysis;
- exploring temperature changes with change of state, on heating ice through water to steam;
- measuring lung capacity;
- fault diagnosis in an electrical circuit.

The Third International Mathematics and Science Study (TIMSS) data (Harmon *et al.* 1997) show that considerable progress has been made in England and Wales in teaching fair testing investigations. In some investigations, however, procedures of fair testing, such as predicting the effect of one variable on another whilst controlling other variables, are inappropriate.

Teachers are concerned that the National Curriculum has led to a restricted set of investigations and that some kinds of investigations are not adequately represented in schemes of work used in schools. Fair testing investigations dominate to the exclusion of other valuable work. Furthermore, the inappropriate application of fair testing procedures distorts other kinds of investigations when they are included:

> School science is at present enslaved by the perceived need to contrive a situation in which pupils' investigations can be squeezed into the 'fair test' strait jacket.
>
> (Tytler and Swatton 1992)

This chapter proposes a framework of six different kinds of investigations and these can be used both to describe the type carried out and to provide a basis for selecting what should be done. The chapter is based on an article published in *School Science Review* (Watson *et al.* 1999).

Categorizing investigations

As part of the work of the ASE-King's College London Science Investigations in Schools (AKSIS) project, we have considered hundreds of investigations and carried out a structural analysis of them in order to develop descriptions of six different kinds. This chapter draws on our work with three focus groups of teachers (thirty-two teachers of Key Stage 2 and 3 children) and responses of over 1,000 teachers in a national questionnaire survey.

In the focus groups, we asked each teacher to keep a detailed record of their planning, implementation and reflections about one of their investigations which they each carried out with one class. Teachers looked at one another's investigations and were asked to identify the features of the practical work that allowed them to be classified as investigations, or other practical work. There was a fairly strong consensus as to what was meant by an investigation and this was used to formulate a description of investigations used in the national questionnaire survey:

- In investigative work, pupils have to make their own decisions either individually or in groups: they are given some autonomy in how the investigation is carried out.
- An investigation must involve pupils in using investigational procedures such as planning, measuring, observing, analysing data and evaluating procedures. Not all investigations will allow pupils to use every kind of investigational procedure, and they may vary in the amount of autonomy given to pupils at different stages of the investigative process.

The structural analysis, used to differentiate kinds of investigation in this paper, could also be used to analyse more closed, practical activities which involve little pupil autonomy. The focus in this paper, however, is on what teachers in England and Wales understand by investigations and how the varieties of investigations can be described.

Many previous categorizations of investigations have been for the purposes of teaching (e.g. Lock 1990; Watson *et al.* 1990) or assessment (e.g. Gott and Murphy 1987; Ruiz-Primo and Shavelson 1995; Swain 1991; Taylor 1990) and so have concentrated on pedagogical characteristics that affect pupil performance (Song and Black 1991; 1992). Pedagogical characteristics include: the aims of the investigation, whether it is open or closed, whether it is a part investigation or a whole investigation, its length, its context, its place in the curriculum, individual or group investigations, pupils' response and the level of teacher support. These characteristics are not discussed in this chapter. The purpose of the categorization described here is different. It is to represent the range of investigations to which pupils are exposed and to consider whether this range is adequate in terms of learning experiences of science and whether it is based on the inherent characteristics of investigations, and not on their means of delivery. This paper describes six kinds of investigations which have different structural characteristics.

Kinds of investigations

The six kinds of investigations proposed in this paper are:

- Classifying and identifying
- Fair testing
- Pattern seeking
- Exploring
- Investigating models
- Making things or developing systems.

The first three categories have been derived from a classification suggested by Ruiz-Primo and Shavelson (1995). Three further categories have been added: investigating models which appears in much current science education literature (e.g. Roth 1995) as 'authentic' or 'open-inquiry' investigations; technological investigations which involve pupils in using scientific knowledge or procedures to make things or develop systems, and a group of investigations which we call 'exploring'. The kinds of investigations are described below.

Classifying and identifying

Classifying is a process of arranging a large range of phenomena, either objects or events, into manageable sets. Identifying is a process of recognizing objects and events as members of particular sets, possibly new and unique sets, and allocating names to them. Classification and identification both involve pupils identifying features, tests or procedures that discriminate between things or processes that are being studied.

Scientific classification is carried out for particular scientific purposes. Biologists recognize patterns of similarities and differences in the characteristics of the diversity of living things and arrange the organisms in hierarchical sets. Classification is a process which allows biologists to generalize and it provides a framework from which to predict structures and behaviour. Similarly, chemists classify chemicals in order to highlight chemical characteristics that both enable chemicals to be grouped and patterns of behaviour of a chemical within a particular group to be predicted.

Identification involves recognizing a specimen as a unique example of a particular set. For example, in qualitative chemical analysis, students have to use their knowledge and understanding of science in order to be able to select appropriate tests to apply to an unknown chemical. The basic idea is to change the chemical in such a way that it exhibits characteristics that are unique to that chemical by using tests to successively discriminate between chemicals. Standard sets of procedures for identifying common chemicals are available in texts, but the application of even standard techniques requires a fairly high level of understanding of chemical concepts in order for them to be applied meaningfully. When pupils are given less guidance about what procedures to use, a higher level of knowledge and understanding is required.

Fair testing

Examples of classifying and identifying investigations are:

- What is this chemical?
- How can we group these invertebrates?
- What kind of water weed is this?
- Classify objects according to whether they are conductors or non-conductors of electricity.

These investigations are concerned with observing and exploring relations between variables. The emphasis is on identifying one (or more) independent variable(s) to be manipulated independently of other factors which must be controlled, for a 'fair test'. Systematic changes in the independent variable are compared with changes in the outcome, or dependent variable. The investigation involves developing appropriate procedures to manipulate, observe, measure or control a number of variables.

Gott and Murphy (1987) classify the APU investigations into three types, all concerned with relations between variables: 'Decide which … ', 'Find a way to … ' and 'Find the effect of …'. All three are classified here as fair testing because they are structurally similar and involve manipulating the independent variable (e.g. area of shoe in contact with the ground) and measuring the effect on the dependent variable (e.g. the slipperiness of shoes), whilst controlling other variables (e.g. kind of surface).

Examples of fair testing investigations are:

- What conditions do woodlice prefer ? (choice chamber experiment)
- Which parachute will hit the ground first?
- What is the effect of concentration of acid on the rate of reaction of magnesium with an acid?
- How do the number of layers of insulation around a container affect how much the water in the container cools down?

Pattern seeking

These investigations often involve observing and recording natural events as they occur. They have many similarities to fair testing investigations but have three significant differences: the extent to which variables can be manipulated or controlled; the way in which the investigation is initiated; and the increased importance of selecting a suitable sample size in order to account for natural variation within samples. In pattern seeking, the dependent variable is identified first, i.e. an effect is noticed and the investigation is structured around finding a possible cause for the effect. These investigations are common in ecological studies. For example, a pattern seeking investigation might explore the factors affecting the size of anemones on a seashore. One possibility might be the size of pools in which they live. A reasonably-sized sample of large and small pools could be selected and the sizes of the anemones measured. In this situation, variables which may be difficult to control might be the shape of the pools, the distance up a beach, and the quantity and types of other organisms living in the pools. It is, therefore, difficult to isolate the independent and dependent variables and a more holistic approach, in which observations and recordings of several variables are made, may be needed. It is still important to identify variables to observe and measure but the investigator has less control over them and has to use values of the variable that are available naturally.

Another type of investigation involving pattern seeking is a survey. Surveys are often used in areas such as genetics, epidemiology, psychology, sociology, meteorology, astronomy and ecology. As in other kinds of investigation, the aim is to compare data sets to identify patterns of relationships and propose causal links. For example, the relationship between smoking and lung diseases has been established by epidemiological studies based on surveys.

Examples of pattern seeking investigations are:

- Is pupil fitness related to exercise habits? Carry out a survey to find out.
- What conditions do woodlice prefer? (ecological sampling)
- Do more daisy plants grow on a football pitch or on the field that is not used for football?
- What factors affect the acidity of rain water?

Exploring

Pupils either make careful observations of objects or events, or make a series of observations of a natural phenomenon occurring over time. As they carry out their observations, they make decisions about exactly what to observe and the number and frequency of observations. Not all explorations are scientific. What determines whether an exploration is scientific is its purpose. An example of exploration is observation of the development of frog-spawn over time. This exploration could simply lead to a description of part of the life cycle of a frog. In the future, pupils would come to model patterns in the life cycles of different animals. Alternatively the focus could be on the relation between the changes undergone by the tadpole and how it is adapted to move in and out of the water at different stages. Other explorations may be to study the movement of leaves of a plant over several days, or to observe what happens when different liquids are added together.

Examples of exploring investigations are:

- What happens when different liquids are added together?
- What do woodlice eat? (by observation over time)
- How do plants get their water? (by observing plants in coloured water)
- Are the small woodlice babies, or are they a different kind from the big ones? (observe whether the 'babies' grow/develop over time)

Investigating models

A fifth category contains investigations that explore models. Scientists develop theories that model aspects of the natural and physical world, for example, the theory of plate tectonics models how the surface of the earth behaves, or Darwin's theory of evolution models how species evolve over time. Similarly, students develop their own models to explain both everyday phenomena and phenomena that they meet in the science laboratory: a student may see wood burning to ash and develop a model that wood is transmuted by heat into ash.

This category of investigations is distinct from the previous four categories, in that it incorporates a stage where pupils have to decide what evidence should be collected in order to test the ideas embedded in such mental models. Testing models may lead on to one or all of the preceding types of investigations, but which approach is chosen depends on decisions made about what would count as evidence to test the model. For example, many students believe that when copper is burnt it is transmuted into carbon. How could a transmutation model of combustion be tested? What are the alternatives? How could they be evaluated? Gain in weight of the copper is consistent with the accepted view of oxidation but is also consistent with the transmutation model: copper has been transmuted into carbon that is a different substance and weighs more. Loss in volume of the air is consistent with the accepted scientific model but could also be explained as the heating process transmuting air to an unreactive gas with a smaller volume. The discussion would then have to move on to what other evidence would distinguish between the models. The process of testing models can give pupils insight into the relationship between evidence and scientific models, in a way that other kinds of investigations often do not.

Examples of investigating models are:

- How can the cooling of a hot body, insulated by layers of material, be modelled? How can the model be tested?

continued on next page

- Observe different kinds of pollen through a microscope. Use the observations to propose models for how the pollen is dispersed. Devise investigations to test your models.
- Why do elephants throw water over themselves?
- Why do the following two lines appear to be different lengths? Devise an experiment to test your ideas.

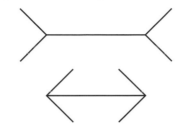

Making things or developing systems

In these technological investigations, pupils design an artefact or system to meet a human need. Scientific investigations use scientific knowledge and procedures to answer questions or solve problems. Some technological investigations have a high scientific knowledge or a strong emphasis on scientific procedures and so can be classified as scientific investigations. For example, making a 'pressure pad' switch involves a working knowledge of an electrical circuit and 'constructing a weighing machine out of elastic bands' involves an understanding of some of the procedures of science in order to calibrate it.

Examples of making things or developing systems are:

- Can you find a way to design a pressure pad switch for a burglar alarm?
- How could you make a weighing machine out of elastic bands?
- Devise a way to determine the water content of an apple.
- Make an efficient model water mill.

Assessing different kinds of investigations

Since the publication of the original article on which this chapter is based, a new version of the National Curriculum for Science for England has been published (DfEE 1999). This is intended to reflect calls from teachers and science educators for a wider variety of kinds of investigations. For this reason, investigations have been renamed 'scientific enquiry' which is meant to be a term which can include the variety of the kinds of investigation described above. Within the new programme of study, more kinds of 'scientific enquiry' are explicitly mentioned. This change in emphasis is reflected in the new level descriptions for the attainment targets. For example, compare the following statements at level 4 in the 1995 and 1999 versions of the National Curriculum:

> Pupils recognise the need for fair tests, describing, or showing in the way they perform their task, how to vary one factor whilst keeping others the same.
>
> (DfE 1995: 50)

> Where appropriate, they describe, or show in the way they perform their task, how to vary one factor while keeping others the same.
>
> (DfEE 1999: 75)

The key difference lies in the words 'where appropriate'. The implication is that in assessing the level of achievement of pupils in a scientific enquiry, it is not necessary that pupils fulfil all the requirements for a particular level descriptor for every enquiry. So, for example, level 4 can be achieved in a specific enquiry, without involving fair testing. What is important is that 'in their own investigative work, they decide an appropriate approach to answer a question' (DfEE 1999: 75).

The way in which the level descriptors can be applied to different kinds of scientific enquiries is illustrated in Figure 7.1 (on next page) using an example of a student's write-up of a 'Making things or developing systems' investigation.

In order to assess this work it has to be matched against one of the level descriptors for attainment target 1: scientific enquiry. The closest match is with level 5 and the Table 7.1 (on page 69) analyses the extent of this match.

Overall the student is just failing to reach level 5 and so a similar exercise is needed to try to match the write-up with the descriptor for level 4. One thing that is clear from the analysis is that it would be very difficult for any one scientific enquiry to match all of the components of level 5: very different activities would be needed to assess whether pupils can 'describe how experimental evidence and creative thinking have been combined to provide a scientific explanation' or whether they can 'identify key factors to be considered' in a fair test.

Conclusion

This chapter has introduced a way of categorizing different kinds of investigations. The method of categorization is useful in discussing the balance of different kinds of scientific enquiry in the curriculum. For example, Harlen (2000: 80–9) has analysed the demands of different kinds of investigations and related them to child development. She uses this analysis to propose the kinds of investigations that are appropriate to use with children of different ages. A way of categorizing investigations is also useful in developing teaching and learning strategies appropriate for different kinds of investigations (Goldsworthy et al. 2000). In this chapter, it has been shown how it can be used to match achievements of students with level descriptors for the National Curriculum for Science in England. The fact that only some of the components of the level descriptors can be met in one kind of enquiry means that, for a balanced curriculum, a variety of kinds of enquiry is needed.

The problem set by the teacher

Design a method to find out the percentage of an apple that is water. This method will be used to study the water content of different kinds of apples.

A student's write-up

The percentage of water in an apple
Introduction

The cells in apples contain water. If apples are kept in a dry place the skin goes crinkly as the cells lose water. This takes a long time and often the apples go bad before they are completely dry. To find out the percentage of water in an apple, we need to find a way of drying an apple quickly. We can weigh the apple before drying and then again after drying to find the weight of water in it.

The skin of an apple protects it and reduces water loss. One way of making the apple dry faster is to cut up so as to remove the protection of the skin. Drying apples can also be speeded up by placing them in the sunshine or in a hot place.

When apples are cut open they turn brown. This is because the air reacts with the apple. This might affect the weight, so when we are drying the apple, we will need to observe any other changes apart from water loss.

Method

Pieces of the apple were dried in different ways, as shown in the table. The results were collected in the table.

Table of results

	Trial 1	Trial 2	Trial 3	Trial 4
Size of piece	1/8th of apple	1/16th of apple	1/16th of apple	1/16th of apple
Weight before drying (g)	1.87	0.92	0.90	0.95
Method of drying	On window sill	On window sill	In oven at 100^oC	In oven at 200^oC
Temperature (^oC)	21	21	21	21
Weight after 30 min (g)	1.83	0.88	0.72	0.67
Weight after 1 day (g)	1.84	0.87	0.11	0.07
Weight after 1 week (g)	1.67	0.63	0.10	0.07
Other observations	Went brown then mouldy after 1 week	Went brown then mouldy after 1 week	Went brown	Went brown after 30 mins. and after one day looked black and burnt

Conclusion

A good way of finding out the percentage water in an apple is as follows:

1. Cut the apple into 1/16ths.
2. Weigh the piece (A).
3. Put the apple in the oven at 110^oC for 5h.
4. Weigh the piece again after 5h (B).
5. Work out the mass of water lost from the slice (A-B).
6. Work out the percentage of water (B-A) x 100 / (A)

Figure 7.1 A scientific enquiry to assess

Source: Adapted from Goldsworthy, Watson, Wood-Robinson, 2000, p.117.

Table 7.1 Does the enquiry match level 5?

Description of level 5	Comments related to the apple enquiry
Pupils describe how experimental evidence and creative thinking have been combined to provide a scientific explanation.	Not applicable. This enquiry is about making a system for doing something.
When they try to answer a scientific question, they identify an appropriate approach.	The write-up matches this criterion.
They select from a range of sources of information.	The enquiry began with a search of various biology books to find relevant information. This was used to write the 'introduction' and has influenced the design of the enquiry. This criterion is matched.
When the investigation involves a fair test, they can identify key factors to be considered.	This is not relevant.
Where appropriate, they make predictions based on their scientific knowledge and understanding.	This is not appropriate.
They select apparatus for a range of tasks and plan to use it effectively.	This criterion is matched.
They make a series of observations, comparisons or measurements with precision appropriate to the task. They begin to repeat observations and measurements and to offer simple explanations for differences they encounter. They record observations and measurements systematically and, where appropriate, present line graphs. They draw conclusions consistent with the evidence and begin to relate these to scientific knowledge and understanding.	These sentences are concerned with the sufficiency of the data collected. Insufficient data were collected to support the student's conclusions about the size of the pieces of apple used, the temperature chosen and the time of drying. There is no explanation about why certain conditions were rejected: it would have been better if the student had stated that 200 °C was too hot as this turned some of the apple to carbon. The student went some way towards meeting these criteria but has not yet achieved it.
They make practical suggestions about how their working methods could be improved.	No evaluation of how the scientific enquiry was carried out. There needed to be an exploration of the level of confidence that could be placed on the conclusions reached and what additional data would have provided more confidence for the conclusions.
They use appropriate scientific language and conventions to communicate quantitative and qualitative data.	This criterion was met.

Acknowledgements

This chapter is based on the work of the AKSIS Project (**A**ssociation for Science Education – **K**ing's College London **S**cience **I**nvestigations in **S**chools Project) which was funded by the Wellcome Trust.

References

Department for Education (1995) *Science in the National Curriculum,* London: HMSO.

Department for Education and Employment (1999) *Science: The National Curriculum for England,* London, HMSO.

Goldsworthy, A., Watson, J. R. and Wood-Robinson, V. (2000) *Investigations: Developing Understanding,* Hatfield: Association for Science Education.

Gott, R. and Murphy, P. (1987) *Assessing Investigations at Ages 13 and 15, Science Report for Teachers 9,* London: DES.

Harlen, W. (2000) *Teaching, Learning and Assessing Science 5–12,* third edition, London: Paul Chapman Publishing Ltd.

Harmon, M., Smith, T. A., Martin, M. O., Kelly, D. L., Beaton, A. E., Mullis, I. V. S., Gonzalez, E. J. and Orpwood, G. (1997) *Performance Assessment in IEA's Third International Mathematics and Science Study (TIMSS),* Boston: Center for the Study of Testing, Evaluation and Educational Policy.

Lock, R. (1990) 'Open-ended problem-solving investigations: What do we mean and how can we use them?', *School Science Review* 71(256): 63-72.

Roth, W.-M.(1995) *Authentic School Science: Knowing and Learning in Open-Inquiry Science Laboratories,* London: Kluwer Academic Publishers, ch. 2.

Ruiz-Primo, M. A. and Shavelson, R. (1995) 'Rhetoric and reality in science performance assessment: an update', paper presented at American Educational Research Association, San Francisco.

Song, J. and Black, P. J. (1991) 'The effects of task contexts on pupils' performance in science process skills', *International Journal of Science Education* 13(1): 49–58.

Song, J. and Black, P. J. (1992) 'The effects of concept requirements of task contexts on pupils' performance in control of variables', *International Journal of Science Education* 14(1): 83–93.

Swain, J. R. L. (1991) 'The nature and assessment of scientific explorations in the classroom', *School Science Review* 72(260): 65–77.

Taylor, R. M.(1990) 'The National Curriculum: a study to compare levels of attainment with data from the APU science surveys', *School Science Review* 72(258): 31–7.

Tytler, R. and Swatton, P. (1992) 'Critique of AT1 based on case studies of students' investigations', *School Science Review* 74(266): 21–35.

Watson, J.R., Black, P.J., Fairbrother, R.W., Jones, A. and Simon, S. (1990) *The Open-ended Work in Science Project: A Task Framework,* London: King's College London.

Watson, J. R., Wood-Robinson, V. and Goldsworthy, A. (1999) 'What is not fair about investigations', *School Science Review* 80(292): 101–6.

8 Data-logging tools for science investigations

Laurence Rogers

Introduction

Of the information handling technologies, data-logging has a special role in science, providing a valuable range of tools for 'hands-on' experience in the school laboratory. At face value, data-logging is merely an electronic method of gathering and recording physical measurements; electrical sensors provide signals which are calibrated and recorded by a computer system. However, the chief value of data-logging to practical science resides not in the process of *automated data-gathering* but in the processes of *analysing and interpreting the data*. This chapter illustrates how investigations can set the context for this sort of activity and considers some of the decisions the teacher has to make when designing it.

The benefits of data-logging

In designing the tasks and framing the context for data-logging, it is necessary to have a clear vision of the expected benefits. The distinction between the properties and potential benefits of data-logging has been discussed elsewhere (Rogers and Wild 1996). Properties are not benefits; they have to be turned into benefits by suitable application. For example, one property of data-logging is to provide 'real-time' reporting where the measurements are presented on the screen continuously while the experiment is in progress. This has no benefit if pupils passively watch the computer gathering the data; indeed this is a 'turn-off' (Newton 1997). The benefit comes from making immediate observations of the data, asking questions about it, looking for links with other information, making comparisons, making predictions and looking for trends. In short, the benefits depend upon the quality of the thinking about the data. Teachers are skilled in prompting pupils to think, and pupils' interpretation of graphs presented with software is an important context for exercising this skill (Barton 1997).

Skills for interpreting graphs

The graph, being a major feature of most data-logging activities, merits close examination as a tool for investigative practical work (Rogers 1995). Experience has shown that, whereas most pupils may become proficient at the reading and plotting of graphs, they are much less successful at interpretation (Janvier 1978). The problem will be discussed by considering several levels of sophistication, and the potential benefits of software. At the simplest level, the graph shape may be viewed qualitatively, identifying trends and interesting features. Progressing to a quantitative treatment, information is obtained from the graph, reading values, performing simple calculations on coordinates, and so on. Beyond this, progression may involve attaching meaning, making generalizations and applying understanding.

Viewing the graph

The most obvious feature of a graph is its shape. Potentially, the shape can immediately convey information in a qualitative manner without concerning the observer with unnecessary detail. Pupils can gain a quick overview of what may be going on in an experiment; they can 'see' gradual or sudden changes, continuity or discontinuity, and can select and give attention to particular interesting features. It is a valuable characteristic of data-logging software that the graph can be built up as the experiment proceeds which makes it more easily associated with the phenomenon it represents.

A generally weak aspect of graphwork tends to be pupils' understanding and use of scale markings. Errors frequently occur when a coordinate does not coincide with a scale marking or grid line. The effect of scales on the shape of a graph also reveals weak understanding. Unfortunately, the time needed to plot a graph manually does not encourage the pupil to repeat the exercise if an unsuitable choice of scale is made. This is a clear case of where the computer can offer distinct advantages. Not only is the plotting accurate, but the speed of plotting enables graphs to be treated dynamically and interactively.

Reading values

Surveys have revealed that pupils tend to find difficulty in reading analogue scales correctly (Swatton and Taylor 1994). The interpolation of values between scale markings, and an understanding of sub-divisions and decimal places are typical casualties. The problem appears to be compounded when two or more readings need to be compared and used to calculate quantities such as gradients and intervals. Using software, reading and calculating data from graphs becomes an almost trivial activity, merely requiring the pupil to manoeuvre a pair of cross hairs to read off values which are displayed in a panel on the screen. This type of facility may be used to gain automatic readouts of coordinates, time intervals, differences, ratios, gradients, areas, mean values, maxima and minima. In the traditional context of graphing skills, it may seem an abuse to deny pupils opportunities to perform these tasks manually. However, by reducing these skills to a low level, higher order skills may flourish, empowering pupils to think more about the science. This has an important impact on investigative and problem-solving approaches to practical science, where service skills such as measurement should be effortless and as automatic as possible (Underwood 1990: 30).

Time-dependent data are the most common in pupils' experience of school science. As a variable, time has a special quality; pupils have a natural 'feel' for it through a sequence of events or changes in other variables. Sometimes, so strong is the feeling of a schedule of events, pupils tend to interpret data in a 'pointwise' fashion rather than in terms of periods of elapsed time; they attach more significance to the time coordinates than the intervals between them (Leinhardt *et al.* 1990: 37). Software can compensate for this and help strengthen the notion of intervals of time by allowing pupils to choose an arbitrary origin for time measurements, and it can also exclude errors in reading intervals correctly.

Describing variables

To describe a variable, pupils need both to obtain information from a graph and also attach meaning to that information. It was noted above that qualitative descriptions may be based on the shape of a graph without any explicit reading of data values. Software can provide useful assistance in making the types of measurements which benefit *quantitative* descriptions, for example, finding maximum, minimum and mean values, the difference or ratio between two values or the rate of change in a variable.

The quantity of data contained in a computer graph naturally lends itself to the study of connections, patterns, and trends in the data. The visual aspect of the graph draws attention to these more effectively than numbers in tables. Indeed, there is evidence that pupils are distracted by obvious numerical patterns in tabulated results, and, instead of making generalized descriptions, describe patterns such as sequences of odd and even numbers, or multiples and differences (Austin *et al.* 1991: 28). Tabulated data encourage this type of stepwise analysis, which misses the continuity in the behaviour of a variable. Even with a graph, when asked to draw a line through their data, pupils often attempt to join successive points with straight lines, again illustrating this stepwise perception. Software can help to move pupils' thinking towards a continuous view of the data by plotting a best-fit curve which emphasizes the underlying trend.

However, even when pupils focus appropriate attention on the shape of the graph, this does not necessarily result in descriptions of a variable; instead, some pupils describe the graph line in terms of its shape, direction or curvature in isolation from what the axes represent (Austin *et al.* 1991: 29). A similar geometrical viewpoint is revealed when pupils interpret a graph as the actual picture of a situation, for example, going up and down hills in distance–time graphs (Leinhardt *et al.* 1990: 39).

Much of this evidence suggests that the process of obtaining scientific descriptions of variables is fraught with distractions. One approach to deflecting attention from numbers, points and geometrical properties is to use software tools for manipulating the data, providing a variety of alternative views and data presentations. For example, data may be smoothed to reduce the effect of 'noise' and emphasize the trend.

Relating variables

Identifying and describing a trend or pattern in the behaviour of a variable marks an important level of sophistication in interpreting graphs, because it indicates a generalization beyond the actual items of data presented. The majority of graphs generated by data-logging software typically show the time-dependence of one or more variables, so the description of a pattern implicitly relates the physical variables to the time variable.

Describing the relationship between variables in a generalized manner is the key to developing scientific ideas from the graph, but pupils often find this difficult. Sometimes their difficulties are linguistic; they are unsure of the type of expression required. As previously indicated, they may find it easier to use geometrical or numerical descriptions rather than referring to the physical variables. Their terminology may lack precision; the use of vague terms such as 'goes up' instead of 'increases rapidly' might imply that they are perceiving variables separately and are not consciously relating them. Even though linguistic considerations may disguise pupils' understanding, it is still a big step for pupils to see the graph as showing the relationship between two variables (Bell *et al.* 1987). Pupils need a teaching strategy which helps them ask appropriate questions and gives them practice in appropriate skills. The tools they need to support this are readily provided in the software.

The shape of a graph gives vital information about the relationship between the variables. A straight line or a curve have distinctive properties which provide insight and understanding of that relationship. There are many alternatives for exploring those properties, but they can involve excessive repetition. The computer's capacity for repetition and multiple calculation can be exploited, so that software tools can make this type of exploratory activity viable and worthwhile.

Making predictions

When a pupil has succeeded in elucidating a generalized relationship between two variables, it will not necessarily indicate that one physically influences the other, but it should make possible interpolation and extrapolation to predict new data values. Thus the interpretation can be put to the test by using it to predict new values. Software tools, such as best-fit curves, support pupils in developing confidence in the concept that the description transcends the items of collected data and enables them to identify values between and beyond these items.

Similarly, pupils might predict data and descriptions of the graph shape for new compound variables, for example, predicting a velocity–time graph from a distance–time graph, or a power–voltage graph from a current–voltage graph. Software provides a variety of convenient calculating facilities for generating new data from the collected data, allowing pupils to test their prediction.

Translating description into mathematical forms

A further stage of refinement of interpreting skill involves translating the relationship into an algebraic representation. Trends may be classified and described more precisely by association with a mathematical function, but unless the pattern is linear, the manual method of identifying the appropriate function usually depends upon transforming one variable and replotting it in the hope of obtaining a linear graph. This process can be convoluted, but software offers a number of alternative strategies:

- Choosing a suitable function to linearize the data;
- Simulating a function, comparing it with the graph of the data, and altering the parameters of the function until the best match is obtained;
- Using curve fitting techniques.

Software curve-fitting facilities generate very attractive smooth curves, but often their mathematical description consists of complex polynomial expressions. In a version called 'Trial Fit' (Rogers 1999), the pupil can choose from three simple general forms of mathematical curve, and experiment to find out the quality of the fit. The tool is designed so that the pupil is allowed to make a judgement of this quality. The virtue of restricting the choice is that pupils might readily associate these forms with simple numerical descriptions. The three forms available have been chosen to identify the most common relationships found in scientific data:

- Linear: used for identifying proportionality, and extrapolating to find off-sets and starting values.
- Power Law curves: used for identifying parabolic, inverse and inverse square relationships.
- Exponentials: used for identifying exponential growth or decay.

As in previous examples, the speed of calculation and plotting of data through software provides an interactive tool. Different types of fit may be tried in rapid succession, and curves may be compared by overlaying so that pupils can look for similarities and differences.

Designing a data-logging activity

Techniques for analysing and interpreting graphs discussed thus far are important to data-logging because the prompt appearance of the graph makes it a starting point for thought. The graph need no longer be regarded as the end product of an experiment, as often occurs in conventional practice. This has implications for the design of classroom activity. It provides new opportunities but also new challenges.

As with any classroom activity, having chosen the curriculum topic, planning must start with the identification of the anticipated learning outcomes. The task will involve posing questions which point the way to such outcomes and using the software tools to find answers. Pupils need purposeful strategies for selecting and using the tools. This requires confidence in using the tools and a vision of the useful information which can be obtained. Figure 8.1 highlights the main factors which contribute to the design of a task.

To show how these principles are put into practice, four case studies will be presented. They also become progressively more sophisticated. At the simplest level, an investigation may consist of simple qualitative observations on the graph:

- Picking out and commenting on notable features;
- Describing a graph as a 'story'.

An example of this simple level is investigating the sound produced by a 'singing' kettle.

The progression from this is to a more quantitative approach which involves obtaining numerical information:

- Finding values for maxima and minima;
- Measuring changes, gradients, etc.

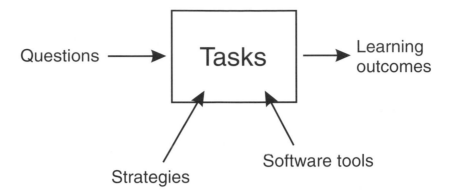

Figure 8.1   *The factors which contribute to the design of a data-logging task*

Here, an example is investigating the rate of a chemical reaction.

At the highest level, groups of observations are linked and relationships are explored:

- Identifying patterns, trends and connections;
- Describing the relationship between variables.

Examples at the highest level include investigating an aquarium and investigating current and voltage in a circuit.

Investigating a 'singing' kettle

Boiling water in a plastic jug-type electric kettle can be a noisy business. The spring loaded switch gives a loud click and as the temperature of the water rises, a roaring or 'singing' sound develops into a crescendo. The sound begins to subside as the temperature nears the boiling point. At boiling, the spring switch clicks off and, as the kettle gradually cools down, various creaks are heard. Placing a sound level sensor near the kettle can record the whole sequence of noises and the resulting graph (Figure 8.2) contains sufficient information to recount the story of the 'singing' kettle. As a simple detective game, pupils can be asked to examine the graph and speculate about the story behind the graph. The sudden peaks, the smooth stretches, the rising curves and the jagged sections all have a significance which contributes to the storyline.

This simple, qualitative exercise in graph interpretation can be applied to a variety of phenomena recorded with the aid of data-loggers. The more variety in the data, the more interesting the story. Other examples include studying the weather, the temperature inside a fridge, the environment inside a motor car during a journey and the temperature of a greenhouse or conservatory over 24 hours. Such informal experiments can teach pupils to think about the symbolism of graphs.

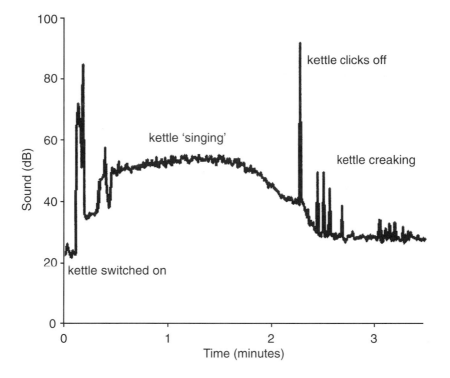

Figure 8.2 *The sound made by a 'singing' kettle*

Investigating a chemical reaction

In experiments to study the rate of change in a chemical reaction, changes can be observed in a variety of ways including colour, temperature and changes from liquid to solid or gas. One of the commonest experiments uses the reaction between sodium thiosulphate and hydrochloric acid, which deposits a sulphur precipitate making the solution go cloudy. In the conventional method, pupils estimate the onset of cloudiness by noting the time it takes for a cross on a piece of paper to disappear, when viewed through the beaker containing the reactants. The ICT method uses a light sensor and a data-logger to record the transmission of light through the reactants. As the graphs show (Figure 8.3), there is no clear cut-off point when the solution becomes cloudy; the process is gradual.

The graphs are a rich resource for exploration, though pupils need a repertoire of suitable questions. Some suggestions for this experiment are:

- How long does it take for the reaction to start after the solutions are mixed?
- Does the reaction proceed at a steady rate?
- How do you know when the reaction has finished?
- How long does it take the reaction to finish?
- If you dilute the solution, how does this affect the reaction time?

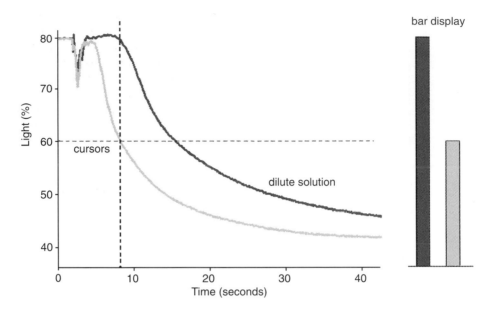

Figure 8.3 The reaction between hydrochloric acid and sodium thiosulphate solution

'Action replay'

As a limbering up exercise, it is often helpful to use the cursors informally to get a feel for the graph as a record of a sequence of events. Cursors (crossed lines which lock on to the data points) not only provide for reading values off the graph, but, used in conjunction with a bar display window, give a visual display of the relative magnitude of the values. Pupils can 'replay the events' of the experiment by slowly sweeping the cursor from left to right across the graph and observing the changing light level indicated by the bar display.

Taking measurements

Using the cursors to take readings from the graph becomes a routine activity with software. In this case, the maximum and minimum light values may be compared, but more interestingly, the time for changes to occur can be measured in a variety of ways. Software provides a convenient tool for measuring time intervals from any chosen starting point on the 'Time' axis, but examination of the shape of the graph shows that it is not so easy to decide exactly when the reaction has finished. The little dip in the reading near the beginning shows when the acid was added but after that there is an 's'-shaped curve with a long tail.

Measuring rate of change

Data-logging software is particularly good for helping pupils observe and measure rates of change. There are several alternatives, each with its strengths and limitations. For this experiment, which is the more appropriate measure: the average rate of change during the reaction or the rate of change at a particular instant? If it is the latter, which instant should be chosen: near the beginning, the middle, or the end of the curve, or the time when the rate of change is at its maximum? If it is the former, what time limits should be chosen for calculating the average rate of change?

Having chosen a strategy for measuring rate of change, the graphs for further trials using different concentrations can be investigated and compared. The same strategy must be applied to each graph so that it constitutes a 'fair test'. It then becomes a fairly small step to draw a conclusion about the connection between the rate of change and the concentration of the solution. Carefully-recorded readings show a linear relationship.

Investigating an aquarium

Recording light, temperature and dissolved oxygen levels in an aquarium over a period of a few days is an ideal task for a data-logger. This is a prime example of the graph as a starting point for scientific investigation. A general strategy might seek to answer these questions:

- What do we know about the conditions of the experiment?
- What can we learn from observations and analysis of the data?
- How can we connect these observations with the conditions?

In this case, pupils' thoughts about the context should include knowledge of the cycle of daylight and the process of photosynthesis. Complete knowledge of photosynthesis is not important; the data collected in this experiment should stimulate questions about the process. Questions about the data can focus on:

- Observing and describing the trends and variations in the data
- Taking measurements and relating them to the context
- Comparing data by considering similarities and differences.

There is a variety of ways of viewing and analysing the data (Figure 8.4). When the graph appears to contain a lot of information, it is a wise strategy to switch off some of the data displayed and concentrate on one variable at a time. Looking at the graph for light only, there appears to be an underlying trend showing as peaks which are not identical, but which seem to repeat in a regular fashion. These peaks show up very clearly when a smoothing function is used (Figure 8.5). Measuring the time interval between the peaks confirms the 24-hour cycle of daylight. There is much information to be explored here.

- Why are the peaks different heights?
- What causes the fluctuations in the 'raw' data graph?
- How does the graph's shape indicate the season when the data was collected?

The graph for oxygen again shows a 24 hour cycle, but the shape of the peaks is completely different from those observed for light. Comparing the similarities and differences between the light and oxygen graphs can prompt further thought about the context.

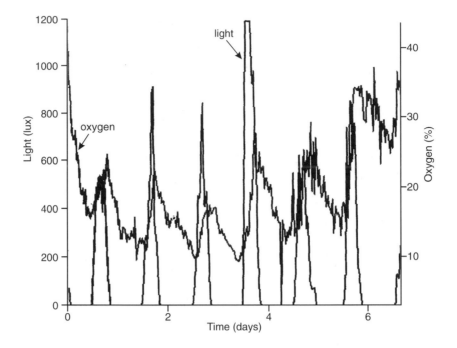

Figure 8.4 Dissolved oxygen and light level in an aquarium

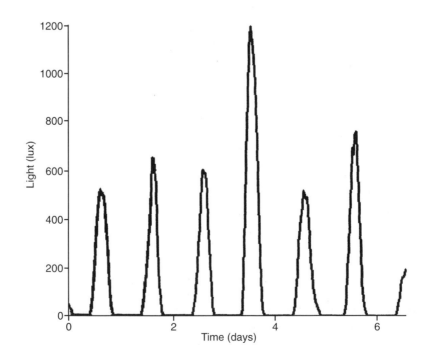

Figure 8.5 Light level in an aquarium (after smoothing)

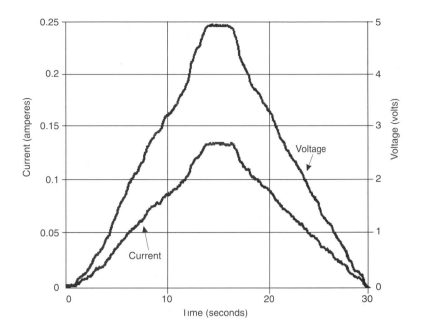

Figure 8.6 *Current and voltage for a simple resistor*

Investigating current and voltage

This is an experiment in which the data-logging method contrasts greatly with the equivalent conventional method, in terms of the quality and quantity of the data obtained, the opportunities for manipulating the data and the broadened range of possible learning objectives. The aim of the experiment is to study the relationship between the voltage across an electrical component and the current through it. The component to be tested is connected in a circuit in which the voltage is first increased to a suitable maximum and then decreased. Measurements of the voltage and current are measured continuously over a period of about 15 seconds and the results immediately displayed as a graph against time. Figure 8.6 shows results for a simple resistor. A considerable time 'bonus' is achieved in comparison with the conventional method which normally involves tabulating about ten pairs of readings over several minutes. How can this time bonus be put to productive use?

Looking for connections

A considerable amount of information can be obtained from the basic graph. From a conventional perspective it is unusual to present the current and voltages against time; it is more common to plot the current against voltage. One of the advantages of the plot against time is the 'action replay' facility described earlier. As the cursor is slowly moved across the graph, the bar display shows one bar for voltage and another for current, and they vary in height according to the sequence of readings. This visual display focuses attention on the apparent synchronization of the changes in each variable; as the voltage rises or falls, the current follows suit in a similar manner.

Furthermore, for any particular voltage, the current can be predicted with certainty. There appears to be a direct correlation between the values of the current and voltage.

Testing for linearity

The connection between current and voltage becomes clearer still when the axes are redefined to show current against voltage or voltage against current. Software makes it easy to set up either type of graph or swap between them. The resulting straight line reassures the tutored eye, but its appearance should not be regarded as the conclusion of the investigation. The implications of the straight line for the relationship between voltage and current should be explored further using the cursor tools. The special properties of the linear relationship can be explored in a number of ways:

- Read off the *values* of current for simple multiples of voltage (say at 1.0 V, 2.0 V, 3.0 V, etc.): the current is also observed to increase in simple multiples.
- Measure the *increase* in current for a given *increase* in voltage, starting at a variety of different places on the graph: equal increases in voltage produce equal increases in current.
- Measure increases expressed as a *ratio*: voltage and current increase in the same ratio, and the ratio of voltage to current is shown to be constant.
- Find the *gradient* at different places on the graph: the gradient is the same everywhere.

Calculating and exploring new data

The investigation may be usefully extended by plotting the electrical power dissipated in the resistor for the range of voltage used. The values for power are calculated as the product of corresponding values of voltage and current. Software makes light work of doing this for about 600 pairs of collected data. In this task, data-logging software has an advantage over spreadsheets in that the result is shown directly as a graph without the numerical tabulation of data. Studies have shown that few pupils can process information equally well from both tables and graphs (Dreyfus, A. and Mazouz, Y. 1992).

As before, when the graph of power against current is displayed, there is still much to be done in exploring the relationship represented by the new curve.

Describing relationships

The explorations described above focus on the numerical properties of the data. Perhaps the most precise method of describing data is to identify the algebraic function which relates two variables. Best-fit facilities producing smooth curves or straight lines through the data are common in graphing software, but they should be used with discretion. The aim should be to maximize the involvement of pupils and prompt them to think about the significance of the fit. This might be done by first challenging pupils to predict the type of line which is likely to fit and then checking their prediction. Additionally, they could have some control over the selection of the function to be fitted and its parameters.

Summary and conclusions

The examples presented here have illustrated how graphs from data-logging investigations can be used to encourage thought about data. Data can be explored in a variety of ways, providing many new experiences and insights. The design of a task requires a clear vision of the learning objectives so that contextual questions can be set. Ideally, tasks encourage pupils to develop the habit of asking questions about the data and making links with their science knowledge. Pupils' familiarity with the software tools can speed up the process of obtaining answers, but they need to be given *strategies* for using the tools and evaluating and selecting the alternatives.

References

Austin, R., Holding, B., Bell, J. and Daniels, S. (1991) *Patterns and Relationships in School Science*, London: SEAC.

Barton, R. (1997) 'Computer-aided graphing: a comparative study', *Journal of Information Technology for Teacher Education* 6: 59–72.

Bell, A., Brekke, G. and Swan, M. (1987) 'Diagnostic teaching: graphical interpretation', *Mathematics Teaching* 119: 56–9.

Dreyfus, A. and Mazouz, Y. (1992) 'Assessing the judicious use of the "language" of certain types of graphs by 10th grade Biology pupils. *Research in Science and Technology Education* 10(1): 5–21.

Janvier, C. (1978) 'The interpretation of complex Cartesian graphs representing situations', Ph.D. thesis, University of Nottingham.

Leinhardt, G., Zaslavsky, O. and Stein, M. K. (1990) 'Functions, graphs and graphing: tasks, learning and teaching', *Review of Educational Research* 60(1): 1–64.

Newton, L. R. (1997) 'Graph talk: some observations and reflections on students data-logging', *School Science Review* 79(287): 49–54.

Rogers, L. T. (1995) 'The computer as an aid for exploring graphs', *School Science Review* 76: 31–9.

—— (1999) *'Insight 3' Measurement Software – Teachers' Guide*, Cambridge: Longman Logotron.

Rogers, L. T. and Wild, P. (1996) 'Data-logging: effects on practical science', *Journal of Computer Assisted Learning* 12: 130–45.

Swatton, P. and Taylor, R. M. (1994) 'Pupil performance in graphical tasks and its relationship to the ability to handle variables', *British Educational Research Journal* 20: 2.

Underwood, J. D. M. and Underwood, G. (1990) *Computers and Learning,* Oxford: Blackwell.

9 Risk assessment in science for secondary schools

Peter Borrows

Introduction

The gradual acceptance of the concept of risk assessment over the last ten years or so has changed the way science departments approach health and safety matters. The status of various publications has also changed, as they have become adopted as 'model' (general) risk assessments.

Initially, teachers' reaction was that risk assessment would impose yet more demands on departments already over stressed by the implementation of the National Curriculum, Ofsted inspections, examination league tables, etc. There was also a fear that the effect would be to restrict practical work even further. In practice, however, risk assessment has been empowering, allowing some once-banned activities to be resurrected, at least in some schools.

There are a lot of myths about risk assessment, in the world outside education as well as inside it. Sometimes, mature entrants to teaching, consultants, or school governors with experience in industry go into schools assuming that the approach with which they are familiar is not only the best, but indeed the only one which is legal. In fact, however, the law tends to be quite general – it is concerned with outcomes not the detailed process.

The term risk assessment is used in two different ways:

- to describe a thinking process, and
- to describe the outcome or record of that thinking process.

These will be discussed in turn.

The law

The main legislation governing health and safety in the UK is the Health and Safety at Work etc Act 1974 (the HSW Act). This tends to be very general but it enables the government to introduce regulations which may be quite specific. The European Union (EU) sometimes produces Directives on health and safety matters. These are usually incorporated into UK law by new or amended regulations made under the HSW Act. Initially, risk assessment was introduced as a requirement of the Control of Substances Hazardous to Health Regulations 1988 (the COSHH Regulations). Contrary to popular misconceptions, these regulations applied to only a relatively limited range of chemicals and microorganisms. Highly flammable liquids, such as ethanol, and explosives, such as hydrogen/air mixtures were not covered, although these have been common causes of accidents in school laboratories in the past. However, the approach was deemed so successful that the concept was extended by the Management of Health and Safety at Work Regulations 1992, which required a risk assessment to be carried out before any hazardous procedure was undertaken. This might include cleaning out locust cages (allergy to their dust and droppings is well known), demonstrations involving exposed conductors which are live at mains voltages (e.g. the transmission line experiment) or climbing on a stool to reach apparatus stored on the top shelf. Both the Management Regulations and the COSHH Regulations have been subsequently revised, most recently in 1999. One effect of changes to the Management Regulations is to require a risk assessment of the hazards from a particular activity to new and expectant mothers, over and above the hazards to the workforce in general.

Other legislation also requires risk assessments. For example, under the Personal Protective Equipment Regulations 1992 (the PPE Regulations) there must be an assessment to determine what type of PPE is appropriate in particular circumstances. Similarly, the Ionising Radiations Regulations 1999 have a risk assessment focus, unlike their 1985 predecessor.

Accompanying many of the regulations is an associated Approved Code of Practice (ACOP). This expands on, explains and interprets what can sometimes be the rather impenetrable language of regulation. The law does not require an ACOP to be followed, but in any legal action it might be necessary to show that what was done was at least as safe.

Hazard and risk

In everyday life, the terms hazard and risk are often used interchangeably (and, indeed, the distinction cannot be translated into some languages of the EU). However, over the last 10 years or so, the Health and Safety Executive (HSE) has tried to encourage a distinction and it is useful to understand this.

A **hazard** is anything with the potential to cause harm. Electricity at high enough voltages is a hazard, as is working up a ladder. Many chemicals are hazardous. The hazard is an inherent property of the chemical: concentrated sulphuric acid is CORROSIVE and nothing can change that, any more than its density or boiling point can be changed. For chemicals, the hazard is defined in the Chemical (Hazard Information and Packaging) Regulations 2000 (the CHIP Regulations). For many important industrial chemicals, the hazards are actually listed in the latest edition of the Approved Supply List. For substances not listed, there are procedures given to allocate a hazard. However, it must be said that this often results in different suppliers classifying the same chemical differently, which can certainly be confusing to schools! American suppliers tend to be more cautious because of the greater tendency to litigation in the USA.

continued on next page

It is important to remember that chemicals are often used in solution and that the hazard will depend on the concentration. Sometimes publishers and worksheet writers are unhelpful when they refer to 'dilute' solutions. Pure liquid H_2SO_4 is classed as CORROSIVE. A 'dilute' solution of sulphuric acid may be LOW HAZARD (if less than 0.5 mol. dm^{-3}), IRRITANT (if between 0.5 and 1.5 mol. dm^{-3}) or CORROSIVE (if 1.5 mol. dm^{-3} or more).

Risk is defined as the probability that a particular hazard will actually cause harm. This depends in turn on the likelihood of something going wrong, the severity of the injury caused and the number of people affected. Clearly, a hand cut off is more serious, i.e. a greater risk, than a cut finger. However, if all the pupils in a class cut their finger, the risk is also significant. In industry and research, it is common practice to put numbers on the likelihood and severity factors. This is not required by law, unless the employer requires it (rare in schools but not uncommon in post-16 colleges). Most experts in the school science context consider it unhelpful. There is good evidence (based on past experience) about the types of accident which do occur in school science and it is more profitable to focus on reducing the likelihood and severity of these than on endless debates on probability.

Control measures are those steps adopted to reduce the risk from a particular hazard. In the school science context, this might involve abandoning a particular experiment or substituting a safer microorganism; using lower voltages, concentrations or temperatures; wearing gloves or eye protection; or using a fume cupboard or a safety screen. Appropriate control measures will depend upon the risk. When using a CORROSIVE liquid, goggles giving chemical splash protection are usually necessary. If the liquid is merely IRRITANT, it is usually possible to get away with safety spectacles. Clearly, chemical splash goggles would give better protection but the risk assessment takes account of both affordability in the school context and difficulties of enforcement with some classes.

The role of the employer

In law, risk assessment is the responsibility of the employer. The employer is the body with whom a teacher or technician has a written contract of employment. For those working in community schools (much the commonest type of maintained school) and voluntary controlled schools, the employer is the education authority. For foundation and voluntary-aided schools, it is the governing body. For post–16 colleges, it will be the corporation and for most independent schools it will be the governing body, or possibly the proprietor or a trust. The responsibility cannot be delegated, although the duty of assessing the risks might be committed to a suitably competent employee, e.g. the head of science. Even so, the employer should be monitoring, from time to time, that this is being carried out satisfactorily.

Model (general) risk assessments

There is clear guidance in the ACOP (Approved Code of Practice) accompanying the Management Regulations for employers that operate on several sites (e.g. an education authority with a number of schools). It encourages them to produce model risk assessments for those activities commonly carried out on these sites. Model assessments may also be produced by employers' organizations or other organizations concerned with a particular activity. In science education, these include:

- CLEAPSS School Science Service (a consortium of almost all the education authorities in the UK outside Scotland);
- ASE (Association for Science Education).

Guidance issued to schools when the COSHH Regulations were first implemented makes it clear that the HSE regards some of the common safety publications used by schools as general risk assessments, later called model risk assessments. Some of the publications commonly used as model risk assessments for school science are:

- *Safety in Science Education*, DfEE (1996)
- *Hazcards*, CLEAPSS (1995)
- *Laboratory Handbook*, CLEAPSS (1997a)
- *Safeguards in the School Laboratory*, ASE (1996)
- *Topics in Safety*, ASE (2001)
- *Safety Reprints*, ASE (1998)
- *Hazardous Chemicals Manual*, SSERC (1997)
- *Preparing COSHH Risk Assessments for Project Work in Schools*, SSERC (1991).

In addition, some education employers may have produced their own, local, model assessments.

Using model risk assessments

For the most part, risk assessment will involve consulting one or more of the above model risk assessments. The school will then need to consider whether some adaptation is necessary to suit local conditions. Table 9.1 summarizes how model assessments can be used to write warnings into point-of-use texts. For example, some schools might want classes to heat lead nitrate. This produces nitrogen dioxide, which is a CORROSIVE and VERY TOXIC gas, with an Occupational Exposure Standard (OES). The OES is a concentration which should not be exceeded. *Hazcards* indicates that lead nitrate could be safely heated in the open laboratory by a class of Year 10 pupils, provided no group uses more than 1 g. *Hazcards* will have reached this conclusion on the basis of calculations involving the amount of nitrogen dioxide produced from 1 g of lead nitrate, the likely number of pupils in the class, the average size of the laboratory and published tables of OESs. A safety margin will allow for large classes in small rooms, but it would *not* allow for pupils who would weigh out 10 g rather than 1 g. For such classes, the school might well decide that the risk from

Table 9.1 Writing warnings into point-of-use texts

How to write warnings from model assessments into point-of-use texts

---

Locate hazards – from experience, safety texts, etc.

Understand the hazards – consult Model Assessments in published safety texts.

Ask yourself the following questions (some of these will have been answered for you by those compiling the Model Assessments).

- Is the activity really worth doing? Should it be carried out at the proposed level? Consult Safety in Science Education, CLEAPSS Hazcards or the CLEAPSS Laboratory Handbook.

- Should substitutes be found or changes made? E.g. for a hazardous chemical, is there a less hazardous alternative? Can it be used in smaller quantities or at greater dilution? Can thinner wires be used so that lighter masses can be used to stretch them? Can the bacterial culture be incubated at a lower temperature? Consult references.

- What safety equipment should be used? Eye protection (what sort?), fume cupboard, gloves (what type?), safety screens, etc.

- What are the emergency procedures if there is an accident? Should any reminders be written on schemes of work or lesson plans? Should any equipment e.g. a fire blanket, be to hand?

- Can risks be minimized by the way practical resources are distributed? Are the instructions to technicians clear on quantities, concentrations, etc.? Can safety be increased by measuring out hazardous chemicals in advance, pre-setting voltages, etc.?

- Are there any risks for technicians preparing, clearing up or disposing of wastes? What instructions should be given to teachers to minimize these? What warnings should be given to technicians?

Write your decisions in the most relevant place.

What to write in the science department safety policy	The texts to be consulted for Model Assessments should be listed, with the procedures adopted on adaptation, on marking point-of-use texts, the need for staff to follow Risk Assessments, what to do if a Risk Assessment cannot be found, etc. Staff with the functions of adapting Risk Assessments, marking texts, etc. should be named.
What to write in schemes of work, lesson plans, instructions to technicians, etc.	Warnings should include the need to look up references, consult other staff about hazards and to try out particular activities in advance. Also, hazard classifications, concentrations, quantities and precautions. Warnings to pass on to students. Instructions for technicians should include warnings about preparation and clearing up after practical work.
What to write on pupil worksheets and/or textbooks	Hazard classifications, concentrations, quantities, precautions. (For younger students, obviously these will need to be expressed very differently from the Model Risk Assessments.)

this hazard would be reduced if the technician provided pre-weighed amounts of lead nitrate. Thus the school would have adapted the model risk assessment to its own situation by deciding, perhaps, that a low-attaining pupil set should be provided with pre-weighed quantities of lead nitrate. Another school might decide that, because of the problems of class control, the activity might be completely unsuitable where there are pupils with emotional and behavioural difficulties in the class.

Recording the outcomes of risk assessment

The regulations require that the 'significant findings of risk assessment' should be recorded. Record-keeping is necessary so that:

- evidence that thinking has taken place is available to HSE Inspectors;
- evidence that thinking has taken place is available to the employer or the employer's representatives (e.g. an LEA health and safety adviser, the head teacher, etc.);
- the thinking does not have to be done afresh every time;
- the thinking of experienced staff can be shared with newcomers.

Clearly, some judgement is necessary in deciding what constitutes the 'significant findings'. The ACOP makes it clear that it is important not to obscure major issues with an excess of information or a mass of trivia. What may be significant in one school may be less so in another. A school with a high turnover of staff and much teaching by non-specialists may find it necessary to spell out more details than a school with a stable staff and largely specialist teaching.

As a general rule, however, it is best to consider what information a newcomer to the profession needs. Even a chemistry graduate with a first-class honours degree may, until confronted by a Year 11 class, never have dropped sodium into water, nor, until encouraged by that Year 11, ever have considered how large a piece might be safely dropped into the water. As well as being reminded that sodium is CORROSIVE and reacts violently with water to produce an EXTREMELY FLAMMABLE gas, that newly-qualified teacher perhaps needs to be told to:

- use a piece of sodium no bigger than a 3 mm cube;
- carefully clean off the oil;
- avoid trapping the sodium under water;
- surround the reaction vessel with safety screens;
- place the safety screens very close to the reaction vessel;
- have pupils seated at least 2–3 m away;
- ensure pupils are wearing eye protection;
- check that the water is not too hot, if repeating the demonstration.

The hazards must be pointed out along with the essential control measures. Dropping sodium into water is perhaps exceptional in the amount of detail spelled out. This may be a case where a department decides that hands-on training is preferable. In that situation, all that needs to be recorded is that:

- staff must have hands-on training before carrying out this activity; or perhaps
- equipment and chemicals for this activity will only be issued to staff on the approved list.

In a lesson on testing for sugars in food, the significant findings of risk assessment might be:

- do not use Fehling's solution (CORROSIVE); Benedict's solution is far safer (LOW HAZARD)
- remind pupils how to heat a test tube safely using a water bath
- eye protection for all!

In a lesson in which pupils are learning how to wire up a three pin plug, significant findings might be:

- to avoid accidents if pupils attempt to insert a (badly-wired) plug into a socket, make this impossible by disabling the plug by bending the earth pin or by drilling it and inserting a bolt.

Of course this might be seen as a reminder to the technician preparing the lesson as much as to the teacher.

Good and bad practice

A good risk assessment will give just the right amount of information, in a form useful to readers, and it will be recorded where teachers (and technicians) are likely to see it, without too much inconvenience.

Some consultants, usually without much experience of the way schools actually work, may suggest completing detailed risk assessment forms. The forms they provide rarely make any provision for the most important factor – the nature of the pupils in the class. Often, after completion such forms reside unread in a filing cabinet. The risk assessment has been 'done' but it has no impact on day-to-day practice.

Most science departments have some documentation which outlines what is to be taught on a lesson-by-lesson, week-by-week basis. It may be called a scheme of work, a collection of lesson plans or it may be the teachers' guide for a published teaching scheme. This is the documentation which teachers will consult daily in order to know what they are to teach next. This is what they will take home to plan tomorrow's lessons. This, therefore, is where the significant findings of risk assessment need to be recorded because then they will be read as the lessons are being planned. In some places these are referred to as 'point-of-use texts'. An example is shown in Figure 9.1.

Other examples of point-of-use texts might be a technician's guide for a published scheme or a technician's index card for a particular activity (Figures 9.2 and 9.3). Equally, worksheets for pupils' use might include warnings about the hazards of particular chemicals, reminders about eye protection, or an illustration of

Chemical Patterns and Changes: Lesson 1, Elements and Compounds

Equipment	Student instruction sheets available covering a circus of three decomposition experiments. Refer students to pages 6 and 7 of *Chemistry Counts* which are to be read for homework.
Plan	The students' notes are comprehensive so go through them carefully with the students, reinforcing safety and assessment arrangements during the course. At the end of the lesson, leave plenty of time to go through their class results and homework so that they can round off the lesson satisfactorily. (Time is short on the course so it may be difficult to go over the work later.)
Homework	Complete the Results Table. Write word equations for the reactions. Read pages 6 and 7 in *Chemistry Counts* and answer the questions.
Risk assessments	*Rehearse* experiments first. Experiment 1: *Suck back* is possible so demonstrate to students to remove limewater if this happens or lift out delivery tubes. Experiment 2: Use no more that 0.3 g **(small spatula)** of copper (II) nitrate as nitrogen dioxide gas is **Toxic.** *Open window.* *For bottom set*, technician to weigh out samples. Experiment 3: Hydrogen peroxide should be rinsed off the skin and clothes if spilled because, at this concentration (20 volume), it is an **Irritant.** Arrange for: Benches 1 and 2 to start with experiment 1; Benches 3 and 4 to start with experiment 2; Benches 5 and 6 to start with experiment 3.

Figure 9.1 Teachers' lesson plan

Source: CLEAPSS (1997b)

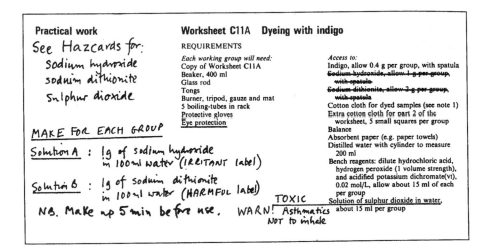

Figure 9.2 Instructions from a published course

Source: CLEAPSS (1997b)

Apparatus list   Please submit 3 days in advance

Period: *Tuesday 5*   **Room:** *L4*   **No. of groups:** *12*   **Class/teacher:** *11A Jones*

Chemical matter   Soap making   Section 5.4 p 39

NB **THIS ACTIVITY IS NOT SUITABLE FOR STUDENTS WITH BEHAVIOURAL PROBLEMS**

beaker, 250 ml	2 test–tubes fitted with bungs
evaporating basin	test–tube rack
2 measuring cylinders, 10 ml	castor oil, about 50 ml in bottle with dropper
glass stirring rod	5 M sodium hydroxide solution **(CORROSIVE – face shield – see recipe card)**
spatula	1 wash bottle (distilled water)
filter funnel and paper	**Goggles, NOT safety spectacles**
	Gloves
Note	10 ml of the sodium hydroxide solution for each group in one of the measuring cylinders. To be left in prep room until requested during the lesson.
	Include sodium hydroxide *Hazcard* with equipment.
	CARE when washing up.

Figure 9.3 *School apparatus sheet*

Lesson 1   Name ....

Decomposition

If a substance breaks down to produce two or more different substances, it is said to be 'decomposing'. Heating is one way of making substances decompose.

You are going to carry out three decomposition reactions. **Wear goggles!**

Light the Bunsen burner. **Keep the flame yellow when not needed.**

1. Zinc carbonate

Place one spatula of zinc carbonate in test tube.

Attach the delivery tube.

Clamp the tube horizontally, with the delivery tube in the lime water as shown.

Heat the zinc carbonate in the test tube over a hot Bunsen flame.

Record the observations below.

Observations

2. Copper nitrate *etc.*

Zinc carbonate   Clamp here

Heat

Lime water

Beware of suck-back!

Figure 9.4 *Students' worksheet*

Source: CLEAPSS (1997b)

how to heat a test tube safely (Figure 9.4). These would all constitute the significant findings of risk assessment, recorded at a point when technicians or pupils are most likely to see and act upon them.

Sometimes, a scheme of work or other text may simply say, for example, 'See *Hazcard*'. Inspectors of the HSE are *not* likely to consider this a very satisfactory record of the significant findings of risk assessment. They will need evidence that the science department has actually thought about the content of the *Hazcard* and considered whether any local adaptation is needed. At the very least, they will expect to see a few key phrases extracted from the *Hazcard*, even if the reader is told to 'See *Hazcard* for further information'. Even if it is normal practice for the technician to bring the relevant *Hazcard* into the laboratory with a tray of equipment, it seems unlikely that the teacher will have much chance to read it as thirty children walk through the door. It should have been read when the lesson was planned.

It is not uncommon for experienced teachers to consider that risk assessment does not apply to them. Merely because a rather dubious activity has been carried out safely once a year for each of the last 35 years does not mean it will be carried out without accident next year! Once a school has an agreed scheme of work (or equivalent), properly risk assessed, there should be an expectation that staff will not deviate from it. Of course, creative teachers will come up with new ideas, perhaps picked up from journals or old books. Creativity is certainly to be encouraged, but it must still be tempered by risk assessment. The bright idea must be checked against the accepted model risk assessments. Sometimes, they will not help much – unusual chemicals or microorganisms may be required, or the suggested procedure may be quite novel. Again, the employer should have given guidance. In some cases, the school may be able to deal with it internally e.g. following guidance in *Preparing COSHH Risk Assessments for Project Work in Schools* (SSERC 1991). Mostly, however, it is likely to involve getting an outside agency, such as CLEAPSS or SSERC, to provide a Special Risk Assessment.

Risk assessment by pupils

The National Curriculum and some examination syllabuses (e.g. GNVQ) require the pupils to identify the hazards in their work, or, sometimes in wider contexts. They are then expected to assess the risks and suggest suitable control measures to reduce them. Many teachers will, of course, routinely expect pupils to go through such thought processes as a prelude to all practical work, not just investigative work. Pupils who have thought about the hazards and developed some understanding of the risks from them are more likely to adopt the control measures than if they are simply told what to do by the teacher.

On the whole, most of the model risk assessments listed earlier were written with teachers and technicians in mind, not pupils. In some cases, the language will be too demanding, there may be a surfeit of information and perhaps some of it you would not want pupils to read in case it puts ideas into their heads! The only resource deliberately written for pupils is the *Student Safety Sheets* (CLEAPSS 1997c and later). This is a pack of photocopiable sheets, which teachers are encouraged to modify to suit the needs of their pupils. Whilst most of the sheets cover chemical hazards, there are some with a physics or biology focus. Opportunities are taken to include contexts outside the school laboratory.

Even if pupils are assessing the risks themselves, for example in an investigation, this does not absolve the teacher from the necessity to check pupils' risk assessments before they are allowed to proceed with practical work.

Acknowledgements

Many of the ideas and earlier versions of some of the examples first appeared in Tawney (1992) and are also available in *Safety Reprints* (ASE 1998).

Table 9.1 and Figures 9.1–9.4 are taken with permission from the guide *L196 Managing Risk Assessment in Science* (CLEAPSS 1997b).

References

ASE (1996) *Safeguards in the School Laboratory*, tenth edition, Hatfield: Association for Science Education.

ASE (1998) *Safety Reprints,* Hatfield: Association for Science Education.

ASE (2001) *Topics in Safety*, third edition, Hatfield: Association for Science Education.

CLEAPSS (1995) *Hazcards,* Uxbridge: CLEAPSS (also updated in 1998 and 2000).

CLEAPSS (1997a) *Laboratory Handbook,* Uxbridge: CLEAPSS (also later updates).

CLEAPSS (1997b) *L196 Managing Risk Assessment in Science,* Uxbridge: CLEAPSS.

CLEAPSS (1997c) *Student Safety Sheets*, Uxbridge: CLEAPSS.

DfEE (ed.) (1996) *Safety in Science Education*, London: HMSO.

SSERC (1991) *Preparing COSHH Risk Assessments for Project Work in Schools,* Edinburgh: Scottish Schools Equipment Research Centre.

SSERC (1997) *Hazardous Chemicals Manual,* Edinburgh: Scottish Schools Equipment Research Centre (also CD-ROM version 1998).

Tawney, D. (1992) 'Assessment of risk and school science', *School Science Review* 74(267): 7–14.

10 Using critical incidents in the science laboratory to teach and learn about the nature of science

Mick Nott and Jerry Wellington

Introduction

This chapter describes a range of 'critical incidents' which we have used with experienced and trainee teachers in order to promote discussion and reflection on the nature of science. We hope that they will stimulate readers to think about their own views of science. If these or similar incidents should subsequently arise in the 'heat of the classroom' we hope that this chapter will illustrate how teachers could use them to teach pupils about the nature of science.

> We define a **critical incident** as an event which confronts teachers and makes them decide on a course of action which involves some kind of explanation of the scientific enterprise. For example, it may be an event like some practical work going wrong, or it may be an event that raises moral and ethical issues about scientific knowledge or the conduct of scientists. In this chapter, we concentrate only on incidents arising during practical work.

Pupils saying and doing things often stimulate critical incidents but they may also arise through the action of the teacher, particularly when a demonstration goes wrong. We are not talking about deliberately arranged events where a teacher may plan for and engineer a debate or argument amongst children – part of the criticality of the events is their spontaneity. Another part of their criticality is that they evoke responses from the teacher which provide an insight into the teacher's view of science as well as matters to do with teaching and learning.

We discuss the ways in which we have used the incidents. The incidents themselves are included and we encourage you to respond to them before you read the responses other teachers have made. We finish with our interpretation of what the responses tell us about teacher knowledge of the nature of science and consider a few of the implications for good practice.

Subject knowledge and 'teaching' knowledge

Science teachers have a body of subject knowledge that they bring to the classroom and another set of knowledge which is developed and learned from their classroom experience. These two ways of knowing one's subject have been called, respectively, subject content knowledge and pedagogical content knowledge (Shulman 1986 and 1987). The two sets of knowledge interact and inform each other. At the start of a teacher's career, the pedagogical content knowledge is fairly thin, but studies have shown that student teachers recognize the rapid acquisition of the knowledge (Wilson *et al.* 1987) and the mismatch between their subject content knowledge and their pedagogical content knowledge. We would like to argue that, as teachers progress through their careers, the pedagogical content knowledge increases in size and importance in relation to the subject content knowledge, and that the two inform each other. We think that considering critical incidents in advance of classroom experiences, and later experiencing them in a real setting, can develop a teacher's pedagogical knowledge. It can also improve a teacher's awareness and understanding of the nature of science.

The critical incidents

We believe that the incidents we provide make teachers draw on their understanding of the nature of science because they:

- relate closely to classroom practice;
- promote reflection and discussion when used;
- explore teachers' implicit understandings and help to make them explicit;
- illustrate and probe teachers' knowledge-in-action (Schön 1983) and their practical wisdom rather than 'academic knowledge'.

This last point is perhaps the most important. The critical incidents can probe understandings from the domain of pedagogical content knowledge as well as subject content knowledge. The critical incidents selected and listed in Table 10.1 come either from our own experiences, those of teachers we know, or from our own reading.

Our experience has been that secondary science teachers, whatever their classroom experience, relate to the critical incidents in that they have experienced similar or analogous incidents in their own teaching. Read each incident in turn and think about what you *would* do in response (the immediate, 'knee-jerk', *probable*, reactions). Then spend a little longer thinking of all the kinds of things you *could* do as a science teacher in response to the incident. These responses could be divergent from your likely behaviour but should be *possible* reactions that you could have as a science teacher.

Table 10.1 Critical incidents for consideration by science teachers

A

A class of Year 9s is heating magnesium ribbon in a crucible with a lid. The purpose of the lesson is to test the consequence of oxygen theory that materials gain weight when burnt.

At the summary at the end of the lesson four groups report a loss in weight, two groups report no difference and two groups report a gain in weight.

List the kinds of things you would and could say and do at this point.

B

A class of Year 7s is working with microscopes and you want them to observe and draw onion skin cells.

They set up the slides and you check that they have focused the microscopes competently and then they start to look and draw.

You find their drawings to be nothing like your image of onion skin cells.

List the kinds of things you would and could say and do at this point.

C

You have set up a demonstration of the production of oxygen by photosynthesis with Canadian pond weed.

Just before the lesson when the class is to look at the apparatus again, you notice that there is a small amount of gas in the test tube but not enough with which to do the oxygen test.

List the kinds of things you would and could say and do when the lesson starts.

D

Year 7 children are doing experiments with circuit boards.

With two lamps in series, many find that one is lit brightly whilst the other appears to be unlit.

List the kinds of things you would and could say and do at this point.

E

You are demonstrating wave phenomena using a ripple tank.

The children are unable to observe refraction clearly and frankly you find it hard to see with the apparatus available.

List the kinds of things you would and could say and do at this point.

continued on next page

Table 10.1 Critical incidents (cont.)

F

Below are two episodes from lessons.

1　A teacher is doing the starch test on leaves. For inexplicable reasons the tests are indecisive.

2　A teacher is demonstrating the non-magnetic properties of iron sulphide. However the freshly made sample sticks to the magnet.

In both responses pupils say the following, 'But science experiments never work. Anyway, we'll believe you, if you'll tell us the result.'

List the kinds of things you would and could say and do at this point.

How the incidents have been used

We have used the incidents as an interactive, social, group activity; colleagues have used them with students individually and then shared responses. We gave them to small groups of teachers and classroom-experienced student teachers to discuss and then to offer their responses. Each response was thrown open to the larger group for discussion. Responses were noted from the lists and the discussion. The next section gives an account of the responses from these events.

You can compare your responses with the examples we provide and move on to reflect on the nature of science you convey to the classes you teach.

Teachers' responses to the critical incidents

Responses to the incidents where practicals 'go wrong' appear to elicit three categories of response. These are 'talking your way through it', 'rigging' and 'conjuring' (Nott and Smith 1994).

'Talking your way through it'

The majority of responses are in the category of 'talking your way through it'. Before you read the examples given below, we must stress that these are statements that teachers have actually made. We do *not* offer them all as examples of good practice.

When science teachers talk their way through practicals going wrong, they often engage the children in a critical evaluation of practical work. It may be criticism of the apparatus:

Blame the fact that the light bulbs aren't identical.

or of the practical procedures:

Assume the experiment with pond weed has been done wrongly.

Check the weighing procedures with the magnesium ribbon.

But the talking can also be explanations and interpretations of the reproducibility of practicals and the way that practical results are negotiated.

(With the magnesium ribbon) stress the need to repeat experiments.

(With the onion skin slide) get the children to agree what they see by consensus.

Get them to see that negative results can be positive results.

Get the class to discuss why it could have gone wrong with the magnesium ribbon.

Analyse and average the results – perhaps average the data.

With the onion skin slide, show them a drawing of a slide and ask them if they can see something like that.

(I) would have to tell them the prediction otherwise they wouldn't learn any-thing (but) say if it's wrong, it's wrong for a reason.

By talking their way through it, teachers are conveying the following messages about science. Science is an activity where:

- practicals need to be evaluated and that this involves repeating experiments;
- the null result is as important as the positive result;
- doing science involves sharing results and collectively criticizing, negotiat-ing and deciding procedures;
- sometimes, to learn from and to do practical, you need to have an idea in your head before you start;
- there are reasons why experiments go wrong; there is a rational explanation.
- results need to match to previously accepted knowledge.

'Rigging' practical work

Many teachers learn to rig practicals. These are simply legitimate strategies that teachers have learned over the years to ensure that the apparatus or procedure works:

Ensure the lamps are the same voltage and power.

Have a good slide ready to use.

Put sodium bicarbonate in the water to ensure that enough oxygen is produced.

We are still unsure as to whether teachers explain rigging to their pupils – our guess is that a few do and most don't. Rigging can allow science teachers to use and exercise the scientific knowledge that they have but pupils do not – a form of authority.

'Conjuring' in practical work

The last category is 'conjuring'. This is where the teacher produces the correct 'matter of fact' (Shapin and Shaffer 1985) by sleight of hand. The alleged procedure has *not* produced the result.

(With the pond weed) spike it and it always works.

Cheat, use oxygen from a cylinder.

Add oxygen yourself – to make sure it appears to work.

Put my thumbs on the scales to ensure that there is a gain in weight.

There seems to be a small set of experiments in the repertoire of science experiments that appear to be conjured. With the pond weed incident it appears that the result is often conjured. Children are not told about the conjuring. We have found that student teachers can start to conjure spontaneously or are inducted into it by science staff and technicians. We suggest that conjuring is a practice which teachers should discuss and challenge.

The following explanation is offered for 'conjuring'. In science research, fraud can be attributed to various motives, such as a need to maintain or acquire status or research grants or a blinding commitment to a particular paradigm. But teachers also have a commitment to a particular paradigm – the science content as set out in the National Curriculum, examination syllabuses and textbooks (Millar 1989). Science teachers often maintain a particular knowledge claim and ally the children's support for that knowledge claim by producing the matters of fact necessary to support it.

If the desired learning outcome is the matter of fact then the teacher may resort to 'conjuring'. Practicals can be fickle and the correct result is not always unproblematic to produce especially with school apparatus and the school conditions. Teachers 'conjure' to ensure the production of the matters of fact necessary for the knowledge claims in the science curriculum.

Conclusion

A teacher's responses to critical incidents indicate something about that teacher's knowledge of the nature of science and their attitudes to the connections, and differences, between science and other ways of knowing the world. The use of the critical incidents in this way provides insights into teachers' views of science that would not have been revealed by other means.

We hope you have enjoyed reading this. We have presented reactions to the incidents that teachers have actually made – we recognize that some of them may be 'dubious practice'. However, by discussing these incidents and their responses with us, teachers have reflected on their practice. Some of you may well have 'conjured' in your teaching experience or experience as a science undergraduate, and some of you may well have 'conjuring' explained to you by teachers and technicians. 'Conjuring' is deviant behaviour for a scientist. So far, we have asked you to consider what you *would* do and what you *could* do. Teaching science, like doing science, is a moral activity in that there are choices about what actions one *ought* to take. Think back about your possible reactions to the incidents: what is it you *should* do the next time a similar incident occurs when you are teaching?

The aim of this chapter is to help you make sense of some of the things that happen in your science classrooms. It should also illustrate the wealth of opportunities that exist for you to discuss with your pupils and explain the nature of science; critical incidents such as the ones above should be seen as opportunities rather than crises. As your teaching experience (and pedagogical knowledge) grow, you will build up a repertoire of understandings, explanations and responses. Even so, and despite the best planning, the unexpected will still happen!

References

Millar, R. (1989) 'Bending the evidence', in R. Millar (ed.) *Doing Science: Images of Science in Science Teaching,* London: Falmer, pp. 38–62.

Nott, M. and Smith, R. (1994) '"Talking your way out of it". "Rigging" and "Conjuring": what science teachers do when practicals "go wrong"', *International Journal of Science Education* 17(3): 399–410.

Schön, D. (1983) *The Reflective Practitioner,* New York: Holt Rinehart.

Shapin, S. and Shaffer, S. (1985) *Leviathan and the Air Pump*, Princeton: Princeton University Press.

Shulman, L. (1986) 'Those who understand: knowledge growth in teaching', *Education Researcher* 15(2): 3–14.

—— (1987) 'Knowledge and teaching: foundations of the new reforms', *Harvard Education Review* 57(1): 1–22.

Wilson, S., Shulman, L. and Richert, A. (1987) '150 different ways of knowing: representations of knowledge in teaching', in J. Calderhead (ed.) *Exploring Teachers' Thinking,* London: Cassell.

Further reading

Collins, J., Hammond, M. and Wellington, J. (1997) *Teaching and Learning with Multimedia,* London: Routledge.

Nott, M. and Wellington, J. (1996) 'Probing teachers' views of the nature of science: how should we do it and where should we be looking', in G. Welford, J. Osborne, and P. Scott (eds) *Research in Science Education Research in Europe,* London: Falmer Press, pp. 283–94.

Nott, M. and Wellington, J. (1996) 'When the black box springs open: practical work in school science and the nature of science', *International Journal of Science Education* 18(7): 807–18.

Nott, M. and Wellington, J. (1999) 'When does normative scientific behaviour start?', in M. Bandiera *et al.* (eds) *Research in Science Education in Europe,* Dordrecht: Kluwer Academic Press, pp. 299–304.

Wellington, J. (ed.) (1998) *Practical Work in Science: Which Way Now?*, London: Routledge.

—— (2000) *Teaching and Learning Secondary Science,* London: Routledge.

3 Imagined worlds

Introduction

'No practical work today, I'm afraid. It's just a theory lesson.' It is not uncommon to hear such a remark made by science teachers. Not uncommon, but perhaps a little sad because it reflects an impoverished view of both science and science teaching. It is after all *theory* that makes science what it is, what makes it powerful and what makes it interesting to learn. Indeed, so charged is the word 'theory' with negative associations that we avoided it in the title of this section, instead using the term 'imagined worlds' - but more of that later.

Seeing colour changes when chemicals are mixed in a test tube may be fascinating for a young child, but for older children the fascination soon wears off. What gives point to continuing to mix chemicals in test tubes and what makes it interesting is that pupils can seek explanations for the phenomena, can test out their ideas and be surprised, can make predictions and inferences, and propose new ideas - in other words, think with theories. This kind of work - using practical work as a way of developing theory - is the day-to-day stuff of science classrooms, even though the word 'theory' is less commonly used explicitly.

In the past, science teaching has tended to use a relatively restricted range of teaching strategies. Perhaps the negative associations of 'theory work' are because of the ways that 'theory' is too often taught, when stripped of any supporting practical work; for want of more imaginative approaches, theory work becomes synonymous with copying from the blackboard or out of a textbook - strategies that are both dull *and* ineffective. With appropriate teaching, learning about theory can be interesting and motivating with or without practical work, and indeed much of this book is concerned with exploring how a range of teaching strategies can be used appropriately to support effective learning. There should be no necessity to apologize for not doing practical work.

As pupils' learning in science progresses, they move from their first-hand *experience* of phenomena to an understanding of how science *explains* these phenomena. These explanations involve pupils in coming to know about a variety of theoretical entities - atoms and molecules, genes, forces, and so on. These entities inhabit the 'imagined worlds' of our title. We have called these '*imagined* worlds' to stress that, in coming to a scientific explanation of a phenomenon, *someone* had to do the *imagining*. These ideas are not waiting to be 'discovered' in the natural world, and they do not emerge simply and solely from the scientist's, or the pupil's, direct experience of the physical world. Indeed, it is well known that in trying to understand the world around them, children construct for themselves their own ideas or 'imagined worlds' which may be very different from those of science. It is an important part of teaching science to understand these alternative ideas and how pupils can be helped to imagine the world in the way that science sees it.

In choosing to follow a section on practical work by a section on 'imagined worlds' we have created an artificial distinction - deliberately so - in order to draw attention to the connections between them. In the previous section, we saw how practical work must be justified in terms of its contribution to scientific understanding; as Robin Millar put it, 'If we do practical work "because science is a practical subject", then it is equally true that we do it "because science is a theoretical subject"'. The 'imagined worlds' of this section are not just 'fantasies'; we cannot imagine theories to be whatever we wish. As pupils' learning progresses, they should increasingly be aware and understand that theories are justified in terms of evidence, and that as more evidence becomes available then theories may change.

- The notions of 'experiment' and 'theory' are clearly central to a scientific understanding of the world. What do pupils understand by these terms and the relationship between them? In the first chapter of this section, Jonathan Duveen, Linda Scott and Joan Solomon report the results of research into this question, following the development of pupils' ideas during science courses that included illustrations of real scientific enquiry.
- Models are used in science teaching to make what is difficult to imagine more accessible. They provide a bridge between what is observed and what is imagined. Richard Boohan discusses the potential of a variety of different models in science teaching, including computer models, and some of the difficulties. A central aspect of learning science is understanding the relationship between the real word and the imagined worlds that we express with models.
- Jon Ogborn, Gunther Kress, Isabel Martins and Kieran McGillicuddy continue their discussion of the nature of science teachers' explanations. They see explanation as being in some ways like stories in which the 'entities of science' play out their roles. Some of these entities may be rather obvious and familiar, but there are conceptual entities too. Through their explanations, teachers need to 'bring these entities into being' for pupils.
- As pupils' understanding of science develops, they progress from qualitative to quantitative explanations. It is, after all, mathematics that we use to manipulate the entities of the 'imagined worlds' in order to make predictions. Graham Lenton and Brenda Stevens examine some of the difficulties associated with using mathematics in science, and stress the need for teaching approaches that emphasize conceptual understanding rather than the rote application of formulae.
- It is all too easy to produce tests that assess superficial understanding, such as factual recall; what requires more thought is how to assess real understanding. John Oversby considers what we mean by conceptual understanding, and how concepts can be understood and assessed at different levels. He gives some examples of assessment techniques that can offer greater insights into pupils' understanding.

11 Pupils' understanding of science
Description of experiments or 'a passion to explain'?

Jonathan Duveen, Linda Scott and Joan Solomon

Introduction

Science is certainly about investigating, but if the essence of being scientific were really no more than carrying out technological tests on absorbent paper or slippery slopes, would we ourselves ever have become enthusiastic science students, let alone science teachers? A scientific investigation is so much more. It is an enterprise which searches for explanations about why phenomena happen in the way they do, using previous knowledge, new observations, imaginative analogies, and carefully designed experiments. As Einstein once said, scientists are people *'with a passion to explain'*. That is the appeal of science.

In the National Curriculum, Sc1 makes references to 'evidence', 'scientific explanations', 'role of experimentation', and 'creative thought'. That shows some of the real flavour of science, and shows that our pupils can be learning about the nature of scientific explanation at the same time as they are learning science content. In order to teach about the nature of science it is important to have some understanding of where our pupils are starting from and how they learn. We have carried out research in which we worked alongside science teachers in five Key Stage 3 classrooms, talking to the pupils and following their progress. The science being learnt was contained in the school's schemes of work, but to teach about the nature of science it also needed some illustrations of real scientific endeavours from contemporary work or historical developments. We provided a book of resources (Solomon 1991) from which the teachers chose one or two units for each term to fit in with the pupils' work.

Teachers have long been aware that everyday meanings for scientific words can be a great obstacle to learning. From our research, we soon found out that there were similar language-related problems in learning about the nature of science. There were numerous examples of pupils holding different meanings for such fundamental terms as 'describe' and 'explain', and for 'theory' and 'experiment'. The younger pupils' notion that the outcome of an experiment is quite unpredictable probably comes from everyday remarks like: 'We had no idea what would happen, so we just had to experiment'. Similarly the idea that theory is no more than a simple everyday prediction is conveyed by offhand comments like: 'I've got a theory that it's chips again for tea!'.

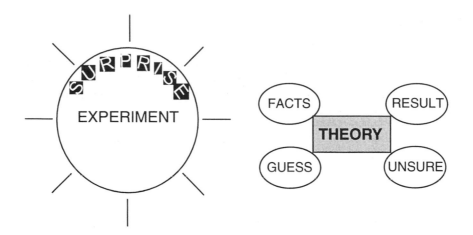

Figure 11.1 *An experiment is an isolated, unsupported, unpredictable event*

The disconnected realms of experiment and theory

What are experiments?

For many pupils at the start of Key Stage 3, there is no connection at all between theory and experiment. They seem to occupy two different worlds. Experimental results are unpredictable and a complete surprise. In this extract, a Year 7 pupil is talking to the interviewer at the beginning of the year.

Interviewer   Do scientists know what they expect to happen when they do an experiment?

Asko   No, otherwise they wouldn't do the experiment if they knew what would happen.

This was a surprisingly common response. Pupils often used the word experiment in its everyday sense of venturing into the completely unknown – unless they thought that the experiment had been done before.

Karen   No, they can't predict what is going to happen in an experiment because anything could happen. If they tried it out before they might know what happens, but if they are trying a new experiment they probably won't know what happens.

This notion of experiment was not confined to what 'scientists' do. Some pupils answered in a similar way about their own experiments in school science. Most pupils who hold this view of an experiment as no more than a 'shot in the dark', have no firm idea at all what a scientific theory is (Figure 11.1).

Sometimes pupils agree that scientists might at least be thinking about what will happen in the experiment they are planning to do. However, as long as they lack any appreciation of the predictability of outcomes and the intentionality of the activity, they can make little progress.

What are theories?

As science is taught in British schools today, this word theory is rarely mentioned. It was not uncommon for pupils to tell us that they never used it at all. From our own work, and from responses to the large-scale survey produced by Durant *et al.* (1990) it seems that pupils, and the public at large, mostly hold one of three views about the nature of a scientific theory:

1   It may be a hunch (guess, or idea) about what will happen.
2   It may be an explanation for why things happen.
3   It may be a fact.

Most teachers would be working to show that the second response is the best description of science. It is the third response which most distorts the nature of the scientific endeavour.

Theories as facts

Many pupils regard science as a process of collecting facts. For them, the purpose of experiments is to uncover yet more of them. Facts are the 'true theories'. This is clearly shown in the following interview with David, a Year 7 pupil.

Interviewer   Scientists have a theory that everything is made up of particles. What sort of theory is that? Is it a guess?
David   No, it's a proper theory. It's true.
Interviewer   How did they make it up do you reckon?
David   They done some tests.
Interviewer   Yes?
David   … and they found out whether it was true or not. And they found that it was.

Sometimes the everyday meaning of theory as not being quite certain still lingers on into this factual view of theory. Established theories are facts, but at earlier stages an uncertain theory or an unconfirmed opinion may need experimentation to find out the 'right answer'. The answer becomes the theory.

Interviewer   When scientists have a theory, what is it?
Dave   It's when they think some things … when they don't know for sure. It's when they think that's what the answer is.
Interviewer   What sort of thing do they think about?
Dave   What the answer is to the experiment.

In this perspective, correctly performed experiments and their results become 'theory', and there is no room at all for either speculation or explanation. It is the most naive form of empiricism.

Theory as guess

This notion seems to be at the other end of the spectrum from the previous meaning, at this level of understanding. It was a very common notion of the word 'theory' at Key Stage 3. The pupils were aware of an uncertainty associated with theories long before they could recall any scientific theory because it is a part of the everyday meaning of the word. One of the units that the teachers used was about Jenner's discovery of smallpox vaccination.

Interviewer How do you suppose that Jenner got his theory?
Sally   It was just a guess.
Interviewer Jenner just had a guess did he?
Sally   Yes, because he wasn't sure.

Two other Year 7 girls took the argument about Jenner's theory and experiment a stage further. In this case we can see a real attempt being made to connect a more scientific notion of theory-as-guess with experiment.

Jennifer   He didn't have any proof or anything.
Natalie   He didn't have much equipment.
Jennifer   And the last time he did it someone died.
Natalie   He didn't have much equipment to do experiments to find out the real answer. He just guessed.

Pupils such as Jennifer show how thinking about guesses in the context of experiment may come to include the concept of proof. Natalie's contribution on the importance of good equipment was a common and interesting response. As the pupils learnt about how new theories had taken over from older ones, their most common general response was that: 'we have better equipment (or technology) now'. This instrumental approach to science denies any role to imagination, model-making, or the cultural context.

Thinking about theory and experiment

Many of our interviews with younger Key Stage 3 pupils showed them holding views of theory or experiment that were so unreflective that we felt forced to identify a transition phase. Here, we could see students just beginning to go beyond these simplistic accounts of theories as facts, or as guesses. They were not yet ready to artic-ulate the connection between theory and experiment in terms of predictions or explanation but they had got beyond the most elementary stage. The key to identi-fying this transition phase was simply that pupils began to reflect on scientific activi-ties, and to attribute the same reflective stance to scientists.

Sometimes the pupils were just dissatisfied with the idea of *theory as a pure guess*.

Interviewer ... so there has to be bit of guesswork?
Adam   Yeah.

Daniel   And it's common sense. I mean if you think of something and it's a wild guess, it's nothing to do with it. It's got to have some sense to it.

Other pupils showed a progression in their thinking while they were answering our questions. Rachael, a Year 8 pupil, gives three different successive ideas in the course of one interview running from 'vague ideas' to what seems like previous knowledge.

Rachael   They've got a vague idea otherwise there wouldn't be much point in doing it …
Well, they've got to have a reason for doing their experiment of course …
We don't just guess, we've got to have something to guess with.

Emma, another Year 8 pupil, puts it even more succinctly:

Emma   A theory is more worked out than a guess.

Other pupils reacted against the idea of *theory as fact* and also began to reflect, audibly and collaboratively, on the problems.

Wali   A fact is something you know to be true.
Sarah   And a theory is, kind of, … I don't know how to explain it but I know what it is.
Wali   Say like you don't know, you think you've got …
Sarah   … pretty good idea of what you're looking for like …
Wali   It's not proven yet, it's not …
Sarah   … It's like you have an idea but aren't sure.

In the next extract, a group of Year 7 students are responding to the question 'After the experiment do the scientists just pack up and go?'

Gavin   No, they talk about the result.
David   No, because they have to talk about it and write it down and everything because they have to keep close records don't they?
Jon   They talk about, explain it.
Gavin   … and explain what they did.
Interviewer   And what about this word theory? Have you any idea what it means?
Nat   It is when they have a guess about why something happens or what is going to happen.

Jon, Gavin and Nat all seem to be on the edge of making a connection between theory and experiment in terms of explanation. However, the problem they all face is that they are not quite clear about the meaning of 'explain' (Solomon 1986). For Jon and Gavin, it is clearly the same as a description. It seems likely that this is also true for Nat who is happy to conflate what is going to happen with why it happens. This problem will be considered again in the last section of this chapter.

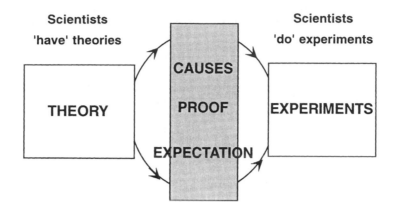

Figure 11.2 Theory and experiments are related

Making connections between theory and experiment

It spite of their more considered answers, none of the previous pupils have managed to make clear a path from theory to experiment via prediction, or from experiment back to theory via explanation (Figure 11.2).

The real shift in understanding comes when they begin to see experiment as following from, as well as testing out, the theory. The theory and the experiment then have complementary functions. After almost a year of using occasional 'Nature of Science' units, Sally and Vicky, both Year 8 pupils, express some aspects of this view.

Vicky   A theory is when you think like 'Oh well, I think so and so' – when you think something and then you do an experiment to find out whether it is right.

Sally   You estimate what is going to happen. (Sally consistently uses the word 'estimate' as meaning prediction.)

This connection between experiment and theory is also seen in the following interviews with Year 8 pupils.

Richard   They did experiments to find out about.
Nigel   They saw things happen and they tried finding out why they happened.
Richard   And they had a theory before they did the experiment and they were just trying their theory out.
Interviewer   So that is the order is it? Nigel you said …
Nigel   They saw something and then they have a theory and then they test it out by doing an experiment.

Most of the ingredients of the 'scientific method' – observing, explaining, predicting and describing, were present in that short extract.

For some pupils, however, the way seems to be blocked again by the same confusion between explanation and description that we met before. If the pupils cannot make this distinction they will have major problems in understanding theories as explanations.

Robert	An explanation is something that is certain, that you know about. A theory is an explanation about what you think might happen.
Interviewer	Sorry, you used the word explanation in both of those, I think you might have got your words muddled up.
Robert	An explanation is when you say something has happened, like, say, a jug flew through the air. You could give an explanation like it was the cat knocking the table or something.

Robert is using explanation in two different senses, as people do in casual talk. 'Explain how you carried out the experiment' is quite a common, and misleading, school instruction to pupils. During our research, some of the teachers emphasized to the class the difference between explanation and description. Their pupils then had little difficulty in recognizing and using the distinction being made (Solomon *et al.* 1994).

Identifying the direct causes of happenings is one of the easier types of explanation. Others are more sophisticated, such as the use of a mental model – like particles in a gas, or genes on a chromosome. Learning to explain in this especially scientific way involves making an analogy and manipulating the model in the imagination. Just a few of our Key Stage 3 pupils had begun to do this. In the following extract Katy, a Year 8 pupil, is describing how she thinks about her experimental results.

Katy	Sometimes I just guess, but most of the time you can imagine what's going to happen.

Katy is starting to use theory as a predictive mental tool. In other cases, pupils begin to learn how to use a model from one of the special units being used and, as one of the Year 7 pupils remarked, 'It was a hard lesson'. Others commented that the models we showed them 'made it easier to imagine' what was going on. In general, however, we found that using a model to explain natural phenomena, from particles in solution to the behaviour of polymer molecules in polythene, was too difficult for most Key Stage 3 pupils.

A feedback loop?

After a year, the majority of pupils had managed to make sense of the connection between experiment and theory in terms of explanation. They did this of their own accord in response to the new kinds of lessons. We asked them again at the end of the year, 'Why do you think scientists do experiments?' and let them answer in one of three different ways. Table 11.1 shows the large movement towards 'Testing out their explanations for why things happen'.

Table 11.1 Why do you think scientists do experiments?

	Year 7 %	Year 8 %	Year 9 %
Making discoveries	50 (33)	53 (18)	60 (33)
Testing explanations	38 (64)	38 (71)	40 (67)
Making helpful things	11 (2)	9 (11)	0 (0)

Note
Pre-course responses, post-course in brackets

There were two further aspects of the theory/experiment connection which we wanted to explore. One was in what philosophers of science often call the 'context of justification', the other was the 'context of discovery'.

Context of justification

This concerns the effect of the experimental result on the standing of the theory. If the result was as expected, did it validate the explanation? More importantly, if the result was contrary to expectation, did it completely negate theory? Two Year 9 boys are talking about this.

Interviewer How do they know if they're right?
Steven They make a hypothesis.
Interviewer And they test it with the experiment.
Steven Yes.
Interviewer What happens if the experiment is wrong, or comes out with a different set of results from what they expected?
Steven They try it again.
Tariq But in a different way. Different hypothesis.
Interviewer And if it still comes out different?
Steven They got to try a completely different (method) or forget about it.

Reference to this kind of crude Popperian falsification occurred quite often in the Key Stage 3 pupils' interview responses at the end of the year. In only a handful of cases did it seem that pupils might be considering a less drastic feedback where the explanation being tested might be modified rather than totally jettisoned.

Context of discovery

How do theories arise? Pupils who referred to the Jenner story told us about the evidence he had collected about the milkmaids not getting smallpox. A few others, like these Year 9 girls, could give full and general responses.

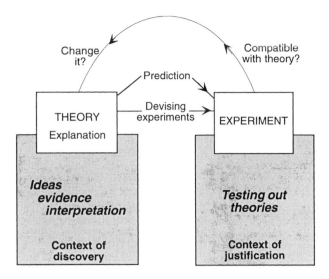

Figure 11.3 The feedback perspective

Interviewer	Where do the scientists get what 'they think they know' from?
Natasha	From other experiments that they've done, so they put other different things together and they hope to make something (theory) with other things that have happened, like, near to this then …
Interviewer	Right.
Natasha	… they do that.
Gina	Or they research it.
Interviewer	OK. What does research give them?
Natasha	Information.
Gina	They give them ideas.

This acceptance that experimental results, along with other observations, contribute to new and more comprehensive theories, forms the other end of the feedback loop. The experimental outcome informs theory as well as being explained by it. By the end of the year in which we carried out our research in Key Stage 3 classrooms, just a few of the pupils had moved beyond the view that theories just led to experiments and towards this view of the scientific process as a feedback look (Figure 11.3).

Summary

When we began work on pupils' understanding of the 'Nature of Science' there was very little previous research to guide us apart from some by Carey *et al.* (1990) based on one special unit of work, and others (Brickhouse 1989; Lederman and Zeider 1987) which showed that teachers' private views influenced what their pupils thought. From interviews, questionnaire response, and action research in the classroom, we have shown the following points:

1   The everyday meaning of 'experiment' suggests an unthinking activity with surprising results.
2   The everyday meaning of 'theory' suggests uncertainty and guessing.
3   Scientific theory may be considered a fact or just the (correct) experimental results.
4   Progress may be attributed entirely to technological improvements.
5   Understanding the explanatory nature of theory is often inhibited by lack of clarity about the meaning of 'explain'.
6   Unanticipated outcomes to experiments may be taken to falsify the whole theory.
7   The role of imagination and evidence in theory building and using a model is rarely understood.

Our pupils seemed to start from a position where the scientific enterprise had little connection with any intention to explain. Slowly, and with difficulty which seemed to be associated with the operation of causal and analogical explanation, they made progress. We have seen this process continue in further work which we have carried out with Key Stage 4 pupils (Solomon 1995). Eventually, perhaps, a new generation of young scientists will begin to appreciate and share in Einstein's *passion to explain*.

Acknowledgement

We are grateful for funding from the NCC and the Nuffield Foundation which made this work possible.

References

Brickhouse, N. (1989) 'The teaching of the philosophy of science in secondary classrooms: case studies of teachers' personal theories', *International Journal of Science Education* 11(4): 437–49.

Carey, S., Evans, R., Ellis, J., Giese, J., Parisi, L. and Singleton, L. (1990) '"An experiment is when you try and see if it works": a study of grade 7 students' understanding of the construction of scientific knowledge', *International Journal of Science Education* 11: 514–29.

Durant, J., Evans, G. and Thomas, G. (1990) 'The public understanding of science', *Nature* 340: 11–14.

Lederman, N. and Zeider, D. (1987) 'Science teachers' conceptions of the nature of science: do they really influence teaching behaviour?', *Science Education* 71(5): 721–34.

Solomon, J. (1986) 'Children's explanations', *Oxford Review of Education* 12(1): 41–51.

—— (1991) *Exploring the Nature of Science*, Glasgow: Blackie.

—— (1995) 'Higher level understanding of the nature of science', *School Science Review* 76(276): 15–22.

Solomon, J., Duveen, J. and Scott, L. (1994) 'Pupils' images of scientific epistemology', *International Journal of Science Education* 16(3): 361–73.

12 Learning from models, learning about models

Richard Boohan

Real and imagined worlds

When you listen to people talking about science, or read about it in a book, you may be struck that it is about two different kinds of thing. There are things that are recognizable from the everyday world – water, rust, microscopes, springs, and so on. But there are other unfamiliar things which seem to belong to a different world – a 'scientific world' – such as atoms, entropy, genes, potential energy and ecological niches. This notion of a 'different world' can be helpful in understanding what science is like. In order to understand the real world, we make models of it – or 'imagined worlds' – to try to represent what the real world is like. There is a lot that we do not know about how the real world behaves. But in the imagined worlds that we have created, we can talk with certainty – we know because we created them. Many pupils are attracted to science because of this apparent certainty. Many pupils are put off it for precisely the same reason. What is often lost in the way that science is presented is that scientific models are the results of creative acts of the imagination. This chapter will explore the use of models, including the role of computer models, in science and in learning science.

Pupils are familiar with model cars, train sets or dolls. These models are 'cut-down versions of the real thing'. A model car is not like a real car in many ways – being a lot smaller and lacking a working engine are two obvious differences – but it is sufficiently like a car in other ways, that it fulfils a role in the child's imaginary world. Models are *simplified representations* of the real world. But why 'make do' with simplifications? Why not make them as complex as the real thing?

Simplification

In essence, models are simplifications because this is what makes them *useful*. And by useful we mean that we can use them to make *predictions*. Some examples will illustrate this idea.

A scale model of an aeroplane used in a wind tunnel   Like all models, in some ways it is like the real thing, and in some ways it is different. It is clearly smaller than the real thing and lacks many details. What is the same is its *shape* – the important feature being tested.

A dummy used in a car crash experiment   This, too, models some of the physical features of the real thing. The dummy should be the same size and the same weight as a human being, and have joints that move in the same way.

A rat used for testing medicines   Like the dummy, a rat can be used as a model of a human being, but it attempts to model different aspects. One objection made by people opposed to using animals in research is that they are not good models of humans, since they do not react in the same way.

A map of Britain   All of the models so far have been *physical* models. A map is rather different since it is more like an *idea*. It may happen to have been drawn on paper, but it could equally well exist as a slide projected onto a screen, or as a file on a CD-ROM, or even inside someone's head. Just as the car crash dummy and the rat are both models of a human being, so Britain can be modelled by more than one kind of map. Each would simplify the country in different ways, and each would have its own particular uses. It is a model's *simplicity* that makes it *usable*. Lewis Carroll talks of a map which is exactly the same size as the real world and shows everything on it. It is beautifully detailed, but the problem is finding space to spread it out!

A computer model used by the Meteorological Office for weather forecasting   Like a map, a computer model is a kind of *idea*. It *could* be put down on paper, but it would take a long time to do the calculations by hand, so the advantage of a computer is *speed*. Weather forecasters usually get their predictions right (more often than many people imagine), so their model must correspond quite closely to the real world. Because they do sometimes get it wrong, we know that the model is not perfect.

These models appear to be very different, but each is a simplified version of something in the real world. They help us to make predictions, and may help us in bringing about things we want to happen in the real world.

Models and learning science

Using models, however, is more that just making predictions. It is through models that people try to make sense of the world by finding out 'the why of things'. Models are about helping to make *explanations*. For example, you don't need a model to predict that copper can be bent and shaped. This has been known for thousands of years. But *why* does copper behave like this? An explanation might be that when it is bent, the atoms slide over each other, and that gaps in the regular arrangements of the atoms can help to make this slipping easier. The explanation of the phenomenon is in terms of a model that we can easily visualize or make a physical model to represent.

Physical models are powerful tools for learning science because of the way that they can make 'imagined worlds' seem more real to pupils. They can be seen and manipulated. They convey strong verbal messages and leave memorable images. However, this is a double-edged sword. Models can also be misleading for pupils since they may pay attention to features which are not intended to correspond to the object or phenomenon being modelled. These incorrect correspondences are rein-

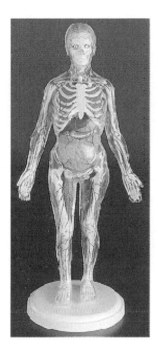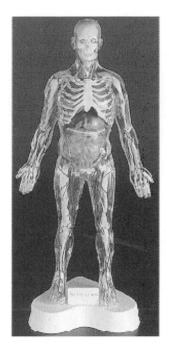

Figure 12.1 Anatomical models

Source: 'anatomy-resources.com' website (http://www.anatomy-resources.com/sh740.htm)

forced by visual messages which are just as powerful as those for the correct ones. Some examples will illustrate this.

Figure 12.1 shows two anatomical models. These physical models are in a certain sense quite like the real thing. They are clearly recognizable as people, though they are simplified in a number of ways, not least in being transparent. In this case, pupils are sufficiently familiar with human beings to know that transparency is simply a feature of the model. However, there are other aspects of these kinds of models which are not so straightforward. Through the exaggerated or artificial use of colour, for example, certain features are made to stand out. These embody *theoretical interpretations* about the way the body is constructed and functions. The circulatory system is an idea which was constructed; it was not at all obvious to the many people who had dissected bodies before this idea was known. In contrast, these models almost seem to shout 'Look at me! I am a circulatory system!'. Similarly, when pupils look through a microscope at an onion skin, they find it very difficult to see the cells. When they see a simplified diagram or model showing the structure, the 'real cells' become more apparent under the microscope.

Physical models can also help to make sense of the very large or the very small. Figure 12.2 shows a model of the sun, earth and moon, though this is not immediately apparent at first glance. It is a mechanical device that represents the relative positions of the three bodies, and of the rotation of the earth, and it can be used as a model to support explanations about the seasons and about day and night. It does, of course, give a very misleading impression of the relative sizes of the bodies and the

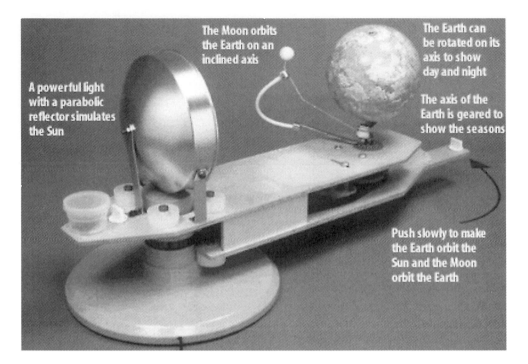

Figure 12.2 A model of the sun, earth and moon

Source: 'Cochranes of Oxford Ltd' website (http://www.cochranes.co.uk/BFXWD03/teller.htm)

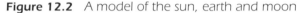

distances between them. A commonly held belief is that the reason it is hotter in the summer is that we are nearer the sun; a model like this could easily reinforce this incorrect idea. When using models like this with pupils it is, therefore, very important to make explicit those aspects of the system which are represented in the model and those which are not. A different kind of model of the sun/earth system would be a *scale* model, constructed, for example, by going out into the playground with appropriately-sized cardboard discs. This is a memorable experience – the earth seems very tiny and very alone in space. Of course, unlike the first model, this second one does not represent the *orbit* of the earth. Different models then may be useful for different purposes by representing different aspects of the same system or phenomenon.

This point is strikingly illustrated in the series of models shown in Figure 12.3, which, in different ways, may all represent water molecules. Figures 12.3a and 12.3b both represent single water molecules; space-filling models give a better impression of the shape of molecules, while ball-and-stick models are better for understanding the structural relationships between atoms. When Watson and Crick built their first model of DNA, they constructed only the skeleton. In a space-filling model, it is not easy to identify the double helix. Similarly, in school science, ball-and-stick models are commonly used to illustrate the structure of sodium chloride. Unless the convention is explained to pupils, they may believe that there are spaces between the ions and wonder what keeps them apart (is it really the sticks?). The idea that atoms themselves consist mainly of empty space creates more potential for confusion.

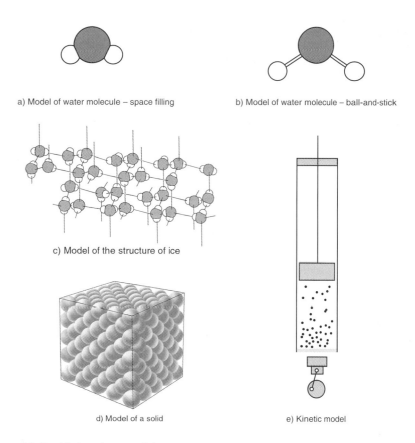

a) Model of water molecule – space filling

b) Model of water molecule – ball-and-stick

c) Model of the structure of ice

d) Model of a solid

e) Kinetic model

Figure 12.3 *Molecular models*

Models of various kinds are essential for pupils to understand the arrangements of particles in solids, liquids and gases, and what happens during changes of state. Figure 12.3c shows a model of ice representing the hydrogen bonds between water molecules. This would be appropriate for more advanced work. For younger pupils, the model shown in Figure 12.3d would be more appropriate when introducing the idea that ice consists of water molecules arranged in regular, fixed positions. Here, a space-filling model is needed to show how the particles are close together in the solid, and to model what happens to them as the solid changes into a liquid and into a gas. The final example, shown in Figure 12.3e, is a little different from the others in that it is a model that can be 'run', and so bears some similarities to the computer models discussed later. It is a model commonly used in school science to represent the behaviour of the molecules in a gas. It consists of a perspex tube and a piston. At the bottom, a motor causes a diaphragm to vibrate and this makes the ball bearings inside the tube move around. Increasing the speed of the motor represents 'raising the temperature of the gas'; the ball bearings move faster and push the piston up. Pushing the piston down 'compresses the gas'; when the piston is released it rises up again. In such ways, it models the *behaviour* of a real gas.

All of the models discussed so far have been three-dimensional, physical models. But models can also be found in the pages of textbooks. The cross-sectional diagram of the eye is a simplified representation of a real eye, and the diagram of the electron configuration of an atom is a representation of an entity in an imagined world. These two-dimensional models may complement three-dimensional models; for example, a diagram of the digestive system emphasizes the *sequence* of the organs, while a physical model shows better the *spatial relationship* of these organs. Other kinds of diagrams may be more abstract, showing models of processes or of classification, for example. Using such models in conjunction with textual or verbal explanations can help learners to construct their own mental models, and shift their performance from a reliance on verbatim retention towards a better conceptual understanding (Mayer 1989). Examples of a wide range of models and how they may be used in science education can be found in Gilbert (1993).

Analogies are widely used in science teaching to facilitate learning, and they are related to models. An analogy essentially says 'think of A as being like B'. For example, in the case of the kinetic model of a gas discussed above, it says 'think of a gas as being like a collection of randomly moving ball bearings'. The model then represents one part of this analogous relationship. In this example, the model is represented physically, but many analogies are used in explanations without necessarily any kind of physical or diagrammatic expression. Examples include thinking of the heart as a pump, of sound as ripples on a pond, or of electricity as a flow of water. In trying to understand new ideas, learners try to find something familiar to which they can link the new. The power of analogies is that they explicitly make these connections. However if the supposedly familiar (the source domain) is not well understood by the pupil, there will be problems in learning the new ideas (the target domain). For example, the difficult concept of potential difference in an electric circuit might be explained by analogy to pressure differences in an arrangement of water pipes and pumps. However, probing pupils' understanding of the flow of water in pipes reveals as many difficulties as with their understanding of electrical circuits. In using analogies effectively, it is important to know about the learners' prior knowledge of the source domain, and to explain the relationship between the source domain and the target domain (Dagher 1995).

As well as their role in learning, analogies have also played an important part in the development of scientific ideas. In developing his theory of the flow of electricity, for example, Ohm drew by analogy on the existing theory of heat flow, which in turn was based on the analogy of water flow. Metaphors, too, have contributed much to scientific thinking. They are more than verbal ornaments; metaphors shape the way we perceive and think about the world. Whereas an analogy says 'think of A as being like B', a metaphor suggests that 'A *is* B', and it is this that gives a new metaphor its capacity to surprise, to impress on the memory, or even to shock. To say that your word-processed file contains a self-replicating computer program does not sound quite so alarming as to say that it is infected by a computer virus. When the metaphor 'virus' was employed to describe this kind of program, it carried with it a whole set of meanings with which people were familiar because of their knowledge of real viruses. Much of scientific language is metaphorical, though through continued use, the roots of metaphors become less apparent. The origins of 'computer virus' are clear, and with a little thought, it is not difficult to see that an 'electrical current' might once have brought immediately to mind an image of flowing water. Largely forgotten are the roots of the 'cells' in living tissue (from monks' rooms in a monastery) and electrical 'batteries' (from the guns of an artillery unit).

Laws, theories and mathematics

As pupils' understanding of science progresses, we have seen how they move from simply observing and describing phenomena, to explaining these phenomena through representations or imagined worlds. They also progress from qualitative descriptions and explanations to quantitative mathematical approaches. How does mathematics fit into this story about imagined worlds? Here we look at the relationship between laws, theories and mathematics.

As a simple sketch, laws summarise the patterns found in data, while theories try to create imagined worlds that attempt to explain the way the real world works. This is an oversimplification, since finding a law needs some kind of theoretical assumptions in order to know what data to collect, and making a theory involves knowing some real world data. An example of *finding a law* comes from the seventeenth century. A familiar feature of the school science curriculum is the relationship between the pressure and volume of a fixed mass of gas:

$$PV = \text{constant (Boyle's Law)}$$

Robert Boyle found this relationship through systematic measurement of the behaviour of air when it was compressed and rarefied. He went rather further, however, than simply finding a relationship. He attempted to explain *why* the law should be like this by proposing that air consisted of 'springy' particles that could be squeezed together.

In the nineteenth century, a different, and more successful, theory was proposed. The 'kinetic theory of gases' assumed that a gas consisted of a collection of particles that were in constant random motion and which collided with the walls of the container. The kinetic model described earlier is a physical representation of this theoretical model. The success of this theory lies in its predictive and explanatory power. From a mathematical treatment of the behaviour of this collection of moving particles, Boyle's Law could be derived, along with many other known relationships about gases.

What the mathematics is doing in this example is breathing life into the imagined world of the moving particles. It is one thing to imagine a gas as consisting of moving particles, but quite another to think through the consequences of how a collection of randomly moving particles would behave. One way to do this is to represent these imagined entities mathematically by writing down algebraic equations. These mathematical representations may be manipulated, and predictions made which can be tested out by experiment. Of course, these algebraic manipulations are too demanding for pupils and this is why we use a perspex tube and ball bearings to demonstrate to them how the imagined world behaves.

This illustrates a central problem in science education. Scientists propose theories about the way the world may work. By manipulating theoretical entities, they make predictions that can be tested by manipulating physical entities in the real world. It is through this comparison between models and evidence that theories are modified and new ones developed. However, for pupils, manipulating theoretical entities is difficult, and so school science tends to overemphasize the manipulation of physical entities. In other words, they do practical work, with insufficient attention paid to theoretical interpretation or testing out ideas. Perhaps computer models have a powerful role to play here; they can allow pupils to manipulate directly the imagined entities of science, while leaving the computer to do the mathematics that brings these imagined worlds to life.

Computer models

Alongside the more traditional models, computer models are increasingly being used in schools. These have enormous potential for allowing pupils to explore and interact with ideas in a way that was not previously possible. There are many different kinds of software which use computer models, and it is useful to start by making a distinction between 'simulation' and 'modelling'. Here, the term 'simulation' will be used to mean 'model made by other people', while 'modelling' is an activity which pupils do themselves in which they create or modify models.

There are many simulations which are commercially available to support learning in particular topics – for example, simulations of circuit boards to construct electrical circuits, of the operation of a nuclear power plant, of different coloured lights and filters, of predator–prey populations, and so on. In studying science, it is essential that pupils gain first-hand experience of phenomena. A key question when deciding whether to use a computer simulation is 'How will pupils learn more by using this simulation than by studying the real thing?' There are a number of ways in which simulations can complement first-hand experience.

Some simulations are intended to be rather like the real thing. For example, Figure 12.4 shows a simulation of the Haber process, in which pupils can see how altering the temperature and pressure affects the yield of ammonia. The image portrayed on the screen gives a powerful sense of a 'real' industrial plant. There are many simulations of laboratory activities or industrial processes which can give pupils experiences which would otherwise be impracticable because of cost or safety. Simulations can also be used to explore the very fast or very slow. In a book which gives interesting insights into the role of simulation, Khan (1985) puts this strikingly as being able to operate 'outside the viscous flow of time in which we perform our own mundane tasks.'

This use of simulations as a 'virtual laboratory' makes them potentially very powerful learning tools. Of course, they cannot be a substitute for real experience – a computer cannot provide anything which compares with watching a crystal growing or seeing an evacuated can being crushed by atmospheric pressure. But by being able to interact with simulations, altering factors easily and exploring the effects, pupils can gain insights which practical work cannot always give them.

A word of warning is necessary, however. The ease with which a simulation can be used can be misleading if pupils confuse it with reality. Experimenting in the real world is a difficult and messy business. Factors may be very difficult to control and to manipulate, and the effects may not be clear to see or interpret. This is an important lesson of science, and one which pupils should learn through their own investigative work. But by teaching them explicitly about the nature of a simulation, pupils can learn not just about a particular topic, but about the way science is done. Pupils

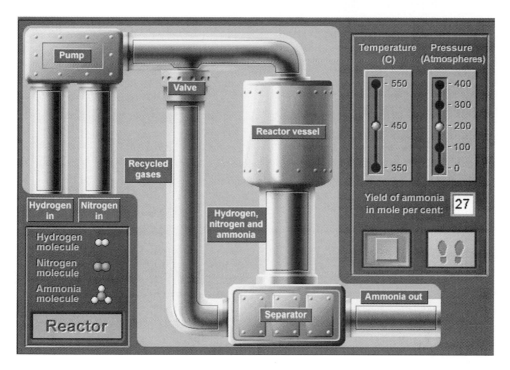

Figure 12.4 *A simulation of the Haber process*

Source: 'Haber Process' CD-ROM, Multimedia Science School

should understand that simulations are an essential tool of *science itself*. A simulation of a nuclear power plant may be a way of learning something about nuclear physics, but it can also be a way of gaining an appreciation of how computer models are used in science to make predictions and to develop understanding. These models are human constructions, based on assumptions and simplifications, so this can lead into broader social and controversial aspects of science – for example, the disagreements over the predictions made about global warming.

Not all simulations aim to be close imitations of the real thing. In Figure 12.5, a deliberately 'stripped-down' version of reality is presented in this simulation of the behaviour of an object thrown in the air. Throwing objects is not a difficult thing to do in reality. The simulation offers more, however. Over the 'stripped-down reality', it adds a layer of *conceptual interpretation*, by showing the directions of the *velocity* and the *force* acting on the object. A very common difficulty that pupils have is thinking that a force always acts in the direction of motion. What this simulation shows is that the force on the object while it travels through the air is always downwards (the force of gravity).

Most simulations used in learning science add these kinds of layers of conceptual interpretation, and they can be very powerful tools. While we encourage pupils to think about conceptual entities when they are doing practical work, and to use these ideas in interpreting what they observe, simulations can make these conceptual entities visible and available for manipulation.

Creating a model of something is a very powerful way of gaining an understanding of it (Mellar *et al.* 1994). There are a number of programs designed specifically for

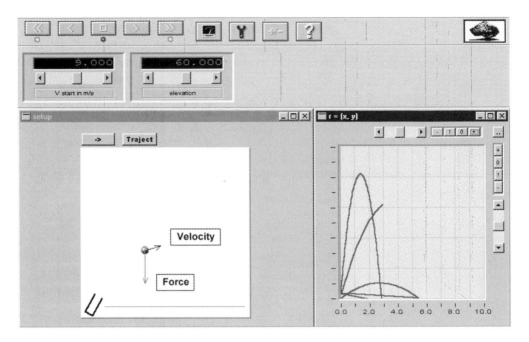

Figure 12.5 A simulation of projectile motion

Source: Albert software 'Projectile motion' (Albert Version 1.00) [NB: Labels 'Velocity' and 'Force' have been added]

creating models, but a convenient and popular choice is to use spreadsheet software. This has the advantage of being widely available, and pupils will also be developing the skills required to use it in other areas of the curriculum. A key difference between using a simulation and making a model, is that *the model is made explicit to the pupil*. In a commercial simulation of, for example, predator–prey populations, the equations of the model are hidden from the user and all they can do is to alter the values of the variables. But in a spreadsheet model, the model is explicit (pupils can see the equations), and the *model itself can be changed by the user*. It is this aspect of modelling which can potentially bring enormous benefits to pupils in their understanding of scientific concepts and relationships.

The models that pupils are able to make themselves are clearly going to be much simpler that the models which are used in commercial simulations. A very simple model that a pupil may make, for example, is to create a spreadsheet to perform a calculation based on the formula 'Time for a journey = Distance travelled/Velocity'. They can then enter different values for distance and for velocity, and see how this affects the time taken. Not the most exciting model in the world perhaps, but nevertheless, it still poses some challenges. But instead of calculating just one value, the model could be extended so that a number of different values are calculated, for example by keeping the distance constant and changing the velocity. The results can be plotted on a graph. Or two lines could be determined, representing different distances. Now there is a lot to be explored, and in engaging with such a model, pupils can understand a great deal about the nature of the relationship.

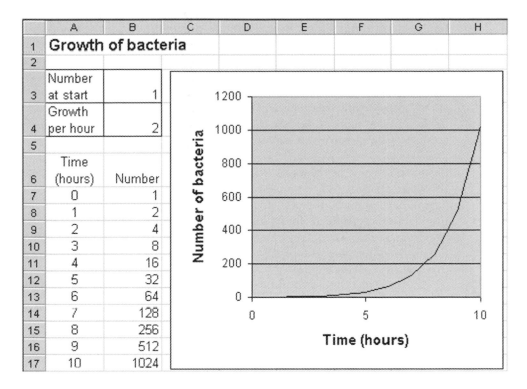

Figure 12.6 A spreadsheet model of bacterial growth

Simulations often follow how something changes over time, and a spreadsheet also allows these kinds of dynamic models to be built. Figure 12.6 shows a model that allows exploration of the exponential growth of bacteria. Many examples of more complex spreadsheet models suitable for science lessons can be found in professional journals for teachers (e.g. Brosnan 1989; Carson 1996; Diament and Clemenson 1996), and Tebbutt and Flavell (1995) offer a wealth of suggestions for using spreadsheets in science, including modelling activities.

Although spreadsheets have many advantages, they were not designed as modelling tools and can be cumbersome to use. There are, however, a number of purpose-built modelling programs which offer better graphical interfaces and other powerful features (Boohan 1994). While simulations are generally very intuitive to use, using a modelling program is more demanding in terms of the technical skills required, and the investment of time in learning these is an important consideration in choosing which software is appropriate.

Simplification revisited

We have seen throughout this chapter that making models is about creating simplified representations of the real world.

A physicist, an engineer, and a psychologist are called in as consultants to a dairy farm whose production has been below par. Each is given time to inspect the details of the operation before making a report.

The first to be called is the engineer who states: 'The size of the stalls for the cattle should be decreased. Efficiency could be improved if the cows were more closely packed, with a net allotment of 275 cubic feet per cow. Also the diameter of the milking tubes should be increased by 4 per cent to allow for greater average flow rate during the milking periods.'

The next to report is the psychologist who proposes: 'The inside of the barn should be painted green. This is a more mellow colour than brown and should help induce greater milk flow. Also, more trees should be planted in the fields to add diversity to the scenery for the cattle during grazing, to reduce boredom.'

Finally the physicist is called upon, who asks for a blackboard and draws a circle. 'Assume the cow is a sphere ...'

(Krauss 1994)

This is a clear case of simplification gone crazy! Or is it? Maybe a good way of increasing milk production would be to breed a 'supercow', the same shape as a normal cow, but just twice the size in each dimension. This would mean that its volume (and so its mass) would increase eight times, but the cross sectional area of its legs would only increase four times. It would have problems in supporting its own weight on its legs. Thinking about the cow like this suggests there would be a problem with a supercow. The model cow seemed like a joke at first, but maybe it can be a useful way of thinking about real cows. So, even apparently crazy ways of simplifying things can help us to a better understanding of the ways things are. Perhaps we should remember this when we ask pupils to imagine such crazy things as atoms, energy and genes.

References

Boohan, R. (1994) 'Interpreting the world with numbers: an introduction to quantitative modelling', in H. Mellar, J. Bliss, R. Boohan, J. Ogborn and C. Tompsett (eds) *Learning with Artificial Worlds: Computer-based Modelling in the Curriculum,* London: The Falmer Press, pp. 49–58.

Brosnan, T. (1989) 'Teaching chemistry using spreadsheets: equilibrium thermodynamics', *School Science Review* 70(252): 39–47.

Carson, S. R. (1996) 'Foxes and rabbits – and a spreadsheet', *School Science Review* 78(283): 21–7.

Dagher, Z. R. (1995) 'Review of studies on the effectiveness of instructional analogies in science education', *Science Education* 79(3): 295–312.

Diament, A. and Clemenson, A. (1996) 'Spreadsheet simulations of physical phenomena', *School Science Review* 78(283): 29–35.

Gilbert, J. K. (ed.) (1993) *Models and Modelling in Science Education*, Hatfield: Association for Science Education.

Kahn, B. (1985) *Computers in Science,* Cambridge: Cambridge University Press.

Krauss, L. M. (1994) *Fear of Physics: A Guide for the Perplexed*, London: Cape.

Mayer, R. E. (1989) 'Models for understanding', *Review of Educational Research* 59(1): 43–64.

Mellar, H., Bliss, J., Boohan, R., Ogborn, J. and Tompsett, C. (eds) *Learning with Artificial Worlds: Computer Based Modelling in the Curriculum,* London: The Falmer Press.

Tebbutt, M. and Flavell, H. (1995) *Spreadsheets in Science*, London: John Murray.

13 Making entities
Jon Ogborn, Gunther Kress, Isabel Martins and Kieran McGillicuddy

It has been common to think of classroom talk in science as 'inducting students into scientific discourse' or as their learning to 'talk science'. In our work on understanding the nature of science teachers' explanations, we treat the same issues as a matter of how 'entities of science' are *brought into being* for students (Ogborn *et al.* 1996). This reflects our preference for going beyond the realm of words and what they refer to, and to stress the role played by *action*, real and imagined, by and on *material things*. And we extend this preference to *conceptual 'things'*.

This view is inspired by some current philosophy of science, particular Harré (1985) and Bhaskar (1978). We take from them the idea of explanation as resting on 'how things are', as being stories about how a set of entities can produce the phenomenon to be explained. This conception makes space for analogy and metaphor in explanation (Rosch and Lloyd 1978; Lakoff and Johnson 1980; Lakoff 1987). We are also influenced by Piaget. In his later work, he offers an account of how the meanings of entities are constructed through action, through what they can do, what you can do to them and of what they are made (Piaget and Garcia 1987).

Scientific explanation

What makes a scientific explanation be something that *explains*? If I ask why water is falling from the sky and you tell me it is raining, I have only been given a label for what I see. Quite a lot of science teaching involves this kind of naming. If you tell me that it is raining because it rains a lot in April, I have been told only that raining is usual and needs no further explanation. But a story about a depression coming across the Atlantic and bringing wet air with it begins to do the job. Such an explanation tells how something or other comes about. This makes a scientific explanation very much like a story, even though it may not be told like a story. Some vital features of a story are that:

- there is a cast of protagonists, each of which has its own capabilities which are what makes it what it is;
- members of this cast enact one of the many series of events of which they are capable;
- these events have a consequence, which follows from the nature of the protagonists and the events they happened to enact.

In this light, let us consider some examples of scientific explanations:

How a river came to be polluted An explanation might be that farmers fertilize their crops, that rain washes fertilizer into the river and that the fertilizer makes plants in the water grow rapidly so that the water becomes full of decaying matter. The cast is farmers, fertilizers, rain, plants, and so on. Most of the things in the story are familiar.

The origin of coal This also uses common knowledge, but the story extends over hundreds of millions of years. The need for scales of time outside any possible experience demands imagination to think of the explanation as what 'really happened'.

The transmission of disease Since Pasteur, we live with a new world of invisible microscopic agents – bacteria and viruses. Although bacteria are visible in the microscope, explanations about them involve belief in a world, just as real as the everyday world, but on a scale too small to see or act upon directly.

The mechanism of heredity This introduces novel actions of novel entities. A mother and father passing characteristics to their child turns into a story about DNA. Possessing brown hair becomes possessing a set of chemically coded sequences in DNA. The story involves unfamiliar objects which do unfamiliar things in an inaccessible world.

How television works We are again in the realm of unfamiliar new imagined entities – magnetic and electric fields. Fields, talked of as existing in the real world, are also clearly something which someone once just thought of, a construction of the mind.

It is clear that scientific explanations rely on the existence of worlds of protagonists whose possible behaviours make up the story. But it is also clear that these worlds of protagonists are often far from everyday common sense. Such explanations make no sense until we know what the entities involved are supposed to be able to do or have done to them.

In one important respect, scientific explanations are *not* much like imaginative tales. Scientific explanations insist that their protagonists are to be taken as real things, existing beyond the closed world of one story and acting independently of our thinking and wishes. We can't wish things into existence in one context and out of existence in another, as it suits us. And we get more confident of the reality of imagined entities the more we can act on them or get them to act on other things.

Scientific explanations also rely on formal, sometimes mathematical, constructions. Thus the protagonists in explanation-stories must also be thought of as including such entities as harmonic motion, rates of change, differential coefficients, exponential decay, negative feedback, vectors, and so on. It may seem artificial to treat these formal entities on a par with material entities. Are they not just part of the law-like patterns of behaviour of material entities? The answer is that formal entities may begin life as law-like patterns, but they often develop a life of their own in explanations.

New things from old

A teacher, David, is talking about teeth:

David   Your teeth are part of your digestive system, your teeth take the food, smash it up into tiny bits, bite it off, smash it, make it into tiny bits.

What's going on here? Several accounts are possible: David is explaining the function of the teeth; he is explaining a part of the process of digestion; he is developing 'the concept of the digestive system'. But what strikes us most about it is that the teacher is trying to change what 'teeth' are for the students. The students already know a lot about teeth, from early childhood and beyond. They have been constantly reminded to clean them. They may remember losing milk teeth. They know – not necessarily consciously – that teeth are important in smiling. But now the teacher wants them to imagine teeth differently, not now as a part of the mouth, and not now in relation to feelings, but as a component of a biological system. Words like 'chew' associated with intentional action are avoided; instead the teeth are presented like machinery ('smash it up into tiny bits'). So, our account is that the teacher is busy *constructing a new entity,* the entity 'teeth in the digestive system'. Teeth are being given new meaning, just as (say) 'banks' are given new meaning when considered by an economist as part of the invisible economy, instead of as a place in the high street where one gets money.

There is a reason to change their world, a reason which derives from the nature of explanation. The everyday explanation of eating is that food is nice as well as neces-sary, sociable as well as personally satisfying. It satisfies wants. The biological expla-nation tells a story in a different world, made of organs, juices and biochemical processes. The biological actors in the story of digestion are not at all the social human actors of the everyday business of having lunch. So, to get to the biological explanations, the resources needed – the relevant biological entities – have to be constructed.

Making a new conceptual entity

The teacher in the extract below, Tom, has the perhaps unenviable task of intro-ducing his relatively low ability and sometimes difficult Year 9 class to 'the concept of density'.

Tom   Right, listen, what we want to do now is have a chat about, mmm, what this word means, density.

Student   *I* know.

Tom   Now, I'm going to tell you what density means, and then we're going to go and have a look at how you can measure it.

Student   Is it the same as on a disk?

Tom   No, well, in a way, what, you mean like a computer disk?

Student   Yeah.

Tom   How much information you've got? In a way it is.

Again, these students are encountering something new. As yet, 'density' is just a 'word' to them. For the term to develop, the teacher will have to perform a lot of work, over a long period of time, and the students will have to be active participants in that work. Already, one student is seeing if he can create his own tentative understanding, building by analogy. Others are likely to be doing the same even though they merely seem to listen.

Soon, the teacher moves from words into *activities* which seem quite different. In fact, he stops talking about density and puts pieces of wood and metal before the class, discussing which is heavier and which is bigger, and he *does* things together with the students, having them weigh various objects, and *look at* the objects to make guesses of their size. The work is directed at *things*, not at a *word* any more.

Over the span of a whole lesson, 'density' is gradually constructed. The teacher finally arrives at the form 'how many grams of stuff are there in every centimetre cubed'. This is rehearsed through repeating this form of words in several successive examples by questions of this kind:

Tom	Let's have a look and see if you know what to do. Meesha, what do you think is, has got more grams for every centimetre cubed, the piece of lead or a piece of wood?
Student	Piece of lead.
Tom	Piece of lead okay.

The repetition of these examples 'says' that these are all parallel cases; that the new idea is to be used in the same way in each. It repeats one of the things one can do with the entity density, namely deciding which of two things is more massive.

'Density' will continue to be transformed. Over several years it will be implicated in a wide variety of relations with other entities – floating ships, 'floating' continents, gases, mercury and barometers, the atmosphere and the weather. It will participate as an entity in a multitude of explanations. In all this, as it becomes related to other things, it will be undergoing yet further change. The students will be learning more of what you can do with this entity. For example, when eventually the density of a gas is considered, both 'gas' and 'density' will be changed into something else. Density will now apply to seemingly intangible things. And a gas will, as a result, come to seem more tangible, more substantial.

Why 'entities'?

In the discussion of David's lesson, we referred to the teeth as an 'entity'. For Tom's lesson, we have also, and with less obvious justification, called density an 'entity', as if it were to be thought about in the same way as the teeth. Why insist on it as an 'entity', implying that it is constructed in the same way as others? There are several reasons.

- We do not find it helpful to distinguish 'explanations of material things' from 'explanations of concepts'. Certainly, verbal forms of definition play a role in the latter, but the discussion of material things in the classroom also involves a lot of definition.

- The distinction between the material and the conceptual is not at all clear-cut in science itself. A chemical bond or a wave are conceptual and real at the same time. Forces and accelerations are concepts, but they are also talked about as things which affect one another.
- By thinking of all the elements that enter into scientific explanations as 'entities' of some kind, we can give a uniform account of explanations. We can think of explanations as being like stories in which actors play out their roles, and we can think of the actors (the entities) as the things about which the student has to learn.
- Meanings are constellations of possibilities; they are what something can do, can have done to it and what it can be made from or make. Of course *what* can be done with 'density' is not the same kind of thing as what can be done with 'teeth'. But learning their meaning is, in many ways, the same kind of job.

Resources for explanations

Much of the work of explaining in science classrooms concerns the resources out of which explanations are later to be constructed. Protagonists have to be described, by what they can do and have done to them, before any story which explains a phenomenon can be told. Before we can explain how batteries light lamps we have to tell about electric currents, voltages and resistances. Before we can explain respiration we have to tell about lungs, blood, oxygen, carbon dioxide and haemoglobin.

For these reasons, much of the work of explaining in science classrooms looks like describing, labelling or defining. It has to provide the material for explanations. The entities which are to be used in explanations have to be 'talked into existence' for students.

A simple example is where Steve is teaching a Year 7 group about melting:

Steve	Shamir?
Shamir	It's liquid.
Steve	Right. Okay, it's a liquid, like water, it's a liquid like water. Can you just explain what you mean by that.
Shamir	It's like, umm, it's runny.
Steve	It's runny. You can pour it, *(teacher picks up test tube)* you could pour it out of the tube. It's a liquid.

'Liquid' is much more than the 'correct scientific term' for runny things, though that may be how it seems at that moment. 'Liquid', along with 'solid' and 'gas', will gradually be transformed into 'states of matter'. And the reason to do that is not at all a matter of terminology. It is that different kinds of explanation are appropriate for accounting for these different states. Thus the 'terms' solid, liquid and gas are pointers to different kinds of explanation.

Providing resources to be used later obviously has its problems. It may seem to students too much like a case of 'medicine today, jam tomorrow'. For this reason, teachers need to provide effective motives. In the example below, the motive is provided by putting the 'entity-coming-to-exist' to use in a partial explanation of something familiar. The teacher is building up the entity 'hormones', but makes time for some examples of the working of hormones, in this case about what happens when you get a fright:

Leon	Umm, okay, umm, so, umm, that's another gland called the adrenal gland, A–D–R–E–N–A–L. Adrenal gland. *(writes 'Adrenal gland' on the whiteboard.)*
Student	That's what makes adrenalin?
Leon	Yes, well done, Myra. Ad–re–nal gland and it produces adrenalin, yeah.
Student	Is this for girls *and* boys?
Leon	Yeah, well, well everybody does this one, yeah. Yeah, the boys get frightened just the same as girls.
Student	Ohhh.
Leon	What's it for? [ ] Why would you want, your lungs, why would you want your rib cage to sort of come up to about here, and your diaphragm to go down to about there and then come back again? What are you trying to get a lot of?
Students	Air.
Leon	Well particularly [?]
Students	Oxygen.
Leon	Oxygen, yeah, and your heart instead of just going, *(makes small gestures over his chest)* toom, toom, toom, goes *(makes very large gestures across his body)* fe-toom, fe-toom. What are you trying to get round your body?
Student	Blood.
Leon	Lots of blood, which contains [?]
Students	Oxygen.
Leon	Oxygen, and [?]
Student	Food.
Leon	Food, right? What does that sound, like you're trying to get ready to do?
Student	Spree.
	(Student laughter.)
Leon	It sounds as though you're trying to get ready to do [?] Nasma, it sounds as though, you're trying to get, you're going to get ready for something pretty active, yeah?

As always, not one but many constructions are going on at the same time. The teacher's talk is crucial, as an example of how to talk, indeed of how to think. The very point of constructing entities as resources is that they need to become, not things to think *about*, but things to think *with*. This is the importance of teachers demonstrating in their own talk how to think with and manipulate one's knowledge.

Entities and their parts

So far we have mainly looked at the construction of meaning for entities in terms of what they can do and what can be done to them. A further aspect remains to be examined. It is 'what they are made of': the parts they have, and the other entities of which they are part.

In some cases, the parts of entities are straightforward, physical sub-components. The lungs have parts such as air passages and blood vessels, and are themselves part of both a physical thing, the body, and part of a conceptual entity, the respiratory system. All these facets contribute to the meaning packaged up in the entity 'lungs'.

One expects an organ like the lungs to have parts, but some entities have parts much less obviously. Here is Leon, stressing to Year 8 that lack of obviousness in the case of light itself being made of colours:

Leon	Have you, did you ever have one of those Barbie dolls? Yeah? Okay. Right, excuse me, if you, if you, take this leg off, and this leg off, and this arm off, excuse me, this arm off and the head off, right? You've got all the parts, yes?
Student	Yes.
Leon	Stop … the Barbie doll, you took the bits off, yes, and it's just like parts now. What happens if you, put this leg on and this leg on and this arm on and this arm and it's head on?
	…
Leon	It's a Barbie doll. So if you've got white light, yes, and you can separate it into all its colours – red, orange, yellow, green, and blue and violet, what happens if you put red, orange, yellow, green, and blue and violet back together again?
Students	They're white.
Leon	OK, right, that's how it works. I didn't think you'd get that one 'cause it's a hard one, okay.

Leon enforces the un-obvious idea that white light can be 'taken apart' into colours and then 'put together again' by the analogy with a doll which can obviously be taken apart and put together again. The analogy is not one which says anything about what light *is*. It is one which says something about what can be done to it.

Just as entities, in our way of thinking, are not at all restricted to physical entities but can be conceptual, so parts can also be conceptual. A lesson on sound may introduce the conceptual parts 'amplitude', 'wavelength' and 'frequency', or magnetic fields may be constructed as 'made of' lines of force. Amongst other important kinds of entity with parts are crucial tabular and diagrammatic knowledge structures such as the Periodic Table or the carbon cycle.

Prototypical explanations

Particular explanations use particular entities to account for a given phenomenon. But learning science is just as much learning about *kinds* of explanation, which differ in detail but are similar in form. For example, stability in biological organisms is accounted for in terms of controlled checks and balances between the actions of various influences. This scheme is used to explain the control of body temperature, of hormone levels, and even of the rate of breathing. It may be termed a prototypical explanation. In this way, an entity which fills a certain role (e.g. control) in one such explanation, for example a hormone, becomes more than a hormone. It is also a regulator – a general class of entities. And, of course, a hormone is already a class of entities, whose members include progesterone and testosterone.

Much of schooling in science necessarily concerns such prototypical explanations and classes of entities. Teaching about electric circuits is not teaching about 'this circuit here now', but is about how *a* current is produced by *a* voltage across *a* resistance. Teaching about gravity is about *a* force exerted on *a* mass. Later on, this is expanded to gravitational, electric and magnetic fields in general. While pupils mixing chemicals in test tubes may be talking about changes in temperature or colour, the teacher is trying to move the talk towards types of change in general.

To conclude, we return to the subject matter with which we began – digestion – to illustrate that general prototypical kinds of change need not just to be abstracted but also to be instanced. Here is the teacher, David, making sure that 'digestion' does not remain *only* a prototype; that what 'digestion' is in particular is also made vivid, immediate and concrete.

David   So right – here *(points at dissected rat)* here is the stomach – yeah? – and the food, when it's liquid, gets squirted into the first little bit of the tube there, which is called the duodenum … the duodenum is where extra digestive enzymes get squirted onto the food to help – to make – digestion continue.

Summary and conclusions

The variety of scientific entities needing to be brought into existence for students is large. Some are invisible or intangible – for example, microbes or waves. Some are patterns – for example, the Periodic Table. Some are abstract – for example, a sinusoidal graph. They may be real but newly minted objects (atoms), instruments (an oscilloscope), relations (Ohm's Law), classifications (fluid or gas), processes (melting or freezing), special objects of science (pendulum), or formal structures (straight line graphs). And, of course, they once all had to be brought into existence in science itself.

Why do we call them all 'entities'? One reason is that they are all new chunks of meaning. Just like real objects, abstract or formal ones get meaning from what they can do, what can be done to or with them, and what they are made from. The other reason is that they all enter into scientific and classroom discourse in a similar way, as 'things' with which or about which to think. They are different, but the fundamental work of constructing and using them looks much the same.

The distinction 'about which to think' versus 'with which to think' is crucial. Many scientific entities have to become tools for thought, even if to start with they are only things to think about. They have to become entities which are part of explanations, not things which are explained. So the construction of entities is also the construction of future explanations.

References

Bhaskar, R. (1978) *A Realist Theory of Science,* London: Harvester Wheatsheaf.

Harré, R. (1985) *Varieties of Realism,* Oxford: Blackwell.

Lakoff, G. (1987). *Women, Fire and Dangerous Things*, Chicago: Chicago University Press.

Lakoff, G. and Johnson, M. (1980) *Metaphors we Live by,* Chicago: University of Chicago Press.

Ogborn, J., Kress, G., Martins, I. and McGillicuddy, K. (1996) *Explaining Science in the Classroom,* Buckingham: Open University Press.

Piaget, J. and Garcia, R. (1987) *Vers une Logique des Significations,* Geneva: Murionde. (Translated 1991, *Toward a Logic of Meaning,* New Jersey: Lawrence Erlbaum.)

Rosch, E. and Lloyd, B. B. (1978) *Cognition and Categorisation,* New Jersey: Lawrence Erlbaum.

14 Numeracy in science
Graham Lenton and Brenda Stevens

The National Numeracy Project published by the DfEE (1998) produced a number of positive responses from different subject areas. Schools involved in the pilot project noted 'staggering' results, with improvement figures of up to 9 per cent for Key Stage 2 (7–11-year-olds) (Rafferty 1997). Whilst this project was focused through the core subjects of English, maths, and information and communication technology, it is clear that the National Numeracy Strategy will be of vital importance in many other subjects, such as geography (Davidson *et al.* 1998) and science. Although there appears to be a general lack of confidence in numeracy throughout the general public, this lack is perhaps not so evident in teachers of science, almost all of whom will have had some mathematical training, irrespective of their degree specialism in science.

Numeracy and the National Curriculum

The report on standards at Key Stage 3 (11–14-year-olds) by the Qualifications and Curriculum Authority (QCA 1998) points to the poor interpretation of graphs by pupils in this age range. It gives the example of only half the pupils in the 1997 National Curriculum Key Stage 3 science assessments being able to correctly interpret a graph showing colour changes with time as tea dissolves in water. It was suggested that some of the errors in their responses to this question resulted from a failure to read correctly the scale on the vertical axis.

Derived variables such as speed also cause pupils difficulties. In the same QCA science assessment report (1998), 60 per cent of pupils were able to calculate distance from speed and time; however, a further 25 per cent of pupils attempted to do this by dividing speed by time. In a more demanding question in the same test, only a quarter of the pupils were able to use the information provided to calculate time from speed and distance. (Compound measures are placed at level 7 in both the mathematics and science National Curriculums (DfEE/QCA 1999), whilst the interpretation of time-speed graphs is level 8 in science.)

At first sight these levels may appear higher than teachers might expect of their pupils, which could perhaps account for some of the difficulties described at Key Stage 3. However, there does seem to be some progress in using such information: comparisons of the 1996 and 1997 tests show certain areas of improvement.

Many of the ways in which science teachers handle number in science lessons demonstrate that they perhaps do not differentiate between ensuring an understanding of a particular concept and simply teaching the skill to produce a result. If children learn how to achieve a result from a conceptual viewpoint, rather than only working to a set of rules (the skill), then we may find that mathematical understanding and its use improves.

Why consider numeracy?

Numeracy (as defined below) is important in science because so much science relies upon an understanding of the underlying mathematics. It is therefore essential that science teachers are aware of the inherent difficulties that some pupils have with conceptual understanding in mathematics. This is particularly important in those areas that relate closely to science and underpin understanding of science concepts. Some science teachers may have their own conceptual difficulties with mathematics. Recent observations of student teachers in science by the authors have supported this assumption.

Many pupils exhibit anxiety when confronted with using mathematical ideas in science. There may be a number of reasons for this. The language of mathematics uses many conventions and symbols that can inhibit pupils' understanding and handling of concepts. Often pupils will manipulate data or perform mathematical tasks effectively in maths lessons but when confronted with the same or a similar task in science will not be able to transfer the skill. This may be due to the use in science of a different term, a different approach to a problem, or a lack of confidence in the pupils.

What is numeracy?

Many student teachers have a narrow perception of numeracy. They also often do not realize how important it is to appreciate that pupils often have a fear of maths; they have an in-built barrier when anything mathematical is proposed, or when calculations are expected during science lessons.

Numeracy is defined by the National Numeracy Project as more than knowing about numbers and number operations. It includes an ability or inclination to solve numerical problems, and familiarity with the ways in which numerical information is gathered and is presented in graphs, charts and tables (DfEE 1998). Numerate pupils should:

- be confident enough to solve problems without going to others to seek advice or help;
- have a sense of size of number;
- be able to calculate accurately, both mentally and on paper;
- have strategies to check whether their answers are reasonable, and be able to suggest suitable units for measuring;
- be able to estimate to a reasonable degree of accuracy.

Numeracy and science

An enormous number of areas of science rely upon the use and understanding of mathematical concepts. The use of ratios and fractions, scale factors and place value, representing data in graph and table form, equations, derived variables such as density and speed, are just a few examples. Below we look at some of these more closely to investigate problems associated with their use in science.

Ratios and percentages

Ratios and percentages present enormous problems for many children and yet the use of percentages is a common practice and understanding is assumed in the teaching of many science ideas. Children can, for example, have difficulty in translating percentages into real figures. Calculation with percentages is level 5 in National Curriculum maths (DfEE/QCA 1999), whilst calculating using ratios is level 6.

The following example is from the DES Assessment of Performance Unit research (APU 1985).

> Anthracite is composed of the elements carbon, hydrogen, nitrogen and oxygen in the following proportions by mass:
>
> carbon = 93.3%; hydrogen = 3.0%;
>
> nitrogen = 1.0%; oxygen = 2.7%.

There was only a 59 per cent success rate when pupils were asked what mass of carbon is contained in 100 g of anthracite, a 46 per cent success rate when asked what mass of oxygen was contained in 200 g of anthracite, and only 34 per cent success rate when asked how many grams of anthracite contained a combined mass of 12 g of hydrogen and nitrogen.

The number system

The understanding of decimals can be problematic. When some 15-year-old children were asked to choose the number with the smallest value from a series of numbers with decimal places such as 0.625, 0.25, 0.3753, 0.125 and 0.5 (APU 1983), 36 per cent chose the number with the largest number of digits (i.e. 0.3753) irrespective of the value of the number. This shows that they may have a misconception regarding the meaning of the decimal point. The use of superscripts to define the power of a number leaves many pupils mystified: they cannot relate it to the same number with a decimal point (e.g. $0.1 = 10^{-1}$). Similarly, zero and negative numbers produce misunderstandings. Often pupils have difficulty in handling zeros, especially when subtraction is involved. However, it must be remembered that some of these skills are considered level 8 in National Curriculum maths (DfEE/QCA 1999).

Graphs

Graphs present a number of problems. First, interpretation of graphical information often produces poor or misconceived responses (Taylor and Swatton 1990). When transferring data to graphical form, pupils often do not choose the best representation. For example, a group of children observed (by us) in a science lesson on heartbeat rate had taken their pulse readings before and after exercise. They had taken readings at 2 minute intervals after exercise and recorded the pulse rate for about 15 minutes, until the heart had returned to the normal rate. They were asked to plot their results on a graph (no mean feat, in view of having to place the records at the appropriate point on the time axis). Some pupils asked if they could use a bar chart rather than a line graph, clearly showing a misunderstanding of the use of these two forms of graph. These skills are considered level 5 and 6 in science and level 6 in mathematics, whilst producing graphs with lines of best fit is level 7 in science.

Measures and scales

Pupils studying science are regularly expected to read scales for collection of data during investigations (level 4, maths and science). Rulers, thermometers and balances each involve their own particular problems (Strang 1990). Invariably accuracy of reading or manipulation of the reading needs careful consideration. Tare-balance reading often produces further problems, such as, when to use the tare and how to handle the reading on the balance once the tare has been used. Yet many top-pan balances in laboratories have this facility.

Once a reading has been taken the interpretation of that reading may have further implications. For example, if a thermometer has risen from 20 °C to 40 °C, has the temperature doubled? Many pupils and student-teachers will say yes to this question (our observations). One might ask in what sense is this doubling or not doubling? It may not be possible for a teacher to fully explain the answer but it is well worth raising the issue for pupils to consider the difference between interval scales (e.g. temperature in °C) and ratio scales (e.g. as in length). Offering pupils a comparison which is clearly an example of doubling (e.g. 6 cm is twice as large as 3 cm) may help to clarify the issue.

Without practical experience of estimation, children will inevitably do it badly. How much does a pencil weigh? – 0.4 g, 4 g★, 40 g, 400 g? (★correct answer). They could be asked to hold a pencil to experience the feeling of 4 grams, not just be told that it is that mass. Approximately how long is a million seconds? – 1 hour, 12 hours, 1 day, 10 days★, 25 days, 1 month, 1 year? (★actually 11 days). They could be asked to sit silently for, say, 2 minutes to gain a perception of 120 seconds.

The use of derived variables (compound measurements) such as speed and density relies on the conceptual understanding of the interaction of two variables. Concrete examples such as holding two blocks of metal (e.g. aluminium and iron) of similar size but of different density can alleviate this difficulty.

If a sheet of paper is rolled in two different directions (Figure 14.1) and pupils are asked if the two volumes enclosed by each cylinder are the same, many will say that they are. In fact, they enclose very different volumes, obvious when trialled practically. Pupils who have answered 'yes' to the question may hold a misconception: the conservation of surface area does not necessarily determine conservation of volume.

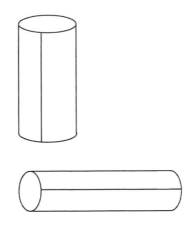

Figure 14.1 An A4 sheet of paper rolled in different directions to demonstrate the different volumes enclosed

Statistics

All children need to be able to use everyday statistics and to interpret common representations of statistics in our daily lives. Some basic statistical terms, such as average and mean, median and mode, are not generally well understood and can be used to misinform unless the reader/listener is fully aware of the differences. A manager might use the most favourable average wage of the workforce by selecting from the median or mean to demonstrate what people earn in a company, whilst the union representative would almost certainly use the mode company wage (a lower figure) if a pay rise was requested. Both could be said to be average wages but could be very different figures. Bar charts are commonly used in daily newspapers and by financial institutions selling investments. These can often misrepresent data if the reader misreads the vertical axis, the axis starts above zero or a large scale is used for an axis. Pie charts have their own problems (level 6 in maths and science).

In science, pupils often find the terms discrete and continuous difficult to apply to variables. If the terms 'counting' and 'measurement' are applied to the two terms, respectively, then there is usually no problem, but it is important for teachers to help and direct in these matters.

Clearly there needs to be an emphasis by the teacher on interpretation of these sorts of statistics for developing numeracy through science.

Facts and skills versus concepts

Many of these difficulties with mathematical concepts arise through not distinguishing between the teaching of facts and skills and teaching through conceptual understanding. In many schools today some mathematics may be taught by non-specialist teachers. Equally, science teachers may not have had a mathematical background. These teachers may not be aware of the nature of the conceptual problems that pupils have and, indeed, may even hold them themselves. It is important to teach from a conceptual point of view rather than from a rote-learned formula or process.

Most children can easily calculate an area if given the dimensions but very few have a conceptual image of a hectare or of a thousand square metres, for example. Many, children can draw a graph from data but find it difficult to interpret a graph presented to them.

Children often have their own successful ways of solving problems mathematically but may be forced into using methods (skills) that the teacher has used themselves. On the other hand, sometimes children form their own generalizations, that do not always apply, and then arrive at incorrect answers simply because they do not understand the underlying concept. For example, applying the 'rule' of the addition of a zero when multiplying by ten works well for whole numbers but when applied to decimals ($2.3 \times 10 = 2.30$) it fails (Askew and William 1995). These generalizations can thus be counterproductive. Unless the teacher makes specific efforts to uncover them they will remain hidden.

Too often, textbook examples assume too much of the learner. An example from a currently used textbook on acceleration is given in Box 1. The calculation is clearly shown, but then it continues to show how the force needed can be calculated from the acceleration. Although each step is clear to a mathematically competent person, to an average 13/14-year-old it may not be. Each step may need to be discussed and support and guidance is clearly needed from the teacher. A possible alternative approach is suggested in Box 1.

Another textbook showed a nutrient list of vitamins measured in μg and mg, but there was nothing to say what a μg was or how it related to a mg. Points such as these can easily muddle pupils and be detrimental to their understanding. Surely all that is needed in this case is a statement explaining that a μg is 1/1000 of a mg, followed by support from the teacher stating that μ is always 1/1000 of m, whatever the unit? Perhaps also somewhere in the text, not necessarily at that particular point, there should be reference to the size of a μg in terms of everyday masses or units. For example, the mass of a 20p coin (5 g) is five million μg – and there are one million seconds in 11 days.

Ways forward

It is important that we, as science teachers, do not reinforce the negative messages about numeracy so often apparent amongst children and adults. The emphasis should always be on positive encouragement, and teachers should enthuse about the importance of using these skills to help understand science. It is also important that science teachers know what is being taught in the mathematics department in their school and how and when common skills are being taught, so that pupils can see some commonality in the subjects. We need to talk with pupils to find out what they understand and how they use their numerical skills and concepts to solve problems. Only by knowing what they are doing and how they are thinking can we help them to understand, use and apply numeracy effectively.

As science teachers we need to clarify to pupils:

- what needs to be remembered by them (facts, conventions);
- what they must practise (skills);

- what they can come to understand for themselves (concepts);
- when they have to make decisions about the approaches to use (strategies).

So, facts and conventions need to be learned and remembered. We need to make sure that pupils gain the skills of manipulating formulae and give them practice to become fluent. Pupils need to experience concepts in order to understand them and be given opportunities to solve problems so that they have to make decisions and learn which strategies are best to employ. Only by giving them time and opportunity to estimate, calculate. interpret, and discuss with each other and with the teacher, will they really gain a full understanding of the numerical and other mathematical concepts within science.

Box 1   Teaching facts and skills versus conceptual understanding

Textbook example of teaching facts and skills

A rugby player of 130 kg runs at 10 m/s. He needs to be stopped by another player or he will score. He can be stopped within 2 seconds. What is the force needed to stop him?

Calculation

The velocity change is 10 m/s to zero in 2 seconds.

$$\text{Acceleration} = \frac{\text{final velocity} - \text{starting velocity}}{\text{time taken}}$$

$$= \frac{0 - 10 \text{ m/s}}{2 \text{ s}}$$

$$= -5 \text{ m/s}^2$$

$$\text{Force needed} = \text{mass} \times \text{acceleration}$$

$$= 130 \times (-5 \text{ m/s}^2)$$

$$= -650 \text{ N}$$

How would the force differ if it took 3 s to stop him?

$$\text{Force} = 130 \text{ kg} \times \frac{0 - 10 \text{ m/s}}{3s}$$

$$= 130 \text{ kg} \times (-3.33 \text{ m/s}^2)$$

$$= -432.9 \text{ N}$$

Alternative version for conceptual understanding

This example is about the notion of velocity and acceleration (**concept**).

A rugby player weighing 130 kg runs at a velocity (remember this is speed in one direction) of 10 metres per second (m/s). He needs to be stopped by another player tackling him or he will score. He can be stopped in 2 seconds. What is the force needed by the tackling player to stop him?

Calculation

You will need to **remember** that if the player is stopped the velocity change from 10 metres per second to zero will be **negative** since he is slowing down. This slowing down is often called **deceleration**. The **convention** is that we use a negative value for deceleration (remember this).

$$\text{Acceleration} = \frac{\text{final velocity} - \text{starting velocity}}{\text{time taken}}$$

$$= \frac{0 - 10 \text{ m/s}}{2 \text{ s}}$$

$$= -5 \text{ m/s}^2$$

Working out this formula is a **skill** you must be able to carry out.

So the answer is −5 metres per second per second. This is a difficult unit and means that after each second he is going 5 metres per second more slowly. So in 2 seconds he will have slowed down to 0 over a distance of 10 metres.

This is the **concept** of deceleration (imagine yourself slowing down – what does it feel like and what happens?).

Now the force calculation

Force is mass × acceleration (another **concept** that you will come to understand). Since our calculation (**skill**) for acceleration is a minus figure the force will also be negative (**convention**).

$$\text{Force needed} = \text{mass} \times \text{acceleration}$$

$$= 130 \times (-5 \text{ m/s}^2)$$

$$= -650 \text{ N}$$

So the figure −650 newtons means that to stop the rugby player a force of 650 newtons must be applied in the opposite direction to that in which the tackled player is running.

How would the force differ if it took 3 seconds to stop the player instead of 2 seconds?

$$\text{Force} = 130 \text{ kg} \times \frac{0 - 10 \text{ m/s}}{3 \text{ s}}$$

$$= 130 \text{ kg} \times (-3.33 \text{ m/s}^2)$$

$$= -432.9 \text{ N}$$

So this means in this case that a force of −432.9 newtons is necessary to stop the rugby player from scoring.

If you were the rugby player would you rather experience the force of −650 newtons or −432.9 newtons? Why?

References

Askew, M. and William, D. (1995) 'Recent Research in Mathematics Education 5–16', *Ofsted Reviews of Research*, London: HMSO.

Assessment of Performance Unit (1983) *A Review of Monitoring in Mathematics 1978–1982, Part 1*, London: Department of Education and Science.

Assessment of Performance Unit (1985) *New Perspectives on the Mathematics Curriculum*, London: Department of Education and Science.

Davidson, G., Stevens, B. and Williams, A. (1998) 'Numeracy through geography', *Teaching Geography* 23(4): 174–7.

DfEE (1998) *National Numeracy Project*, London: DfEE Publications.

DfEE/QCA (1999) *The National Curriculum: Handbook for Secondary Teachers in England (Key Stages 3 and 4)*, London: HMSO.

QCA (1998) *Standards at Key Stage 3: Science: Report on the 1997 National Curriculum Assessments for 14-year-olds*, London: Qualifications and Curriculum Authority.

Rafferty, F. (1997) 'Real Maths wins praise', *Times Educational Supplement* (12 December).

Strang, J. (1990) 'Measurement in school science', *Assessment Matters 2*, London: SEAC (EMU).

Taylor, R. M. and Swatton, P. (1990) 'Graph work in school science', *Assessment Matters 1*, London: SEAC (EMU).

15 Assessing conceptual understanding
John Oversby

What counts as understanding?

If you look at many of the books written about science education, you will find wide discussion of ideas such as misconceptions, concept maps, conceptual progress and concepts of learning. Surprisingly, there is much less attention paid to explaining what a concept *is*. For the purpose of this chapter, I am going to use the term 'concept' to mean a mental generalization about a class of instances or specific examples. The mental generalization serves to distinguish the concept from similar concepts, to test whether a new instance is an example of the concept, and to use the concept to construct a network of related concepts or a schema. Many concepts can be constructed directly by generalizing from experience of many instances. Often, though, concepts are presented directly and then exemplified.

As an example, to make this process clear, let us consider the concept of 'acid'. It is common practice in school science to establish this concept by asking learners to investigate the attributes of materials named as acids. Given samples of fruit acids, vinegar (ethanoic acid) and mineral acids, their reactions with magnesium or sodium carbonate demonstrate similarity in behaviour. Other materials, such as common salt (sodium chloride) solution, do not behave in this way and so are not instances of the concept 'acid'. In this way, a distinction between examples and non-examples of 'acid' is established. In teaching this concept, the generalization is given but is then exemplified through experiment to clarify when it is appropriate to use the concept and when it is not.

The concept of 'acid' is thus a mental construction. It is used in this case to classify materials into two groups, acids and non-acids. One purpose of the development of this concept is to predict the behaviour of novel materials that are also named as acids. This behaviour can be investigated and the extent to which the material can be described as an acid established. The concept of 'acid' represents an idealization; it contains a description of the behaviour of an ideal acid, even if no real material behaves completely in this way. The concept is made richer by the use of a universal indicator. It is subdivided into a continuum of stronger and weaker acids by observation of the range of colours seen when the indicator is added to various acid solutions. The new concept of 'acid solution strength' is related practically to 'acid' by the use of the indicator.

In some cases, instances of concepts are very difficult to demonstrate or make real. For example, it is easier to exemplify concepts such as 'acid' or solution' than those such as 'atom' or 'molecule'. In order that a concept such as 'molecule' may be more readily established, instances are illustrated by constructing representations or models. A model relates to the original it represents in only some ways. The lack of appreciation by learners of how the models relate to the actual instances can lead to misconceptions, by incorrectly ascribing the attributes of one to the other. For example, learners may believe that 'atoms' are solid in the same way that everyday material can be; they may also believe that the 'atoms' will themselves expand when heated. In this case, the learner has ascribed incorrect properties to the concept, and it is clear that this will lead to inappropriate explanations of phenomena.

I would argue that the learners' 'mental models' (their own understandings of the models) are in a dynamic relationship with the concepts that they understand. As an example, mental models of the ethanol molecule are based on understandings of the concepts of molecule, bond, molecular topology, atom, element, stoichiometry, chemical formula, and other concepts. It is likely that use of the variety of mental models of the ethanol molecule will lead to clarification of many of these concepts. Models and concepts are, therefore, linked with each other in developing understanding.

This chapter considers a variety of ways of assessing conceptual understanding. Real understanding is often disguised by the methods we use to explore it, such as asking learners to recall information, or label a diagram, or explain a phenomenon. We may ask learners to explain why a particular instance is an example of a concept, or to distinguish between two similar concepts. Those who can distinguish very fine distinctions are thought to show greater understanding. However imperfect these methods are, they are in common use in science teaching and are the best we have. Performance in responding to questions or tasks is what is actually measured.

A concept, clearly, is not simply the sum of its attributes. Probing the characteristics of a concept does not mean that we know the concept is well established. We should also admit that some concepts are difficult to describe but can be understood, even by the very young. One of these is happiness!

Developing understanding: the example of dissolving

In order to illustrate how concepts can be understood and used at different levels, I shall discuss the example of dissolving. Dissolving is a central theme in science education with explanations at many levels. The simplest explanations are descriptive. In the 2000 National Curriculum for Science for England (DfEE and QCA 1999) the following statement appears for pupils aged 7–11 years old (Key Stage 2):

> Pupils should be taught to describe changes that occur when materials are mixed *(for example, adding salt to water)*. [Italics in original]

It is traditional for primary children to examine dissolving salt and sugar in water and researchers have studied this extensively (e.g. Johnstone and Scott 1991; Longden *et al.* 1991; Fensham and Fensham 1987). There are serious problems for learners in using these examples, since the dissolved materials are then invisible. It is not surprising that young children readily say that the salt has disappeared, and indeed it cannot be seen any more. Use of coloured solutes, such as tea and coffee and food colourings, is less common, despite their advantage in making it clear that the solute is still there in some form. In a study with which I was involved, a research student (Papageorgiou 1999) showed that using coloured solutes with Greek Cypriot children did help them to understand what the solute was doing. Another student (Gödek 1997) showed that students generally focused on the solute and ignored the solvent. The solvent is often not described in terms of particles but as a continuous material. The solvent is seen as passive, as simply a material that helps the solute to free up (*dissolvere* in Latin means to free up).

The 2000 National Curriculum gives these statements related to dissolving for 11–14-year-old pupils:

Pupils should be taught:

- that mixtures *(for example … sea water …)* are composed of constituents that are not combined;
- that when physical changes *(for example … formation of solutions)* takes place, mass is conserved;
- about the variation of solubility with temperature, the formation of saturated solutions, and the differences in solubility in different solutes.

One activity usually carried out at this level is to investigate the notion of saturation, often through very crude semi-quantitative experiments. Saturation is then described as the solution being 'full up', which is consistent with the notion of the solute 'hiding in the solvent'. A common explanation is that the solute particles slip into spaces that already exist in the liquid solvent. Again, the solvent adopts a passive role. In addition, this explanation encourages a range of misconceptions, such as there being large spaces in liquids, and of the relative sizes of particles in the solvent and solute. These ideas are at odds with simple scientific observations. In the first case, liquids are incompressible, and this would not be so if there were large spaces between the particles. In the second case, the molecules in solutes such as sugar are many times larger than the water molecules, yet sugar dissolves.

Levels of understanding

We have seen that a concept, such as dissolving, can be understood at different levels. This section explores two ways in which these different levels could be characterized. The first is Bloom's taxonomy of cognitive understanding and the second is a progression in explanations related to models. Examples of the kinds of questions related to the various levels are given. These questions could be used directly with learners, for example, in a class discussion, but more fundamentally, they are intended to provide a basis for thinking about what knowledge we are trying to assess, in order to develop assessment tasks. Developing such tasks is the focus of a later section.

Bloom's taxonomy of educational objectives

Bloom (1956) constructed a list or 'taxonomy' of educational objectives. This had a hierarchical structure, in which each category of objectives built on the lower levels.

A modified version of his hierarchy in terms of concepts, with brief explanations, is shown in Table 15.1. Examples of questions that might elicit responses at different levels are also given.

Table 15.1 A modified version of Bloom's taxonomy applied to concepts (from lowest to highest)

Level	How concepts can be used	Questions about dissolving	Other examples of questions in other concept areas
Recognition	The concept has been met before.	Do you know that dissolving happens when we put sugar into tea?	Have you heard of the term 'frequency'?
Recall	The concept can be distinguished from similar concepts and recalled.	When we make tea by putting hot water on a tea bag, the water goes brown. What is the name of the process by which the brown material is extracted from the water?	What do we call animals that have backbones?
Comprehension	The concept can be understood in familiar and unfamiliar contexts.	Grass stains can be removed using white spirit dabbed onto clothing. Explain this using the term 'dissolving'.	Explain what is meant by 'fertilizes' in: Sexual reproduction in plants occurs when the pollen fertilizes the ovule.
Application	The concept can be used in new contexts to develop general ideas.	Caffeine can be taken out of coffee using liquid carbon dioxide. Explain why this takes out only caffeine and not other parts of the coffee.	By considering the forces on a tennis ball thrown into the air, explain its motion from leaving the hand until it hits the ground.
Analysis	The concept can be used to tease out meaning of a set of data or related concepts.	Sodium chloride is quite soluble in water but hardly soluble in hydrocarbons such as hexane. Discuss this difference in terms of solvation energy of the chloride and sodium ions and the lattice energy of the sodium chloride solid.	Using the idea of food, explain how a food chain predicts that there will be fewer carnivores than herbivores in a particular environment.

continued on next page

Table 15.1 A modified version of Bloom's taxonomy (cont.)

Synthesis	The concept is used to integrate a collection of ideas.	When anhydrous blue cobalt chloride is mixed with water, a pink solution is created. How can this be explained in terms of enthalpy and entropy changes?	The biological concept of an organ treats the human body as isolated systems. How effective is this concept in explaining the action of the lungs in respiration?
Evaluation	The concept can be compared with other related concepts for the same phenomena for explanatory power.	The solubilities of salts containing doubly charged anions and cations are generally much lower than the solubilities of salt containing singly charged anions and cations. How far is this true? Can you explain exceptions to this generalization?	Different models of atomic structure exist. In one, balls that move in a system similar to that of a solar system represent the electrons. In another, the electrons are represented as charge clouds that fill up the available space. How good are these two models in visualizing atomic radii?

Thus the lowest level is Recognition, which is simply that the learner has met the name of the concept before. They would be able, for example, to recognize the terms 'solution' or 'solute'.

An intermediate level, for example, is Application. At this level, the concept could be used in a new context, for the pupils, such as the use of forces in throwing a ball in the air. 'Explain why the distance from the ground of a ball thrown into the air changes, even though the gravitational force remains the same.'

The highest level is Evaluation. An example of this level in the context of atomic structure is: 'Different models of atomic structure exist. In one, balls that move in a system similar to that of a solar system represent the electrons. In another, the electrons are represented as charge clouds that fill up the available space. How good are these two models in visualizing atomic radii?' In this example, the student is being asked to reflect on two models, and to evaluate the power of each in explaining a particular characteristic of atoms. Such an argued evaluation is typical of this level.

Ladder of explanations

Another approach is to consider how models are used for explanatory purposes. The difficulties learners have, and the successes they achieve, in understanding science may be understood through a psychological framework of constructing models. By 'model', I mean a representation of a variety of targets that can include an object, an idea, a process, a system, an event or an entity. Representations (models) have a variety of expressions, such as physical objects, drawings, animations, and mathematical functions. The mental models of learners also have correspondences and non-correspondences with expressed models as well as the targets. The scientific community has its own set of consensus models and some historical models that have been discarded. It seems also that particular sets of consensus models are used specifically for teaching purposes.

These models have explanatory purposes which appear to progress in the following order (Gilbert *et al.* 1998a; 1998b):

- intentional
- descriptive
- interpretative
- causal, involving a mechanism
- predictive.

Table 15.2 shows this 'ladder of explanations' with a brief explanation about each of the terms and examples of the types of explanations in the context of dissolving. The examples are discussed more fully below. The idea of ladders of explanations is yet to be explored across a range of scientific contexts before it can be seen to be generally helpful in identifying progression, but it does seem to have some potential.

Table 15.2 A ladder of explanations (from lowest to highest)

Level	Characteristics of explanation	Comments in the context of dissolving
Intentional	These explanations define boundaries between phenomena.	They involve distinguishing, for example, between the processes of dissolving and melting.
Descriptive	These explanations provide information at an observational level.	They relate surface features of dissolving such as colour, temperature changes and homogeneity.
Interpretative	These explanations give a way of looking at reality without intending a cause and effect explanation. In practice, they are often combined with other explanations to make them into cause and effect explanations.	These use a particle model to explore dissolving at a molecular level. At a simple level, entities are represented as (generalized) particles, while more detailed explanations refer to molecules and ions, and solvated species.

continued on next page

Table 15.2 A ladder of explanations (cont.)

Cause and effect	Cause and effect explanations are based on a mechanism. They usually require some generalization across a wide range of phenomena.	Explanations are generalized across a range of solutions, and imply a mechanism. They are normally based on a particle model and deal with forces of attraction between particulate entities such as ions, molecules and solvated species.
Predictive	These explanations are built on a wide range of experimental evidence and are constructed with confidence. Commonly, they are quantitative.	At a low level, they focus on one variable e.g. the effect of lattice energy, the attraction between ions in a lattice. At a higher level, predictive explanations synthesize a range of contributions such as lattice energy, hydration energy, and entropies of solvation to yield an overall prediction.

Intentional explanations

In the context of dissolving, intentional explanations serve to 'fence off' dissolving from other phenomena. This may seem trivial at first sight yet the distinction between dissolving and melting indicates that it is not. For young children, ice cream just simply melts since the availability of thermal energy from warm air is not obvious. If dissolving and melting are identified as changing into a liquid, then it is easy to see how dissolving common solid solutes in water to create aqueous solutions can be perceived as melting. An intentional explanation would include the concept of energy input in melting, and the necessity of two substances, a solute and a solvent, in dissolving.

Descriptive explanations

Descriptive explanations of dissolving include both the formation of a single medium or a homogeneous solution (in the case of complete dissolution), and the formation of two or more phases (in the case of partial solution). In the case of salt dissolution, a saturated solution can be identified if excess solid salt is present in contact with the solution.

Interpretative explanations

The 2000 National Curriculum for Science in England has no direct reference at all to solutions in the statements for pupils aged 14–16. The simple pictures of particles intermingling are interpretative. Physical models such as mixing currants (the solute) with dried lentils (the solvent) are also interpretative. More able children in primary schools may well be asked to explain dissolving in terms of particles. In most cases they will draw simple particle mixtures or make mixtures such as currants and lentils (Oversby 2000), in line with the 2000 National Curriculum statement that dissolving is a physical process.

Causal explanations

Causal explanations arise from some understanding of the dissolving process. It is helpful at this point to think about insoluble materials. If dissolving is simply a matter of particles mingling, it really is difficult to explain why anything should be insoluble. We need to be a bit more thoughtful about what happens in the particulate mixing model. As the solvent particles move in between the solute particles, the solute particles move in between the solvent particles. It is a mutual process. Both sets of particles have to be separated. A satisfying explanation for why sand does not dissolve in water might be that the forces holding sand together are too strong to be separated. We know that these forces are strong because it is very difficult to melt sand, which would separate the particles. This is a very attractive explanation.

Salt dissolving should be very surprising! Salt melts at a very high temperature (801 °C, almost too hot for some Bunsen burner flames), so the particles in salt must be held together very strongly. However, in dissolving, water manages to separate these particles at room temperature. How it manages to do this is explained as follows. The particles in salt are held together very strongly, and water molecules are also held together in liquid water, although nothing like so strongly. As the salt dissolves, some molecules of water become strongly attached to the salt particles. The amount of energy released by this is almost the same as the energy needed to separate both the salt and water in the first place. This can be seen if the temperature is measured both before and after dissolving. The temperature hardly changes.

If the particles in the solute are held together too strongly then the water cannot separate them. The solute will then be insoluble. Limestone (calcium carbonate) is a good example of this. There are many intermediate cases, and usually there is a low limit to how much can be dissolved and the solution easily becomes saturated. It has nothing to do with there being spaces in the liquid being available to be filled up!

Predictive explanations

These are often made but are sometimes too generalized. A common example is to make the statement, in the context of dissolving, 'like dissolves like'. This is taken to mean that ionic and polar solutes dissolve more readily in polar solvents. While this is an over-generalized statement, as can be easily verified by examining the large number of insoluble salts, a converse can be quite useful. Ionic solutes are hardly soluble in non-polar solvents. Thus, we can predict with some safety that potassium chloride will be insoluble in toluene, and the evidence then bears this out.

Techniques for probing understanding

Traditional written tests tend to use a relatively small number of familiar techniques. These include multiple choice questions, sentence completion, labelling, short-answer structured questions, and so on. Below, I discuss three examples of less-commonly used techniques for assessing conceptual understanding. These are potentially valuable since they may be able to give a greater insight into pupils' understanding than more conventional techniques.

> **The experiment was demonstrated to the students in the class before the question was asked.**

> In an experiment, Sam put some solution of copper sulphate, blue, in a beaker. Then Sam put some water on top of the copper sulphate solution, so that it did not mix straight away. It took a whole day for Sam to see that the blue colour spread part way into the water, and a few days for the blue colour to spread evenly through both liquids. At this time, Sam noticed there was only one liquid in the beaker.
>
> From the grid of boxes A–G, choose the box or boxes that give the best explanation. If you choose more than one box, please put the boxes in the best order for your explanation. Write down this order.
>
> Why do you think this explanation is the best?

A. Many liquids can dissolve in each other.

B. Particles in a liquid have little space for movement before they collide with other particles.

C. Particles in a liquid move quite slowly and slip by each other.

D. Liquids are runny.

E. Liquids spread out quite slowly.

F. The particles in different liquids can move into each other's space.

G. Particles in a close liquid are very close to each other.

Figure 15.1 Assessment grid on dissolving

Assessment grids

Typically, objective questions are used to select single correct answers from a menu of four or five possible responses. The alternative incorrect responses are often typical errors made by students at this stage. This type of objective question is closed, with a single valid response. In assessment grids, a variety of data is presented, each of which can be true if it is an explanation. The variety of data that can be provided is very large. Higher level skills can then be assessed using this data. These include:

- selecting relevant data to form an explanation;
- sequencing information to form a coherent and progressive explanation. In this case, students might be asked to select boxes containing the relevant parts of an explanation for a given phenomenon and asked to state the order in which they would use this data to form the complete explanation. As an example, the boxes might contain parts of the process of digestion. The students could be asked to choose those parts that relate to the digestion of a protein, and then to order it as it takes place at different points in the alimentary canal;

- choosing explanations at different levels e.g. descriptive or cause and effect;
- word or concept association through linking a variety of data. (For example, I am thinking of the data in boxes 1 and 2. Of which other boxes might I also be thinking?)

In the case of dissolving, assessment grids could be used, for example, to explore whether the learner is operating at the sub-microscopic or macroscopic level. I have used the assessment grid shown in Figure 15.1 for Year 10 pupils.

The assessment grid responses in this example can be analyzed in terms of predominant working at macroscopic or sub-microscopic levels, or using an indiscriminate mixture of levels. Learners working principally at the macroscopic level may not be ready to form concepts at the sub-microscopic level.

In my work with a class of twenty-five 14-year-olds, almost all students chose descriptive explanations, or an indiscriminate mixture of macroscopic behaviours and sub-microscopic descriptions. These students had not been explicitly exposed to teaching about chemical modelling. In a related activity with a parallel class, students were given a free hand to explain the experiment in prose. The results were similar to those used in the grids.

Question generating

Gunstone and White (1992) have described this tool. Here, a completion of a question is given and the learner is invited to speculate on what the questions(s) might have been. An example is:

… because a metal conducts electricity.

Responses could include:

Why is copper used in electrical wiring?

How do we know that there are mobile electrons in metal silver?

Why do we say that graphite has metallic character?

The form and extent of the questions generated give some idea of the extent of knowledge of the learner. The example here is about the use of models in chemistry, which I have introduced to classes with this story:

The class was talking about pictures of ethanol molecules they had seen. Tam asked the teacher a question but I could not hear what it was. The teacher said: 'because each model shows only one way of looking at what the molecule might be.' Make a list of all the questions that might have been asked by Tam.

Most of the 14–15-year-old children in a survey of one class created questions related to observable characteristics of the particles, for example:

Why are the atoms drawn at such a large scale?

Why are the atoms given these particular colours?

None thought of questions relating to the apparent solidity of the atoms, or what might be in the space between the atoms, or of the shape of the molecules.

A strength of this method is that it gives credit for answers at different levels. It may not be possible to claim that the highest level of a particular individual has been discovered although a brainstorm of all the possible answers that can be conceived will provide a better appreciation of the extent of understanding. The responses can also be used to explore understanding by asking the learners to place them in a list showing the highest understanding at the top and the lowest at the bottom.

This technique can easily be used with many other topics. Here is another example that has been used successfully with learners at all levels.

> The class had been studying the various types of astronomical objects such as stars, planets and satellites. Pat asked the teacher a question but I could not hear what it was. Part of what the teacher said was: 'because stars give out their own light.' Make a list of all the questions that might have been asked by Pat.

Answers given by students ranging from upper primary children to PGCE science lecturers have included:

1   Why is the sun a star?
2   How can we count the stars?
3   Why do we get day and night (the earth spins round each day and is partially illuminated by light from the sun which gives out its own light)?
4   How do we know what the stars are made of (spectroscopic investigation of starlight)?

Concept maps

Concept maps are thought to mirror the structure of knowledge in the brain (Gunstone and White 1992). In a concept map, concepts are linked by propositions (linking statements) and produce a network of ideas (see Figure 15.2 for an example). The greater the number of links, the richer the understanding displayed. A variety of methods has been used to enable individuals or groups to construct concept maps.

- Cards with labels of concepts to be used are given. They can be arranged hierarchically and linked with propositions that are also given.
- Concepts are arranged hierarchically and propositions devised to link the concepts. This can be extended into providing pictures that represent concepts.
- The learners can be asked to generate their own concepts, either on their own or as a class, and appropriate linking propositions, and then to construct the whole concept map from scratch.

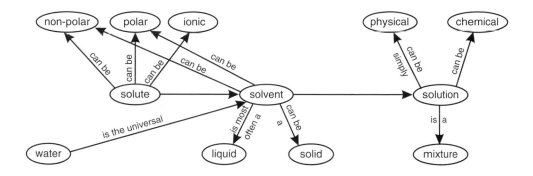

Figure 15.2 A concept map of dissolving

Some people have devised ways of scoring concept maps. Points are given for valid links and more points for appropriate hierarchies of concepts. This approach has a number of drawbacks. In the beginning, it focuses on the outcome rather than the process. The product, the concept map, does not represent the group or individual thinking about sensible formats and appropriate meanings of concepts. What is produced at the end is the final consensus map in which arguments about the format are left out. These may still be in existence in bits of paper left in the waste bin, or may never have been made explicit. Discussions that take place when concept maps are created in groups indicate compromises about placing the concepts and wording the propositions that are not apparent in the final map. The map does not reveal the creation of understanding that takes place when the map is being created.

A concept map gives us much more insight into understanding when we see it being put together. It has much value for the teacher who observes it being created, especially in groups, but much less value when marked away from the learner. It is too easy to make inappropriate inferences from a map in the absence of input from its creator. A concept map may be a better formative assessment tool than a summative assessment tool.

Classroom implications

While science educators have a good knowledge of ways of assessing learners, these are not always clearly related to concept development. This chapter has analysed some ways of assessing performance related to conceptual understanding in terms of two frameworks: a taxonomy of knowledge and a ladder of explanations. In developing pupils' understanding, it is important that teachers should clarify the concepts to be learned or used. In designing assessments of conceptual understanding, key questions to be addressed are:

- Can instances be related to appropriate concepts?
- Can concepts be deduced from instances?

- Can similar concepts be distinguished?
- Can concepts be used in explanations at different levels?
- Can concepts be correctly linked to related concepts?
- Can concepts be modelled?

References

Bloom, B. S. (ed.) (1956) *Taxonomy of Educational Objectives: Handbook 1, Cognitive Domain*, London: Longman.

DfEE and QCA (1999) *The National Curriculum (Science),* London: DfEE/QCA.

Gilbert, J. K., Boulter, C. and Rutherford, M. (1998a) 'Models in explanation Part 1: horses for courses?', *International Journal of Science Education* 20(1): 83–97.

Gilbert, J. K., Boulter, C. and Rutherford, M. (1998b) 'Models in explanation Part 2: whose voice, whose ears?' *International Journal of Science Education* 20(2): 187–203.

Gödek, Y. (1997) 'Models and explaining dissolving', unpublished M.Sc. dissertation, The University of Reading.

Gunstone, R. and White, R. (1992) *Probing Understanding*, London: Falmer Press.

Johnstone, K. and Scott, P. (1991) 'Diagnostic teaching in the science classroom: teaching/learning strategies to promote development in understanding about conversation of mass on dissolving', *Research in Science and Technology Education* 9(2): 193–212.

Longden, K., Black, P. and Solomon, J. (1991) 'Children's interpretation of dissolving', *International Journal of Science Education* 13(1): 59–68.

Fensham, N. and Fensham, P. (1987) 'Descriptions and frameworks of solutions and reactions in solution', *Research in Science Education* 17: 139–48.

Oversby, J. (2000) 'Good explanations for dissolving – even expert chemists find this hard', *Primary Science Review* 63: 16–19.

Papageorgiou, M. (1999) 'Children's ideas about the phenomenon of dissolving', unpublished M.Sc. dissertation, The University of Reading.

4 Communicating science

Introduction

Communicating science means not just talking about it, but reading and writing about it too. Ideas that are written down are less likely to be as tentative and exploratory as those discussed verbally. If they are recorded they can be re-visited and reflected upon in the light of new experience. It is through the more permanent forms of communication that the scientific community externalizes and shares knowledge, not only among scientists, but also with society as a whole. Communicating science to society has perhaps not been something that scientists have done well, and scientific ideas have not been made sufficiently accessible to the public. Understanding what has been written about science, and being able to write about it, is an important part of a science education.

Writing provides learners with the opportunity of refining and communicating their ideas. Just as scientists themselves write for different audiences, learners in school can benefit from using different forms of writing. The enthusiastic pupil moving from primary to secondary school can be de-motivated by always having to write about science in a formal, report style using the passive voice. There is a place for this sort of writing, but it is often overused and becomes part of the ritualized practice of science. This formal writing is unnatural to them, and many find it very difficult. It also has the effect of removing the human dimension from science, which further alienates many children. Worse still, writing may be used as a means of control or as a punishment. 'If you can't be quiet I will stop the practical and you will have to do some writing.' This gives very negative messages about the value of writing and its place in science. Writing for different audiences, considering the needs and characteristics of the target group, brings the human dimension back into science.

How much reading occurs in science classrooms? Studies show that learners are required to do very little reading in science lessons, and the reading they do is low level, such as reading instructions, reading notes from the board or reading questions from text books. It seems that reading is neglected in science and yet it is so central to the subject itself. Just as 'hands-on' practical activity does not necessarily entail active learning, so reading does not need to be passive. Reading can involve pupils as active learners, though too often they read passively, without purpose. There is, however, a range of strategies that teachers can use to engage their learners in textual materials.

Copying what the teacher has written or is saying is a passive activity, but pupils may like copying because it's easy. They copy without thinking, and may even copy the teacher's bracketed instruction asking them to put in some examples of their own. The most common reason teachers give for giving pupils notes to copy is that they have an accurate record in their books from which they will be able to revise. There are several criticisms that can be levelled at this practice. First, copied work is often not accurate, as pupils' minds are not engaged in the ideas. Second, it provides no opportunity for teachers to assess the understanding of their pupils - it is a lost opportunity. Third, if learners have not understood the scientific ideas, they are hardly likely to understand their copied notes when they read them weeks later. Lastly, the work is not their own. Writing involves thinking and clarifying ideas before committing them to paper. If it is closely controlled by the teacher (copying, filling in blanks or dictation) opportunities for creative responses from learners are closed down. Happy, quiet children are not necessarily learning. When pupils progress to post-16 courses and beyond, they will be expected to be able to write for themselves. But this is not a skill developed just by getting older. Pupils need to be provided with the experiences that will help them to develop their writing skills.

- The aim of the National Literacy Strategy is to encourage children to read and write more effectively. In the first chapter of this section, Frankie McKeon provides an insight into the scope and practice of the Literacy Strategy, and the way it is being used to complement primary science. She goes on to argue that this provides secondary science teachers with an exciting opportunity to improve pupils' achievement in science, by using their literacy skills to develop a range of different written materials that build on their prior achievements.

- Undertaking practical work in small groups is a common activity in science lessons, but Jonathan Osborne argues that it is overused. He discusses a variety of activities focused on reading and writing that can be used to generate valuable discussion in small groups. In developing linguistic and conceptual competency, practical work should be seen as just one of a wider repertoire of strategies.

- Brian Hand and Vaughan Prain have written extensively about the role writing has in the teaching and learning of science. In their chapter, they review the research in this area and, based on this, propose guidelines for the effective use of writing to enhance learning in science. Using a range of types of writing helps pupils to clarify, consolidate and demonstrate their understanding of science concepts and some examples of writing tasks that support the learning of science are presented.

- Douglas Newton highlights the various features of textual materials that can support understanding. Much has been written about the words and the sentence construction of texts for science teaching, but as he points out, these are not the only things that matter. He examines some of the other important aspects of textual materials, since, as the title says, There's more to communication than just words.

- ICT offers much potential to support learning in science. Richard Boohan reviews some of the general issues that need to be considered when deciding on appropriate uses of ICT, and in particular, he focuses on how it can be used to support reading, writing and other forms of communication.

These technologies can be used as a more effective means of carrying out traditional activities as well as opening up entirely new possibilities for communication.

16 Literacy and secondary science
Building on primary experience
Frankie McKeon

Language in science

The central role of language in the development of children's scientific under-standing, their problem solving and attitudes towards science has been discussed by many writers (Barnes et al. 1969; Sutton 1989; 1992). They describe an enabling learning environment as one where children are encouraged to be active participants and are given opportunities to become familiar with the language of science, to talk and write about science and to explore their own views and those of others.

As long ago as 1975, the Bullock Report stressed the importance of language development across the curriculum and, as a result, many secondary schools devel-oped language policies in all curriculum areas. Despite the existence of these language policies and suggestions of imaginative language-based approaches to science teaching from science educators (Osborne 1997; Henderson and Wellington 1998) the adoption of language as integral to science teaching has been limited. Yet pupils' learning in science will be enhanced significantly when greater attention is given to language skills (SCAA 1997).

In secondary schools separate departmental planning often limits the links made between science and language work. Also, science teachers feel under enormous pressure to cope with a demanding National Curriculum, without the adoption of unfamiliar language-based strategies which can be time-consuming. There is some scepticism about the value of different approaches to the teaching and learning of science, particularly as many teachers feel that the apparent requirements for success in Key Stages 2 and 3 SATs are best served by a mainly didactic approach interspersed with illustrative practical activities. The benefits of encouraging pupils' reading and writing skills are not immediately obvious. Science teachers do not generally feel well prepared to manage different strategies that appear to be less controlled than their known-and-tested ways of working (Newton et al. 1999).

A new opportunity

Secondary schools in England currently have an exciting opportunity which should make a significant difference to teaching and learning. Through the National Literacy Strategy (DfEE 1998), children are now leaving English primary schools having experienced ways of working with fiction and non-fiction text to develop their literacy skills. This should support the principles of the use of language across the curriculum contained within the new National Curriculum (DfEE/QCA 1999):

> Pupils should be taught in all subjects to express themselves correctly … in reading they should be taught strategies to help them read with understanding, locate and use information, follow a process or argument and summarize, synthesize and adapt what they learn from their reading … in writing they should be taught to organize their writing in logical and coherent forms.

Literacy work will facilitate the active implementation of language-based approaches, increase children's involvement with the use of science language and help to raise their achievement in science.

The Literacy Strategy

In September 1998, the National Literacy Strategy was introduced into all English primary schools. It is designed to ensure continuity of planning across the primary age range so that children learn to read and write with confidence, fluency and understanding. Although the focus is mainly on the skills of reading and writing, speaking and listening are acknowledged to be an essential part of the whole. The Literacy Framework (DfEE 1998) sets out clear teaching objectives in a term-by-term approach to developing literacy skills from reception to Year 6. Implementation has been through the introduction of the daily literacy hour with a prescribed structure consisting of whole-class shared reading and writing with word or sentence work, followed by guided group or independent work with a whole-class plenary session to finish.

Whilst many of the ideas in the National Literacy Strategy are not new, it is different in that it contains explicit guidelines, its detailed objectives are clear and it is compulsory. This means that regardless of their primary school all children should have experienced the same sort of structured work to develop their use and understanding of literacy skills.

Primary science and literacy

The purpose of developing literacy skills is so that children can draw on them when needed. Consequently, literacy should not be divorced from the rest of the curriculum. Ofsted recommended in Standards in primary science (Ofsted 1998a) that:

> literacy and numeracy are supported by and developed in science… the many opportunities for developing and using literacy and numeracy in science should be exploited.

Whilst the literacy hour cannot be used to teach science the focus text can be science-based, thus providing a real context within which children can develop their skills of reading, writing and information gathering:

Where appropriate, literacy should be linked to work in other areas of the curriculum. For example, during the literacy hour pupils might be searching and retrieving from information texts used in science, writing instructions linked to a technology project.

(DfEE 1998)

Literacy work in primary schools is supporting learning in science by developing the skills children need to access science. This is being achieved through explicit use of scientific vocabulary, more overt practice of reading and writing skills and use of stories to develop science. Feasey (1999) has illustrated the role that literacy work can play in improving the quality of science teaching in primary schools and includes many examples of science and literacy being interwoven. The Nuffield Primary Science guide (1998) provides ideas for approaching reading and writing within a science context. Both of these books are well worth the attention of secondary science teachers.

Primary teachers are expected to teach both literacy and science. Developing links between these is economical in terms of planning and provides a cohesiveness that enhances both literacy and science work for children. Can secondary science benefit in the same way?

Benefits for secondary science

Despite the existence of a science National Curriculum 5–16 since 1988, there is still little continuity of experience and learning for pupils as they transfer from primary to secondary school, with consequent dips in achievement (Galton et al. 1999). Ofsted, in its 1999 secondary education review (Ofsted 1998b), identified the need to take account of the science learned in primary schools as still being a major challenge for teachers of science in Key Stage 3:

in many schools the science curriculum at the start of Key Stage 3 has not been modified to allow for pupils' achievements in primary school so their progress is slow. Much can be gained by improving the interchange of ideas and information across the primary–secondary boundary.

A greater awareness of what pupils have done before helps to develop a better sense of the continuous nature of learning from primary through to secondary school (SCAA 1996). Familiarization with the content of the National Literacy Scheme will allow teachers to take advantage of the literacy work that is being done in all primary schools to enhance science teaching and help raise achievement. This will involve recognizing and building on pupils' existing experiences and achievements, providing appropriate activities that make use of their literacy skills in science, and utilizing a greater range of teaching and learning strategies based on use of language. The teaching methods of the Literacy Strategy can be used to make sure that pupils' literacy skills are being utilized to support their learning in science by ensuring that pupils make more effective use of secondary sources of information and that they communicate their science in a variety of ways.

How the literacy scheme can support secondary science

Through their literacy work in primary schools, pupils experience a wide range of learning strategies that are potentially very useful to them in secondary science.

Words in science

The problems pupils experience in using scientific language can be a major block to their understanding in science. There is often conflict between science language and the everyday meanings pupils give to words. Science teachers who are aware of pupils' understanding of both specialist and non-specialist words in science are able to help develop their usage.

Within the Literacy Strategy, words provide a focus from an early stage and their meanings, spellings and usage are made explicit, as illustrated by these extracts from the Year 3 term 3 programme which requires children to learn to:

> infer the meaning of unknown words from context and generate a range of possible meanings;

> use dictionaries to learn or check the spellings and definitions of words.
>
> (DfEE 1998)

This practice can be adopted in science to encourage correct and creative use of language by:

- checking pupils' understanding of words, acknowledging the differences between everyday and scientific use of words (e.g. force, solution) and introducing and explaining new words;
- modelling the use of words, by using them in context and introducing their scientific meaning;
- giving pupils a range of opportunities for using the words to help construct meaning (see Box 1).

Box 1 Words

Use of words Make regular use of word banks, displays, glossaries, dictionaries of science and science-related words. Ask pupils to produce their own version of any of these.

Word games can be fun, are often quick and can be used to support any topic area.

Many can be developed based on familiar formats (e.g. crosswords), or on TV, radio or commercially produced games (e.g. Just a Minute, Articulate, Pictionary).

continued on next page

Card games are easily produced in many different formats, such as true–false games, card pairing (e.g. words with definitions, parts with functions), sorting or sequencing, word bingo, drawing links between words. This can be developed into making sentences and drawing concept maps and developing questioning (twenty questions).

Reading in science

> Since reading is a major strategy ... it is the responsibility of every teacher to develop it.
>
> (Bullock 1975)

Reading is obviously an important access to various sources of information (text, CD-ROM or Internet based) that can provide inspiration and interest for pupils. Learning to read is integral to learning to understand science. However, the reading has to be reflective if the information is to be assimilated and understood. Although most pupils in secondary schools can read, they are often less successful at reading for understanding than for information retrieval. When asked to obtain information from textbooks and CD-ROMs, pupils often end up copying out chunks, even when they realize that they shouldn't be doing so. This may be because they do not know what else to do, or they may not have the necessary text interaction skills (Wray and Lewis 1997). These skills have to be taught.

The Literacy Strategy aims to develop reading skills by identifying the purpose of reading, presenting different types of reading, and utilizing and developing active reading and research skills. It includes a number of approaches for information retrieval using both fiction and non-fiction texts (Box 2).

Box 2   Approaches to information retrieval in the National Literacy Strategy

Teaching specific skills associated with using non-fiction texts in general, e.g. to locate information using contents, index, headings, bibliographies, etc.

Identifying different text styles, e.g. instruction, report, recount and explanation.

Understanding the structure of different non-fiction text types.

Identifying key information (note-taking), using a glossary, diagrams, tables and charts.

Creating summaries, skimming and scanning.

For example, the Year 4 term 3 programme requires children to:

> summarize a sentence or paragraph by identifying the most important elements and rewording them in a limited number of words

and Year 6 term 2 states that children should learn to:

> identify the features of balanced arguments which summarize different sides of an argument; clarify the strengths and weaknesses of different positions and signal personal opinion clearly.

All these approaches form the basis of effective, critical reading needed in secondary schools and can be used effectively by science teachers. The challenge is to develop these, choosing not only the content matter of scientific reading but also strategies that will help pupils to access the information and to interact with it in some way that will encourage reflection. In this way reading will have both purpose and meaning. Various activities, e.g. skimming and scanning, or using Directed Activities Related to Text (DARTs) to make reading more active, can be employed to encourage the further development of pupils' research skills (see Box 3).

Box 3 Directed Activities Related to Text (DARTs)

Activities requiring the text to be analysed

- Underlining text – scan text, search for relevant key words, concepts or ideas and underline or look for text that provides particular information.
- Labelling text – add headings or labels to paragraphs identifying the main ideas or purpose of sections.
- Identifying key points.
- Summarizing with diagram, flow chart or table.
- Writing questions about a text – either questions for someone else or questions raised by reading the text.
- Predicting from a text.
- Applying ideas or information from the text.

Activities requiring the text to be reconstructed

- Word, phrase or sentence completion.
- Table or diagram completion – add labels to diagram (these can be provided or else obtained by scanning the text).
- Alternative representation of text, e.g. diagrams or tables.
- Reconstruction of disordered text to provide a chronological sequence.

All of these can be used to try to ensure that pupils process the information contained within the text. Ideally the opportunity should be taken to set these activities up as small group activities that will also encourage pupils to discuss ideas.

Wray and Lewis (1997) provide many useful ideas for helping pupils develop effective text-interaction strategies. Use strategies such as brainstorming, labelling, concept mapping, discussing and question-raising to activate and establish prior knowledge before reading. Build on this to generate a sense of enquiry and purpose for the reading and ask pupils to make an appropriate record of what they have done and to evaluate the information obtained.

Pupils need to be clear about the nature of the text being used and its purpose (collecting particular information? summarizing? evaluating?). They should have experience of using various text types in science (leaflets, newspaper or magazine articles, adverts, websites) and of using a variety of text-interaction strategies with books or ICT.

Writing in science

Effective writing allows pupils to formulate, reformulate and literally 'come to terms' with their understanding of scientific ideas. Sutton (1992) presents a compelling case for the value of a variety of approaches in scientific writing. Yet much writing in science involves simple recounts of experimental work.

The National Literacy Framework identifies different types of non-fiction text (see Box 4) and helps children to write in a range of different forms using writing to express their ideas.

Box 4   Non-fiction text types identified in the National Literacy Framework

recount (narrative)	to retell events in order to inform or entertain
non-chronological report	to describe a living thing, object or process in a logical way
instructions	to describe how something is done through a series of sequenced steps
explanation	to explain the processes involved in natural and social phenomena or to explain how something works
persuasion	to promote a particular point of view with the intention of persuading others
discussion	to present arguments and information from differing viewpoints

In Year 6 term 2 children are required to:

use the styles and conventions of journalism to report on e.g. real or imagined events

and in Year 6 term 3 they are expected to:

select the appropriate style and form to suit a specific purpose and audience, drawing on knowledge of different non-fiction text types.

Children's writing is developed by:

discussion and modelling, in which a wide range of different types of written text are used in the classroom. Structures and language features of these texts are discussed before and after reading and the way in which different types of writing are used is explained.

provision of support/scaffolding through shared writing, joint text construction and the use of writing frames to prompt and help maintain cohesion in writing (Box 5).

Science provides a rich context for the development of all of these writing types and the approaches used within the Literacy Strategy can be developed if teachers provide pupils with opportunities for use of a wide range of writing (see Box 6).

Box 5   Writing frames

Science teachers often support children's reports of experimental and investigative work by the use of helpful headings to structure their writing (such as: What we are trying to find out; What we think will happen and why; How we are going to find out, etc.). Their use can be extended to encourage and support children to write in other ways. For example, developing a discussion might be helped by headings such as:

There are differing views on

One view is that

This is based on

Another view is

This is based on

Of these views I think

However, writing frames should be considered as a means of support and only used until the children are able to write independently. They are particularly helpful for drafting.

> **Box 6   Possible writing tasks**
>
> - production of class books (e.g. on adaptation)
> - information leaflets, posters or displays
> - stories (both fiction and non-fiction)
> - newspaper or magazine articles
> - review of video
> - provide instructions or flowcharts
> - adverts
> - scripts for news items presenting two points of view
> - responding to other children's writing

The challenge is to be sure that writing is the best form of communication for your purpose. Why are you asking pupils to write (to provide a record; for assessment of their knowledge, understanding or skills; for display)? The pupils should be clear about the purpose of their writing and who their audience is to be. They need to understand the range of written forms available to them so they can decide which best suits their purpose for the task. They may need support with that writing. Many secondary science teachers provide writing frames for Sc 1 activities; these can be extended to other types of writing. Suggestions for 'openers' (e.g. We already knew that … We started with …) and 'connectives' (e.g. also …, however …, this causes …, this explains why …) may also help them to organize their science writing. Model good writing for them and present them with good examples of writing as models for their own. They should be encouraged to use a range of methods to communicate their science and to choose appropriate methods of communication.

All of these need to be used judiciously and appropriately with care to ensure the tasks and products are not superficial, but reflect careful thought by pupils.

Feasey and Siraj-Blatchford (1998) have illustrated a range of imaginative ways of developing children's communication in science with case studies from Year 1 to Year 7 in which children write with a clearly defined purpose for a particular audience. These provide a firm basis for further development within secondary science.

Using stories in science

An important feature of the literacy hour is the use of stories. Do they have a place in science? Stories can be wide ranging and include: stories from children's literature: historical stories; contemporary stories from the media and stories generated collaboratively with pupils. There is plenty of scope for the use of stories in science. They can be used as starting points for pupils' scientific questions, for discussion about issues or to provide the context for investigations. They can be used to introduce new science concepts or to broaden pupils' perceptions of science and scientists. Pupils can create stories based around their investigation or research or use them to explain their scientific ideas.

Summary

An enormous amount of work is being devoted to the development of literacy skills in primary schools. If the Literacy Strategy has its desired effect, a greater proportion of pupils will be arriving in secondary schools with enhanced reading and writing skills. Many of the strategies used in the National Literacy Strategy can be used to the advantage of science teaching. Secondary teachers can benefit from: knowing what has gone before so that it can be built on; being familiar with the quality of work that is done by primary children; and looking at the potential use of literacy skills in science lessons. This will allow pupils' achievement in science to be raised as teachers have more appropriate expectations, provide continuity of experience and capitalize on pupils' achievements. As the Literacy Scheme becomes more established in primary schools, links between science and literacy will become more highly developed. The cooperative teaching of science and literacy will surely foster the development of both. Incorporating strategies from the National Literacy Strategy into science departmental policy and practice has the potential for developing positive attitudes to science and a greater understanding of science. However failure to do so will surely mean an exciting opportunity is wasted!

References

Barnes, D., Britton, J. and Rosen, H. (1969) *Language, the Learner and the School*, Harmondsworth: Penguin.

Bullock Report (1975) *A Language for Life*, London: HMSO.

DfEE (1998) *National Literacy Strategy: Framework for Teaching*, London: DfEE.

DfEE/QCA (1999) *The National Curriculum in England*. London: DfEE/QCA.

Feasey, R. (1999) *Primary Science and Literacy*, Hatfield: ASE.

Feasey, R. and Siraj-Blatchford, J. (1998) *Key Skills: Communication in Science*, Durham: University of Durham/Tyneside Training and Enterprise Council.

Galton, M., Gray, J. and Ruddock, J. (1999) *The Impact of School Transitions and Transfers on Pupil Progress and Achievement*, London: Stationery Office.

Henderson, J. and Wellington, J. (1998) 'Lowering the language barrier in learning and teaching science', *School Science Review* 79(288): 35–46.

Newton, P., Driver, R. and Osborne, J. (1999) 'The place of argumentation in the pedagogy of school science', *International Journal of Science Education* 21(5): 553–76.

Nuffield Primary Science (1998) *Science and Literacy*, London: Collins Educational.

Ofsted (1998a) *Standards in Primary Science*, London: Ofsted.

Ofsted (1998b) *Secondary Review 1993–1997*, London: Ofsted.

Osborne, J. (1997) 'Practical alternatives', *School Science Review* 78(285): 61–6.

SCAA (1996) *Promoting Continuity Between Key Stage 2 and 3*, London: SCCA(QCA).

SCAA (1997) *Science and the Use of Language: Key Stages 1 and 2; Key Stages 3 and 4*, London: SCCA(QCA).

Sutton, C. (1989) 'Writing and reading in science: the hidden messages', in *Doing Science: Images of Science in Science Education*, Millar, R. (ed.) Lewes: Falmer Press, pp. 137–59.

Sutton, C. (1992) *Words, Science and Learning*, Buckingham: Open University Press.

Wray, D. and Lewis, M. (1997) *Extending Literacy: Children Reading and Writing Nonfiction*, London: Routledge.

17 Learning science without practical work?

Jonathan Osborne

> *As practised in many schools, it (practical work) is ill-conceived, confused and unproductive. For many children, what goes on in the laboratory contributes little to their learning of science or to their learning about science and its methods. Nor does it engage them in doing science in any meaningful sense. At the root of the problem is the unthinking use of laboratory work.*

> (Hodson 1991)

Improvements in science education are, in my opinion, most likely to come from making an important distinction between *doing* science and *learning* science. The two are not one and the same thing. The former is necessary to discover and establish new knowledge of the natural and living world but, just as writing poetry is not the best way to learn poetry, neither is the almost ritualistic emphasis on doing science, prevalent in science classrooms, the best way to learn science. In the *learning* of science, practical work only forms one strategy in an extended repertoire. Just as the golfer carefully selects the best club to suit their needs, so in teaching science, particularly in secondary schools, children benefit from teachers who carefully choose *learning strategies* that are demonstrably the most appropriate and effective.

One of the primary purposes of science education is the development of linguistic and conceptual competency within the domain of science. As science teachers we must see ourselves as teachers of language primarily, and that practical work is only one of a number of means of developing such competency *rather than the sole means*.

This chapter suggests some strategies that teachers might add to their repertoire to encourage children to talk about scientific ideas and reflect on their own understanding, based around working in small groups. When most teachers spend their time trying to diminish classroom chatter, why might such activities be beneficial?

Using a variety of strategies

Evidence is beginning to mount that effective teachers select their classroom activities from an extensive armoury, picking those which are most likely to hit their target. In the words of the Scottish HMI (HM Inspector of Schools 1994), the key to success lies in the use of *'a variety of learning and teaching strategies'*. After painstaking and detailed research into effective teaching and learning, Cooper and McIntyre (1996: 131) also concluded that:

Effective teaching, it would seem, is more likely to depend on the teacher's mastery of a wide range of strategies (e.g. from transmission to self-direction) and, importantly, the ability to evaluate circumstances that render the application of a particular strategy appropriate to student requirements. Sometimes a global strategy for whole groups will be appropriate, and may require the teacher to engage in transmission style; at other times more student-directed approaches will be appropriate.

(Cooper and McIntyre 1996: 131)

Whole class discussion

In most classroom discussions, the dominant form of discourse is one in which the teacher asks the questions, a pupil gives a response and then the teacher provides an evaluation with feedback (Lemke 1990; Edwards and Mercer 1987). This form of dialogue is not only severely restricted but, on reflection, somewhat perverse. In the science classroom, questions are asked, surprisingly, not by those who *do not* know, but by the teacher who *does*. This state of affairs is of some concern when viewed in the light of Cooper and McIntyre's findings that the most effective forms of teaching were 'interactive' or 'reactive' styles where pupils' inputs are valued and based on teachers' perceptions of pupil concerns and interest.

Many pupils are naturally reluctant to engage in such discourse in classrooms for fear of exposing their ignorance. In contrast, real science is an exciting, cultural product where ideas are introduced, discussed and explained through dialogue with peers and there is opportunity for critical questioning and elaboration. It is only when you are required to explain a concept in words to somebody else that you really start to understand it. Furthermore, there are many arguments that learning a science is akin to learning a foreign language. Words in science have a set of associated relationships and legitimate contexts. Recognizing the distinction in the meaning of the word 'force' in the sentences 'The force of gravity acts on the apple' and 'May the force be with you', comes only by asking children to use the appropriate language in the appropriate context. What, then, can be done to provide such opportunities for children to engage in open and unrestricted discourse about science in a non-threatening atmosphere?

Working in small groups

It is here that small-group work has a vital role to play. Traditionally, this has been an underused technique in the practice of science teaching. Sands' investigation of the use of group work in school science concluded that:

No opportunity was given to groups to design experiments or interpret results. If there was any imaginative, analytical thought-provoking or enquiry-based thinking it was done by the teacher with the whole class … Rarely was there a follow-up related to the group work involving a sharing of experience. What few follow-ups were observed were used for putting results from each group on the blackboard with a brief summary, or giving instructions about dealing with results and writing up.

(Sands 1981)

Moreover, those interactions that did take place within the groups were at a relatively low cognitive level. Sands concluded that meaningful group work was more of a myth than a reality. Little seems to have changed, as the Office for Standards in Education recently noted: 'small group activities, other than for practical work, are very uncommon' (Ofsted 1995). Despite a major transformation in examinations, the introduction of broad and balanced science and the advent of a National Curriculum with an ambitious and novel model of practical science embodied in Sc1, this aspect of science teaching remains unchanged – evidently a case of 'plus ça change, plus c'est la même chose'.

Small groups provide a context for structured exercises that constrain and conscript children to a well-defined task, easing the management and organizational difficulties of operating within a classroom. Most importantly, they provide an ideal forum for exploring the knowledge of the child and to develop their understanding, for example by exploring the relationship between what they know and the evidence for its justification. It is only when called on to explain, for example, how you know that plants make their own food through photosynthesis, that electric current is conserved in a circuit, or that matter is conserved in combustion, that the crucial significance of experimental evidence is exposed. It is this feature which is at the heart of the rationality of science and which has enabled science to achieve such success. Practising scientific reasoning requires discussion in a non-threatening and non-judgmental atmosphere involving the constructive criticism which only peer-group discussion in small groups affords. Such work provides a valuable opportunity for the child to 'integrate her capacities and interpretations with those of significant others around her' (Bruner and Haste 1987).

Small-group activities

Possibly the most familiar use of small-group work is to produce posters for presentation to peers, explaining either an experimental investigation or the results of research into a set topic. Although time consuming, the seriousness with which children approach such work and the quality of the work can often astonish. The remainder of this chapter explores some other, less familiar, techniques based on small-group work, which share a similar potential to stimulate discussion and *talk about* science. These are:

- Discussion of instances/misconceptions
- Concept maps
- False concept maps
- Key sentences
- Jumbled sentences
- DARTs (Directed Activities Related to Text).

Discussion of instances/misconceptions

The extensive body of literature on children's thinking that has been produced in the past 15 years provides a valuable source of common errors and misconceptions which can be posed to pupils for discussion in small groups (Figure 17.1). Pupils

Statement	Yes	No	Evidence/Reasons
A man lost one of his fingers in an accident. If he has children afterwards, do you think they would have fewer fingers than normal?			
A naturalist carried out an experiment consisting of cutting off the tails of mice along several generations to see how the offspring come out. Over twenty generations, would the tails of the offspring be shorter?			
Mr and Mrs Cross have three boys, they are sure that their next child will be a boy. Would you agree?			
A gardener uses the pollen of a blue lupin to pollinate another blue lupin. Does this mean that all the seeds from this plant will produce blue lupins?			
Is there anything wrong with this statement? 'My father's genes must be stronger than my mother's because I inherit so much of my looks from him.'			
Carol has a flat nose similar to her aunt. Both her parents have prominent noses, but all four of her grandparents have flat noses. Is this possible?			
Is a boy is much more likely to look like his father than his mother?			

Figure 17.1 Statements for discussion

should initially be asked to work through the statements in the left-hand column of Figure 17.1 individually, deciding whether they agree or disagree with the statements. They should also be encouraged to use the final column to provide notes on evidence for their beliefs. Then, having completed the first stage of their task, and only then, should pupils be allowed to discuss their thinking on each of the topics and come to some common agreement. Rarely do they agree and the ensuing discussion is often heated. Pupils should be encouraged to draw on whatever resources are available, such as books, CD-ROMs, posters and models, to help justify their opinions and views so that the activity is a stimulus for learning.

With a little thought, this technique is easily adopted to other areas such as:

- astronomy – 'it is hotter in summer as we are nearer the sun';
- photosynthesis – 'plants get their food from the soil';
- motion – 'a bicycle slows down because it runs out of force to keep it going'.

All that is necessary is to take the many common misconceptions that children have and ask them to discuss whether they are true or false. When the groups have concluded their discussions, they are much more receptive to the scientific view, as they now *want to know* and to resolve any disagreement.

An important aspect of this strategy is that it offers a means of exploring the epistemological question of *how we know*. It is possible to see Sc 2–4 of the National Curriculum as a survey of the facts of science – the 'what we know' of science. It is also possible to teach just this component and justify its importance in terms of the utilitarian value of such knowledge, but to do so is to rely solely on persuasion and authority. Science courses that fail to consider the important dimension of how scientists come to know 'are running the risk of developing students who do not acknowledge the scientist's views as rational' (Duschl 1990), for where is the evidence that justifies the science teacher's beliefs? For instance, everybody knows that day and night are caused by a spinning earth rather then a moving sun, but how many individuals can tell you the evidence for such a belief? Without such evidence, how are the grounds for beliefs discussed in the laboratories of the schools of the developed world any different from the education offered to the child in the African village? As Horton (1967) points out: 'In both cases the propounders are deferred to as the accredited agents of tradition'.

Concept maps

Concept mapping is a technique which sees words essentially as labels for concepts or ideas and asks individuals to define the relationship between them. A full explanation of concept mapping and its use can be found in Novak and Gowin (1984). Typically, a list of words is provided, for example:

Nebula, galaxy, star, meteor, comet, planet, Ursa Major, solar system, satellite, Universe, red shift, red giant, white dwarf, black hole, Meteostat, shooting star, Andromeda, constellation.

The following instructions are then given to groups of 3 or 4 pupils:

1 Write each of the above words in large letters on a small piece of square paper (4 × 4 cm).
2 Sort the squares into two piles – those you know the meaning of and those you do not understand.
3 Discard the pile of words you do not understand.
4 Now lay out the remaining words on a large piece of poster paper. Place related words adjacent to each other.

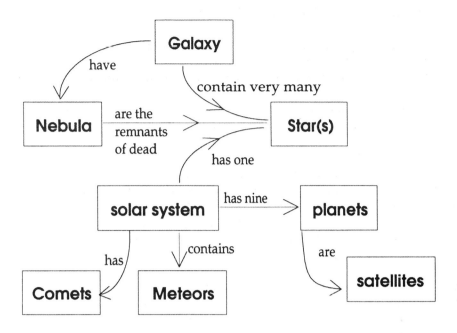

Figure 17.2 Example of a concept map

5 When you are happy with the arrangement, stick the squares down. Draw lines between the terms that are connected.

6 Now add a few words or a sentence to the lines to explain how they are connected. For instance:

7 When you have finished, pin your map up for others to look at.

Such an activity takes 30 to 40 minutes and generates considerable discussion of the ideas and concepts between all participants who are forced to articulate their understanding and justify their reasoning to their peers. A typical product is shown in Figure 17.2.

Contrast this structured activity with the limited opportunity provided for language development by the commonly used question-and-answer strategy, which is both a difficult technique to use successfully for all but the experienced teacher and which, in addition, many pupils find threatening. Recent research (Sizmur 1994) has shown that group concept mapping does provide significant opportunities for children to have elaborated dialogue about science – that is to question each other's ideas and interpret their meaning to one another.

Concept mapping can be clearly used in a range of domains by a different choice of words and with different ages by reducing the complexity of the words and their

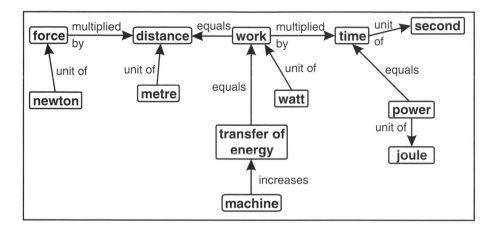

Instructions
Bob Fair, a Year 10 pupil, was given the words in boxes and drew this concept map.
Write down the errors which Bob has made.
Re-draw the concept map correctly.

Figure 17.3 Example of a false concept map

numbers. It has even been used with lower junior children by using pictures rather than words for the concepts. Like all techniques it can be over-used but it makes an excellent activity for revision at the end of a module or a starter activity to explore and elicit children's understanding. The author has made regular use of it on in-service courses with primary teachers and found it to be invaluable for exploring and introducing scientific ideas in a non-threatening manner.

False concept maps

Another valuable technique for promoting useful discussion is to present children with a concept map which deliberately contains a number of fallacious propositions, as in Figure 17.3. Here some of the relations are true and some are false. The challenge to the pupils is to find all the errors in the map, and then to redraw the map correctly. Once again, asking pupils to work in small groups of three or four provides an opportunity to discuss and question the propositions and to justify their reasoning to each other. Such an activity takes 20 to 30 minutes and is valuable as an informal exercise to assess how well a topic has been understood.

Key sentences

Pupils are provided with a list of key words which have a scientific meaning and an everyday meaning. Such a list for energy with GCSE pupils could be:

energy	kinetic	lost
transfer	electricity	heating
potential	conservation	insulator
conductor	sound	light
work	joules	newton
force	metre	stored
power		

The instructions to pupils are:

1   On your own write five sentences. Each sentence must contain at least two of the words in the above list.
2   Now join with three others. Share your sentences with them and discuss whether your sentences are scientifically correct.
3   In your group, pick five sentences, three of which you are sure are scientifically correct and two about which you are not sure. Write these on a piece of paper.
4   Pass the sheet to the group next to your left. With the sheet that is passed to you, discuss as a group whether you think each sentence is scientifically correct. If you think so, mark it with a tick. If not, mark it with a cross.
5   When you have finished, pass your piece of paper onto the next group. Continue this until your piece of paper returns to you.

Clearly the role of the teacher is to pick up the sentences over which the pupils have disagreed and explain and discuss why the sentences are erroneous or correct.

Typically, such a task takes about 30 or 40 minutes. As an activity, it generates considerable discussion about the appropriate scientific use of the words and their specific meaning within this context, helping children to assimilate and understand difficult concepts. Once again, it enables discussion with their peers and the teacher's role is that of an authoritative resource to resolve ambiguities.

Jumbled sentences

This simple technique provides an exercise where pupils have to work out as many correct sentences as they can from jumbled sentences, as in Figure 17.4. They are allowed to pick one word or phrase from each column to make up their sentence which must form a correct scientific proposition. Pupils should work in small groups and discuss the acceptability of the statements they suggest for possible sentences.

Figure 17.5 shows another version with a different focus. The task can be given a competitive element by challenging groups to produce the largest number of sentences they can which adds an additional element of enjoyment for many pupils.

				a	and	
	atom			many	charged	atom/s
All	matter		found	protons	in	nucleus
An	electron shell	is	composed of	in	a/an	particle/s
The	electron	is not	made up of	orbiting	the	neutron/s
A	atomic nucleus			electrons	small	orbit
	neutron			two kinds of	electrons	

Instructions

Make at least seven true sentences by choosing an entry from each column. The same words can be used in more than one sentence.

Figure 17.4 Jumbled sentences

Instructions

Make at least seven true sentences by choosing an entry from each column. The same words can be used in more than one sentence.

An electron	is	the	number	who showed that most of the atom was empty space.
J J Thompson	was	a	Greek	that shows the total number of nuclear particles.
The nucleus	is	a	New Zealand scientist	who stated that matter was made up of atoms.
The atomic number	was	an	atomic particle	that has a positive charge.
Democritus	is	a	scientist	of the atom and is made up of protons and neutrons.
Rutherford	is	a	central part	that is negatively charged and orbits the nucleus.
A proton	is	the	number	that shows the total number of protons.
The mass number	was	a	nuclear particle	who developed the plum pudding model of the atom.

Figure 17.5 Another example of jumbled sentences

DARTs (Directed Activities Related to Text)

DARTs activities are based on the belief that a substantial amount of conceptual understanding comes from the reading of textual materials. Such learning progressively increases through to higher education where the majority of learning is probably from text. Yet learning from text requires a fundamentally different type of reading from that used for normal reading. Normal reading, where the eye absorbs information in a continual flow, is *receptive*. Reading science texts has to be *reflective*, requiring the reader to break, re-read and reflect. Such a style of reading does not come naturally and must be taught with a variety of techniques which enable information from texts to be assimilated and understood.

There is insufficient space to outline the range of DARTs activities generated from the research of Davies and Greene (1984), but three key activities are described. These are text completion and re-sequencing, both of which require the meaning to be reconstructed, and table or diagram completion, which requires text to be analysed.

Text completion

Text completion (also known as a CLOZE procedure) is probably the best known but the most abused activity. In essence it consists of removing selected words from a piece of scientific text and asking the pupil to insert the missing words by deducing the word from the context. The selection of the words for deletion is important and the emphasis should be on scientific words. A typical example for such an activity is shown below.

> Weight is felt as the _____ of _____. If _____ were less, we would not feel so heavy. That is why a 60 kg person would only weigh about 10 kg on the _____ where gravitation is approximately one-sixth of the earth's pull. However the _____ or the amount of _____ in the person's body would be the same. When we weigh potatoes we are only interested in their _____. Indeed, whenever weighing quantities we should talk about _____, not _____. Weight is only a _____ which we use to determine the mass of bodies and physicists insist on limiting the use of the _____ unit to mass only. Weight should be measured in units of force called _____.

Clearly the reconstruction of text requires active intellectual processing, forcing the pupils to read and re-read the passage placing an emphasis on scientific concepts. However, such activities are rarely used in their most effective method – that is as a *group activity* of two to three pupils. This requires the reasoning and justification to be made explicit and the articulation of scientific concepts between peers. Using such exercises with pupils on an individual basis should be avoided. For they then become a dreary, gap-filling exercise where the object becomes one of finding the correct word to plug the gap, rather than a meaning-making exercise of trying to establish the appropriate word for the context.

Such activities are particularly valuable where the subject matter places greater emphasis on the learning from secondary sources, for example, astronomy and the earth in space. In this topic, there is a tendency to produce a plethora of visually attractive books as a resource for project work. But even the simplest scientific text requires reading and re-reading to gain anything useful. A limited set of such exercises is arguably of substantially more value than a wide selection of expensive texts!

Re-sequencing

Re-sequencing of scrambled text requires the teacher to select a piece of text and present it to children as a selection of random sentences all on a common theme. For instance, the previous piece can be arranged as a set of scrambled sentences and pupils asked to reorganize them. Pragmatically, the operation is easier if the sentences are written out on strips of paper by the group and laid out on the table for re-sequencing.

Another valuable use for this activity is with the instructions associated with an experiment. As well as curbing the inevitable rush for equipment, it forces children to reconsider, reflect and hopefully absorb, the procedures for conducting the experiment carefully. White (1991) notes that a teacher using this technique found that students 'accepted responsibility (for their actions), thought about what they were doing, and incidentally reduced the times that they came to her with questions about managerial matters they could work out themselves'.

Table or diagram completion

The third type of exercise uses prepared pieces of text which require careful analysis. The text is read and key aspects are underlined. This information is then used to complete a table or to label parts of the diagram (Figure 17.6). The example shown here involves using text about the eye to label a diagram. Biological information is particularly suitable to this kind of approach.

> The eye is a spherical structure used for seeing. The eye is made of three layers which surround a sticky substance called the vitreous humour. The outermost layer is called the sclerotic layer. This is very tough and holds the eye in shape. The middle layer is called the choroid layer and contains blood vessels. The inner layer is the retina which contains two types of cells that are sensitive to light. The impulses from this layer are taken from the eye to the brain in the optic nerve. The lens of the eye is attached to the choroid layer by the suspensory ligaments. The lens is clear and helps focus the light rays onto a very sensitive part of the retina at the back of the eye called the yellow spot. In front of the lens is the iris which, in people, can be many colours from blue to dark brown. The iris opens in dim light to allow light to enter the eye through the pupil. In very bright light the iris closes to stop too much light entering the eye through the pupil and damaging the retina. At the front of the eye, the sclerotic layer becomes transparent to allow light into the eye. This is called the cornea.

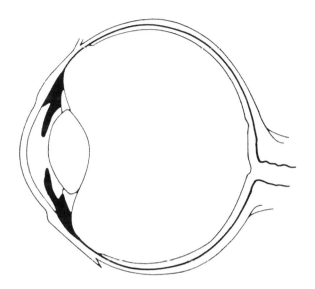

Figure 17.6 A diagram of the eye (for labelling)

Instructions

1 Underline the names of parts of the eye.
2 Double underline any parts of the passage which tell you where the parts are located.
3 Now label the diagram of the eye (Figure 17.6), adding any information you think appropriate.

Conclusions

The message underpinning these examples of alternatives to practical work is a belief that children are curious and will engage with science if they are encouraged to ask questions and discuss possible answers. Watts and Alsop (1995) have argued that the importance of questions is that:

- they can indicate areas of understanding and incomprehension;
- they can show the willingness of pupils to *seek* understanding;
- science itself is based on the asking of questions and the seeking of answers.

Yet, how often do we give pupils the opportunity to ask questions themselves? One simple strategy, often used effectively for the treatment of sex education, but rarely extended to other areas of science, is to have a question box in which pupils can put their questions anonymously. Another useful technique, often used in primary schools, is to have a large outline figure on a noticeboard called 'Professor Question'. Pupils can be encouraged to pin questions to the figure as and when they arise. Just simply starting any topic, for instance, astronomy, with the request for pupils to write down ten questions about the proposed subject of study can be a fascinating insight into children's curiosity.

Providing opportunities for more group work and discussion is one strategy which students themselves have identified would improve their enjoyment of science (Piburn 1993). Whilst science teaching is often dominated by exigencies of the moment and the demands of adjusting to an ever-changing National Curriculum, can we as teachers of science afford to neglect an examination of the range and success of our teaching strategies? Hopefully, this chapter provides a few crumbs as food for thought. Like the addict who tries to give up smoking, offering a lesson with no practical work may be a testing and unnerving experience, but it is my belief that the long-term gains for the health of science education are well worth the short-term pain.

Acknowledgements

I would like to thank Dr Bob Fairbrother for introducing me to the false concept map, an anonymous New Zealand teacher for showing me the use of jumbled sentences and Justin Dillon for comments on an early draft of this article.

References

Bruner, J. and Haste, H. (1987) *Making Sense: the Child's Construction of the World,* London: Methuen.

Cooper, P. and McIntyre, D. (1996) *Effective Teaching and Learning: Teachers' and Students' Perspectives,* Buckingham: Open University Press.

Davies, F. and Greene, T. (1984) *Reading for Learning in the Sciences,* Edinburgh: Oliver and Boyd.

Duschl, R. A. (1990) *Restructuring Science Education,* New York: Teachers College Press.

Edwards, D. and Mercer, N. (1987) *Common Knowledge: the Development of Understanding in the Classroom,* London: Methuen.

HM Inspectors of Schools (1994) *Effective Learning and Teaching in Scottish Secondary Schools: the Sciences,* Edinburgh: The Scottish Office Education Department.

Hodson, D. (1991) 'Practical work in science: time for reappraisal', *Studies in Science Education* 19: 175–84.

Horton, R. (1967) 'African traditional thought and Western science', *Africa* 37(1): 50–71.

Lemke, J. L. (1990) 'Talking science: language, learning and values', in J. Green (ed.) *Language and Educational Process*, Norwood, New Jersey: Ablex Publishing.

Novak, J. D. and Gowin, D. B. (1984) *Learning How to Learn,* Cambridge: Cambridge University Press.

Ofsted (Office for Standards in Education) (1995) *Science: A Review of Inspection Findings 1993/94,* London: HMSO.

Piburn, M. D. (1993) 'If I were the teacher … qualitative study of attitude toward science', *Science Education* 77(4): 393–406.

Sands, M. K. (1981) 'Group work in science: myth and reality', *School Science Review* 62(221): 765–9.

Sizmur, S. (1994) 'Concept mapping, language and learning in the classroom', *School Science Review* 76(274): 120–5.

Watts, M. and Alsop, S. (1995) 'Questioning and conceptual understanding: the quality of pupils' questions in science', *School Science Review* 76(277): 91–5.

White, R. (1991) 'Episodes, and the purpose and conduct of practical work', in B. Woolnough, (ed.), *Practical Science: the Role and Reality of Practical Work in School Science,* Buckingham: Open University Press.

18 Pupil learning through writing in science

Vaughan Prain and Brian Hand

Introduction

For various reasons there has been strong interest in the value of writing for learning in science over the last ten years. In this context, writing is defined broadly to include not only constructing traditional science texts with diagrams, but also engaging with computer-generated programs. Traditional writing practices, such as note taking and reports, were seen as failing to motivate learners or enhance learning, and in some cases as excluding particular groups from success. This has led to extended analyses of the particular demands of writing types or genres in science, their rationale, and teaching methods (Cope and Kalantzis 1993; Martin and Veel 1998; Unsworth 2000). At the same time, new understandings of the key role of language in learning scientific concepts have prompted new approaches to constructing knowledge of science through exploratory talk and writing (Sutton 1992). Writing about science-related issues was also seen as a key way to develop pupils' science literacy (Holliday *et al.* 1994; Kelly and Chen 1999). In addition, the emergence of process and collaborative approaches to writing in other school subjects prompted their use in the science classroom (Sutton 1992; Hildebrand 1998). More recently, researchers such as Cope and Kalantzis (2000) have proposed that multimodal and computer-generated texts, where pupils integrate imagery, sound and writing, should replace a narrow focus on language as the sole medium of learning. Engagement with all these issues has produced strong, contrasting claims about what should count as the main goals, methods, and desired outcomes for effective writing for learning in science.

Approaches to writing for learning in science

Traditional forms of science writing

One strand of research views writing for learning as the process whereby pupils learn about the functions of the particular linguistic features found in traditional forms of science writing, such as the laboratory or research report. The main goal of this approach is to give learners access to the assumptions, procedures, 'hidden' rules, and purposes of scientific writing. This provides the basis for understanding what counts as scientific method, explanation, and justification, as well as the underlying history and rationale of this writing as a practice. From this perspective, learning is primarily defined as the acquisition of this generic knowledge and the ability to interpret, reproduce, and critique this system of meanings. There are several key ideas to emerge from this strand of research. It is argued that knowing the generic rules enables pupils to 'process information deeply' as they 'construct relationships among ideas' (Klein 1999). The specific meanings of scientific terminology are not equivalent to everyday language. While everyday language provides starting points for learning, science literacy must entail pupil knowledge of the exact scientific meanings of words and concepts and their appropriate usage. According to Veel (1996) and others, pupils will learn the rules and meanings of this particular language practice through detailed analysis of examples, joint construction of texts with their teacher, and explicit teacher focus on key textual features. Advocates claim that there have been demonstrable learning gains from this approach over more learner-oriented methods, because tacit knowledge is made explicit in this generic approach (Martin and Veel 1998).

This use of traditional forms of science writing can be argued for and to some extent justified in the research. Learners disadvantaged by class, culture or language need added explicit instruction in the structural features of science writing if they are to succeed in cracking this subject's 'codes' and rules. Much work has been done on identifying the content, strategies, and conventions of scientific writing, but less attention has been paid to establishing the psychological and pedagogical conditions likely to promote engagement of pupils with this learning. At the same time, new technologies have also posed challenges to using a highly prescriptive generic approach. Nevertheless, there are those, such as Hand and Keys (1999), who contend that pupils can benefit from engaging with traditional writing styles, when they are modified to include a new framework that encourages them to be more explicit about their reasoning processes.

Other forms of writing for science

A different strand of research has emphasized the value of expanding the purposes, writing types, and readerships for writing in science beyond induction into the traditional style. Writing here is viewed as one resource among many to enable learners to join a community of practices called 'doing science'. Science learners in classrooms are clearly not professional scientists, but some practices, such as clarifying ideas through notes and diagrams, seeking to persuade others in the team about a particular viewpoint, and disseminating ideas to diverse readerships, may overlap and also be useful for learning in the classroom. Some educators such as Hildebrand (1998), Prain and Hand (1996), Rowell (1997), Sutton (1992) and others have asserted that pupils, in striving to clarify networks of concepts in science topics, should be encouraged to write in diverse forms for different purposes. Gunstone (1995: 15) argues that there are learning gains when pupils write 'translations' of their emerging understandings in a variety of ways, using their own words. Pupil writing is here viewed primarily as a resource for thinking and learning, an interim process or clearing-house by which learners clarify and consolidate conceptual knowledge. The main goals of this approach include the following:

- to encourage learners to see writing in science as a resource for communication, argument, justification and clarification of a viewpoint;
- to provide learners with a tool for learning as well with a means of displaying knowledge;

- to promote pupils' science literacy by developing their interest in and capacity to apply scientific thinking to social issues for the purposes of informed action, where the pupils can learn to cross borders between specialist and more popular genres and readerships.
- to develop pupils' strategies for self-directed learning of science, and provide positive, enjoyable engagement with science for all pupils, not just those who might specialize later in this subject area.

From this perspective, writing in science is not only a means to display knowledge of scientific understandings, procedures, processes and rationale, but also functions as a tool for constructing and clarifying knowledge. This approach assumes that learning occurs when pupils successfully engage in communicating with actual readerships for meaningful and varied purposes. These purposes might include brainstorming initial ideas, predicting and speculating about causes and outcomes, representing their ideas in different forms, explaining or justifying their explanations to themselves or others, persuading others to accept their interpretations, simplifying textbook explanations for other or younger pupils, or modifying their views in the light of additional evidence. When reporting on pupil writing activities in two senior secondary science classrooms, Kelly and Chen (1999) noted there was a surprising diversity of practices beyond traditional note-taking or report-writing, and that such a focus enabled pupils to develop more elaborate conceptual frameworks. It is also argued that the use of everyday language can enable pupils to clarify their understanding of some scientific topics. For pupils who are beginning to learn new concepts, opportunities to write in diverse ways can lead them to connect their emerging knowledge and technical vocabulary with their everyday language and past experiences in a two-way process. In supporting this view, Michaels and Sohmer (2000) also claim that teachers need to provide opportunities for pupils to build connections between their personal meaning-making processes incorporating their everyday perceptions of the phenomenal world, and the official inscriptions and representations of school science knowledge.

Research claims for the benefits of this approach have focused mainly on the positive effects on pupils' attitudes towards and engagement with science (Hand and Prain 1995; 1996). Across a range of studies, pupils have consistently reported that focusing on making sense of scientific ideas and justifying their views helped them to learn. It also promoted a positive attitude towards the subject compared to undertaking traditional writing tasks. These studies also report success with pupils who in the past failed to engage with science, or performed poorly. Critics of this approach, such as Martin and Veel (1998) and Martin (1999), claim that it favours linguistically-able and highly-motivated middle-class learners, but such a criticism can be levelled at any demanding language-centred approach.

Writing for learning

In summary, there is clearly a need to focus on both broad agendas for effective pupil writing for learning in secondary science. Science learners need to become familiar with the rules, rationale, claims, and procedures of traditional ways of representing scientific inquiry and findings. However, writing can also be used as tool for shaping knowledge and they need opportunities to write in ways that allow clarification and consolidation of their emerging understandings. They also need to write to disseminate this knowledge for different purposes to different readerships as part of acquiring science literacy. Such writing can broaden their horizons about the meaning of being a writer of science, or writing to justify a science-informed perspective.

Task design for effective writing for learning

In devising effective writing tasks for pupils, teachers need to be very clear about the following:

- the purpose or purposes of the task;
- the intended audience or readership;
- the key concepts to be addressed;
- the type of writing proposed,
- the method for producing the writing, such as pen or computer;
- whether it will be done as individual or group work.

It is also important that all these dimensions are clear to the pupils, including guidance on what will count as successful task completion, and marking criteria where appropriate. In constructing a framework to guide this decision-making process for teachers, Prain and Hand (1996) proposed the following possible writing purposes that might promote learning:

Purpose for writing

Start of topic	Pupils brainstorm current understandings of the topic for review
	Hypothesize (speculate on explanations)
	Explore first thoughts, preliminary reasoning
	Devise a plan of action
During	Clarify, refine knowledge, sort out understanding
	Reprocess ideas into own words
	Build outlines
	Structure an overview, classify information
	Argue ideas, take sides on an issue
	Revise understanding
	Reorganise and review knowledge
	Redraft to consolidate understanding
	Apply new knowledge to different context

continued on next page

	Consider alternatives
	Explain another writer's ideas
	Persuade others that a particular metaphor provides a useful explanation of a process
	Test the validity of own or others' explanations
	Interpret data or ideas of others
Topic completion	Demonstrate understanding
	Apply learning to new situation or problem
	Test learning
	Revise initial ideas
	Write notes as resource for teaching a topic or part of a topic to other pupils or other group
	Design a solution to a technological problem

A strong focus in learning in any new science topic should be for pupils to write, in order to interpret and understand their own and other writers' ideas on the topic and to process and reprocess these ideas. While much of this work can be achieved through classroom discussion, there is a place for writing where the complexity of the topic warrants and rewards the extra effort of written language for learning. For Sutton (1992: 89), the challenge for the teacher is to 'devise small tasks which will capture the imagination of the learner and give a target audience for whom it is necessary to clarify ideas'. Pupils can write for a wide range of meaningful reader-ships, including themselves, other pupils in their class, younger pupils, the teacher, pupils at another school, parent groups, their own parents, consumers, politicians, or visitors to the classroom or school. For visitors, this writing could take the form of a set of questions to be answered. They can write part of a textbook for younger children, or a guide for next year's class when they tackle a particular topic. They can write as the assessor of other pupils' work, where they explain why they think one answer offers a better scientific explanation than another.

Possible writing tasks can vary from small informal responses and notes, that do not fit any obvious writing style, to tasks that have strong, resolved, generic frameworks and expectations. Examples of the first kind of writing task include the following:

- devising analogies or metaphors to explain a process
- responding to questions that incorporate comparisons, for example, in what ways is cloning similar to, and different from, photocopying?
- preparing a persuasive account of why a particular metaphor is or is not useful for understanding a topic
- producing a map to explain a process or show links between concepts
- giving an explanation of why one account of a topic is more convincing, scientifically, than another account
- producing a sequence of labelled diagrams to explain a process

- explaining a diagram or illustration of a machine in terms of the inventor's intention or purpose
- producing a PowerPoint set of slides as a resource to support an explanatory talk on a topic or process
- writing a summary/revision notes/mind map/hypertext of a topic
- producing a test on a topic for other pupils
- recording predictions, observations, explanations of experiments and excursions
- reporting ongoing reactions to a topic or scientific explanation
- giving personal reflections on how pupils learn in science
- adding captions to diagrams where text is not provided.

Examples of the second kind of task include the following:

Scientific and verbal reports

- report and analysis of experiments and observations
- explanation of a process, structure, or issue, such as health care or causes of disease
- history of famous scientists and their achievements including perceived 'side-tracks'.

Narratives

- stories to show knowledge of a process or a sequence of events, such as the life story of a chromosome or a blood cell
- stories about the interdependence of organisms, the human life cycle
- stories to demonstrate multiple viewpoints through multiple narrators and points of view.

Travelogues

- descriptions of particular sites such as in a geology or ecology topic
- description of a process or a chain of events, as in the topic of energy.

Guidelines and instructions

- guides to the use of materials
- survival manual
- rewrite part of a textbook to clarify the topic for younger readers
- designs for safety labels for use at school
- step-by-step instructions on a process.

Scripts for debates or speech

- debate on a controversial subject such as uses of the environment, scientific experimentation, technology, genetic engineering
- positive and negative issues relating to a source of energy
- performance of a process, e.g.: 'raps'
- scripted dialogue of an interview with a scientist
- new script for a commercial video on a science topic targeting a different audience or purpose.

Posters

- demonstration of knowledge at the completion of a topic
- ordering of knowledge into an appropriate sequence
- representation of knowledge not easily produced as written text.

Brochures

- guides for field work such as geology excursions
- guide for the efficient use of resources
- information to explain a chemical process.

Letters

- persuasive writing on a scientific issue that affects society or the community
- explanation of a topic to a friend.

Implementation strategies

For pupils to learn from these writing activities, various conditions need to be met. The teacher must provide appropriate scaffolding for the task including not only explicit advice on the purpose of the task, but also examples or models of a successful answer or product, and overt guidance on the demands of the task. Such models should not cover the topic of the task directly in order to avoid heavy reliance of the pupils on the content of the model, but rather provide a parallel example to encourage equivalent effort. In this regard, teachers should save copies of all types of successful pupil texts as a key resource for future class analysis and the explanation of tasks. Past experience with writing topics for learning suggests that pupils need considerable exposure to and analysis of different kinds of writing if they are to understand the goals of this work and how to meet them. Pupils also need support with the communicative challenges of different kinds of tasks. For instance, if they are expected to produce a PowerPoint slide show, then they need to understand the effective use of multimodal design features and resources in this technology as well as the number of slides to be used. They also need to be clear about the number of concepts to be covered and the strategies required for making effective use of the limited space on each slide. If pupils are to write effectively for a particular readership then they must be able to anticipate the expectations and needs of this readership, in terms of writing style, appropriate explanations and elaboration, and assumed generic features of the text. For some texts, this entails a focus on the function of introductions, headings, sub-headings, diagrams, illustrations, captions, findings and conclusions.

In setting up the writing task, the teacher also needs to make sure pupils have adequate resources for tackling the task. These include not only, where appropriate, a range of secondary sources such as additional library and internet information, but also opportunities to discuss relevant issues arising from practical work, excursions, and interaction with other resources, followed by pair, small-group and whole-class discussion and reporting. This group work can entail further learning strategies where learners sort collected information and notes to determine which is important for the topic, re-order the information into a conceptual framework, and synthesize this material to identify essential concepts entailed in the topic. In many topics, pupils then need to develop a framework to represent the inter-relationship between the concepts being addressed. Some topics benefit from the opportunity for pupils to share drafts in progress with their teacher or peers to ascertain how successful the draft is in terms of both communication and content. If pupils are attempting to frame an argument they need to determine evidence for the case, make decisions about the concepts to be addressed, and link their evidence to the concepts. Pupils also need explicit criteria of what will count as success in the task. As noted already, some tasks are intended to explore or speculate on an issue rather than produce a 'correct' answer, and this expectation and the relevant criteria for success need to be explained.

Conclusion

The use of different writing types for different audiences requires learners to conceptualize their knowledge from different perspectives. This requires them to rethink their understanding of concepts as they engage with the perceived task demands of the writing. Such a reconceptualization clearly places more demands on pupils than straightforward rote learning, but in clarifying concepts for themselves and for others, they are constructing richer conceptual networks of their knowledge in science, and therefore using writing as a tool for learning.

References

Cope, B. and Kalantzis, M. (eds) (1993) *The Powers of Literacy: A Genre Approach to Teaching Writing,* London: The Falmer Press, pp. 179–202.

Cope, B. and Kalantzis, M. (eds) (2000) *Multiliteracies: Literacy Learning and the Design of Social Futures,* London: Routledge.

Gunstone, R. (1995) 'Constructivist learning and the teaching of science', in B. Hand and V. Prain, (eds) *Teaching and Learning in Science: The Constructivist Classroom,* Sydney: Harcourt Brace.

Hand, B. and Keys, C. (1999) 'Inquiry investigation', *The Science Teacher* 66(4): 27–9.

Hand, B. and Prain, V. (1995) 'Using writing to help improve students' understanding of science knowledge', *School Science Review* 77(278): 112–17.

Hand, B. and Prain, V. (1996) 'Writing for learning in science: a model for use within schools', *Australian Science Teachers' Journal* 42(3): 23–7.

Hildebrand, G. (1998) 'Disrupting hegemonic writing practices in school science: contesting the right way to write', *Journal of Research in Science Teaching* 35(4): 345–62.

Holliday, W. G., Yore, L. D. and Alvermann, D. E. (1994) 'The reading-science learning-writing connection: breakthroughs, barriers and promises', *Journal of Research in Science Teaching* 31(9): 877–93.

Kelly, G. and Chen, C. (1999) 'The sound of music: constructing science as sociocultural practices through oral and written discourse', *Journal of Research in Science Teaching* 36: 883–915.

Klein, P. (1999) 'Reopening inquiry into cognitive processes in writing-to-learn', *Educational Psychology Review* 11(3): 203–70.

Martin, J. (1999) 'Mentoring semogenesis: "genre-based" literacy pedagogy', in F. Christie (ed.) *Pedagogy and the Shaping of Consciousness: Linguistic and Social Processes,* London: Cassell (Open Linguistics Series), pp. 123–55.

Martin, J. and Veel, R. (1998) *Reading Science: Critical and Functional Perspectives on Discourses of Science,* London: Routledge.

Michaels, S. and Sohmer, R. (2000) 'Narratives and inscriptions: cultural tools, power and powerful sense making', in B. Cope and M. Kalantzis (eds) *Multiliteracies: Literacy Learning and the Design of Social Futures,* London: Routledge.

Prain, V. and Hand, B. (1996) 'Writing and learning in secondary science: rethinking practices', *Teaching and Teacher Education* 12: 609–26.

Rowell, P. A. (1997) 'Learning in school science: the promises and practices of writing', *Studies in Science Education* 30: 19–56.

Sutton, C. (1992) *Words, Science and Learning,* Buckingham: Open University Press.

Unsworth, L. (2000) 'Investigating subject-specific literacies in school learning', in L. Unsworth (ed.) *Researching Language in Schools and Communities,* London: Continuum (Cassell).

Veel, R. (1996) 'Learning how to mean – scientifically speaking', in F. Christie (ed.) *Genre and Institutions: The Language of Work and Schooling,* London: Cassell Academic.

19 There's more to communication than just words

Douglas Newton

Introduction

Text used for instruction has a long history. Thousands of years ago, in the Middle East, children attempted to solve mathematical problems set on baked-clay tablets. Since then, the written word has remained a teaching aid and teacher substitute. However, in the seventeenth century, a 64-year-old ex-bishop and teacher, Jan Komensky (better known as Comenius) felt that there was more to communication than just words. Textbooks should be clear, palatable, even enjoyable, and his book, *The World in Pictures* (Figure 19.1), was one of the first 'science' books to use illustrations to achieve those ends. Nowadays, pictures are the rule rather than the exception although sometimes their provision is based more on intuition than on studies of what makes textbooks work. At the same time, these studies have often focused on

Figure 19.1 A page from Comenius's 'The World in Pictures'

the impact of convoluted sentences and difficult words (Long 1991), something that teachers can assess informally and competently without recourse to syllable counts, word counts and sentence analysis (Fatt 1991). In reality, comprehending individual words and sentences may be the least of a reader's problems (Newton 2000). The difficulty is more likely to be in making the words and sentence say something meaningful about the topic in hand. The aim of this chapter is to point to various features of textual materials that can significantly support understanding.

Two sides of the problem

Teaching science has been described as pointing out the uncommon sense of things as effectively as possible (Wolpert 1993). To be effective, teachers' textual materials should be understandable, memorable and, when appropriate, should help readers apply what they learn. It is the job of those who prepare the text, whether it is a book, a worksheet, an instruction leaflet or an examination paper, to do their best to make it work. But this is not always enough to guarantee success – understanding is not won so easily.

Understanding is a constructive process during which the reader creates meaning from the interaction between the text, the situation and their existing knowledge (Myers 1991). In other words, understanding cannot be transmitted; readers have to do it for themselves.

These are the two sides of the problem: what the teacher-writer does to increase the chance of success of textual materials and what the reader does to bring it to fruition.

The first side – choosing and preparing considerate text

Words

First, a few words about words. It is true that long words and convoluted, long sentences tend to make text difficult. Methods of measuring reading difficulty are available that use this association to predict the reading level of prose. These measures, however, are not always successful in predicting the difficulty of science text (Carrick 1978). It is easy to see why. Take polysyllabic words like *thermometer* or *experiment,* for instance. They are familiar to most students but are counted as 'difficult' words by some popular measures. Since such words tend to occur frequently, this inflates the calculated 'difficulty' of the text. At the same time, such measures commonly ignore illustrations, one of the earliest aids to understanding, and do not take mathematical expressions, chemical formulae, tables or the organization of the ideas into account. They are intended mainly for gauging the difficulty of everyday prose and are often unsuited to science text. If used slavishly, there is the danger that they will give rise to writing that is incongruous, boring, fatuous, or even poor science (Duffy *et al.* 1989). For instance, to avoid the four syllables of *thermometer*, would *heat stick,* do?

The general message is to write simply and about one thing at a time. If you call a spade a spade in class, call it a spade in print and not a small-capacity, manually-operated excavating device. Students tend to judge text by how often they stumble over less-common words and are put off when there are a lot of them (Fatt 1991). Such words can also disrupt younger readers' ability to recall the order of events as they are presented in the text (Stahl *et al.* 1989). Unfamiliar scientific terms should at least be explained and preferably be used in class beforehand. If in doubt, test the material before use. One quick and simple way is to spread the fingers of one hand on the page of text and ask a student to explain the words at the fingertips. Motivating students to read can be a concern. Anecdotes and similar asides may catch a reader's interest but they should not be so pervasive that they distract from the key ideas and become counter-productive. For example, the Introduction here was intended to catch attention and set the scene. It could only have been a distraction if it had appeared later. Although brevity can be a virtue, it is not the main concern. What has to come first is making the text meaningful, so you may have to state pre-requisite knowledge, avoid great leaps in an argument and make relationships clear. The result may make the text longer but it should make more sense (Beck *et al.* 1991). Sometimes, what you can do is quite simple. For instance, giving text a 'voice', that is, addressing the reader directly ('you' in the previous sentence), has been found to increase understanding, possibly by increasing the reader's attention (Beck *et al.* 1995).

Organization and structure

By itself, a basic understanding of individual words and sentences is seldom enough for comprehension of the message in science text. This can only be grasped by relating and integrating the meaning of a number of sentences or paragraphs. In other words, the message lies in the whole rather than in the parts.

Before putting pen to paper, you should be clear about your purpose and then keep to it. Watch out for digressions that serve no real purpose. The temptation to allow, say, an account of electrical conduction in ohmic conductors to grow fascinating asides about non-ohmic conductors should generally be resisted when introducing a topic. Select the topic and stick to it.

The selection and organization of the parts and their subsumption by a theme that is apparent to the reader is crucially important (Chambliss and Calfee 1989). Content is made more memorable, and the relationships between the elements more obvious, if it has been appropriately organized or sequenced. One approach is to group content according to how we see it in the world around us. We might, for instance, describe woodland ecology, seashore habitats, or common birds. Another way of organizing material in science is by logical necessity. According to this principle, we would teach speed before acceleration and some symbols for the elements before molecular formulae and chemical equations. However, because things have a natural organization or logic, does not always mean these must provide the teaching sequence. An age-old principle is to proceed from the simple to the complex, the concrete to the abstract and the familiar to the unfamiliar. If you choose to organize content in ways that conflict with this principle, you need a good reason.

The purpose of a passage of text is usually to present certain key ideas. Unless these are explicitly stated, most students, including older ones, may not be able to grasp them unaided. For maximum effect, especially with younger and less able students, it is better if the number of key ideas is small, preferably only one or two. It often helps if the main ideas are stated in simple and concrete terms at the beginning of the passage. Supporting information then follows. Where supporting information is basically a *list* – 'A wide range of animals is found in ponds. For example, on the surface there are water boatmen, in the water there are tadpoles, and on the bottom, there are caddis fly larvae …' – or forms a *sequence* – 'The life of the frog has three stages. It begins as an egg, develops into a tadpole and becomes an adult frog' – these tend to be readily understood. A little more difficult is a *compare/contrast* structure – 'A whale and a fish are different kinds of sea animals. Both are vertebrates but the whale has lungs while the fish has gills …'. A *cause–effect* sequence can present particular difficulties. It is quite common in science and often comprises a chain of logically connected events – 'Burning coal, oil, gas and wood may make the sea flood our coastal towns and cities. Burning coal, oil, gas or wood produces carbon dioxide. Carbon dioxide in the atmosphere traps the heat from the sun, rather like the air in a greenhouse on a sunny day. This is called the Greenhouse Effect. This heat is making the polar ice caps melt. The melted water returns to the oceans and makes the sea level rise. As the water slowly rises, it will flood coastal towns and cities.' The reader has to construct the connections between the statements in the sequence. This can depend crucially on prior knowledge, knowing that making connections is expected and, of course, being willing to make those connections.

Even when the main idea is explicitly stated, younger and less able students may find it difficult to make compare–contrast and cause–effect sequences meaningful (Hare *et al.* 1989). However, the physical deployment of the words on the page can be used to help readers construct meaning (Long 1991). Just as a list or table announces the order in which information is to be taken and points to associations by juxtaposition, text can be arranged to do the same. For instance, in the compare–contrast structure, the text might be set to emphasize similarities and differences:

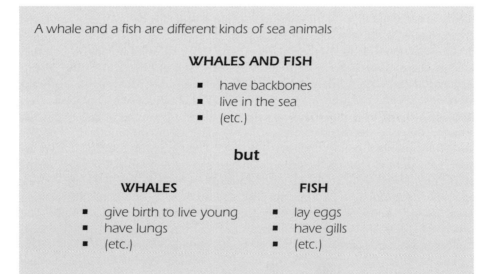

Similarly, a cause-effect sequence might be set as:

Burning coal, oil, gas and wood may make the sea flood our coastal towns and cities

because

1 burning coal, oil, gas or wood produces carbon dioxide
2 carbon dioxide in the atmosphere traps heat from the sun
3 this heat is making the polar ice caps melt
4 the melted water returns to the oceans and makes the sea-level rise, so
5 as the water slowly rises, it will flood coastal towns and cities.

This is called the Greenhouse Effect because the atmosphere is becoming warmer, rather like the air in a greenhouse on a sunny day.

It can also help to point out the structure of the argument at the outset using a *tree diagram* (Gropper 1988). Figure 19.2 shows a tree diagram for the structure of this chapter. *Framing* is another technique that requires an active mental engagement (Guri-Rozenblit 1989). The teacher extracts key information from a passage, section or chapter and constructs a framework that reflects the organization of the content. It could, for instance, look like a tree diagram or be a table or flow chart. A version with blanks is produced for discussion before the text is read. Students consider what could appear in the blanks, as individuals, in groups, or as a class. After the passage has been read, the framework is reviewed and a new version produced (Figure 19.3 is an example). The process helps readers to focus attention on important information, its organization and the relationship between the parts.

Tables, graphs and diagrams

A table is a useful way of presenting information and is common in science. It takes advantage of the way we read, from left to right (in the West) and from the top to the bottom of the page. Trends and associations can be more easily perceived because the information is ordered and what goes together is placed together. Spatial layout is often exploited in diagrams that show process or structure. The parts of the nitrogen cycle, for instance, can be depicted in a circle with stages and interactions shown by arrows (Holiday 1976). In a sense, the parts are like nouns and the arrows like verbs so that the diagram makes a sentence-like statement (Fleming and Levie 1978). Charts and diagrams are good at making information explicit and provide a useful channel of communication. Illustrations, for instance, are particularly valuable when they elaborate some phenomenon by, for example, showing a sequence of events. For instance, the action of glaciation may be depicted with 'before', 'during' and

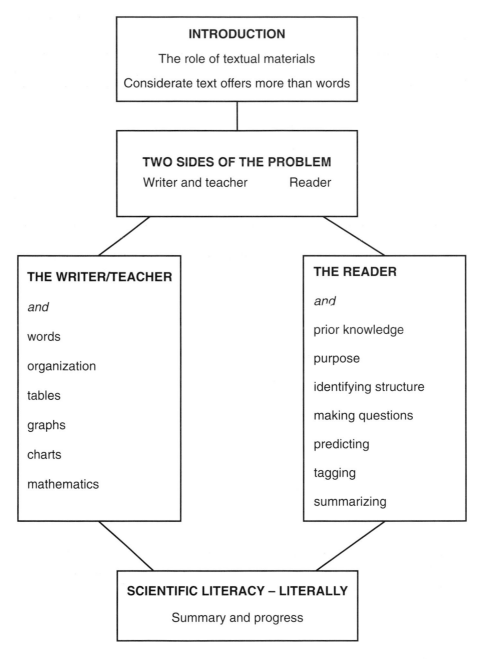

Figure 19.2 A tree-diagram showing the structure of 'There's more to communication than just words'

The flowering plant		
	Important parts	What they do
1		
2		
3		
4		

Figure 19.3 A frame with blanks for use with text about the flowering plant. The text describes stem, root, leaf and flower so the table has four rows

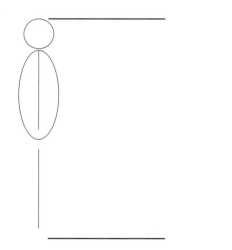

Figure 19.4 Whiz lines used to indicate motion to the left. In the case of people and other animals, posture may clarify the direction of motion. This additional clue is not available for inanimate objects (unless they are anthropomorphized)

'after' diagrams (Holiday 1975). However, like prose, they can become ineffective if overloaded with information and attempt to show too many key ideas at once (Winn 1987). Pictorial metaphor – depicting things that are not naturally visible in a picture, like indicating motion by whiz lines (Figure 19.4) or magnetism by a lighting flash – can also present problems. For example, about 15 per cent of 14-year-old students see the whiz lines in Figure 19.4 as indicating movement to the right when the opposite direction was intended (Newton 1984).

Mathematics

Another feature of science text, especially for older students, is the inclusion of mathematics. Mathematics allows statements to be made in very precise and concise ways. However, its language can be hard to grasp (Newton and Merrell 1994). To make sense of it, the vocabulary, conventions and rules have to be known (Noonan 1991). For instance, *ratio* and *mass per unit volume* are meaningless to many students. These tend to be less familiar than the structures found in everyday prose but, since much of science rests on quantitative study and mathematical modelling, the science student will meet this way of expressing ideas sooner or later. This makes it particularly important that the nature and direction of the argument is made explicit at the outset; that the specialized language is carefully controlled, that steps are clearly labelled and are not too large. Where possible, other support, such as providing an analogy, can be helpful. Our own familiarity with mathematics may lead us to express it too quickly and take short cuts that confuse rather than clarify. 'It is obvious that ...' helps no one.

Mathematics is very economical; a lot can be said in a short space. While this economy might be appealing to mathematicians, it can be impenetrable to those who cannot use it easily. Supporting the mathematics with a gloss can help. This is not to say that a logical development with mathematics has to be translated into prose. A logical sequencing or setting on the page is useful and should be retained, but it can be supported by sliding in explanatory sentences at appropriate points. The aim is to describe what the mathematics is doing in as concrete a way as possible. At the same time, the language of the mathematics itself needs to be considered. It can be so stilted, abstract and full of qualification that it takes several readings to grasp its meaning. Generally, avoid introducing unfamiliar vocabulary without good reason. A definition alone is seldom sufficient to make new terms meaningful. If possible, use the present tense and avoid words like 'if', 'suppose' and 'given that' (Shuard and Rothery 1984). 'Given that a ball weighs 100 g, what is its potential energy relative to the floor if it is on a table 1.5 m above that floor?' might be better expressed as 'A ball weighs 100 g. It is on a table 1.5 m above the floor. How much extra potential energy does the ball have by being on the table rather than on the floor?' Finally, worked examples really do help understanding, provided that the student reads them (Sweller 1989).

To sum up so far, it is unwise to place too much reliance on measures of word and sentence alone. Unlike narrative prose, science text usually includes exercises and activities intended to focus attention, articulate and elaborate what has been described and to practise using what has been acquired. The importance of such aids to comprehension and learning should not be underestimated (Newton 1990). It should also be emphasized that there is not one solution to the problem of preparing textual material, but many – and that none comes with a guarantee. No matter how well written, well organized, well illustrated and carefully supported a piece of text is, it may fail if the reader cannot perceive its structure, ignores tables and illustrations, skips mathematical bits, and does not adopt remedial strategies when understanding fails. This is the other side of the problem.

The second side – the reader and the text

Why does even the most considerate text not come with a guarantee? Why, in spite of your greatest endeavours does your literary masterpiece fall flat? The answer is that readers bring with them knowledge and experience and a reason for reading. These determine what they pay attention to and the meanings they construct. At the same time, skills and abilities need to be applied to construct those meanings. Text has to be read in an active way, noting relationships between elements, distinguishing main ideas from lesser ones and subtracting incidental information to see the thread of the argument. Weakness or deficiency in coping with any of these makes the construction of meaning less likely. Teachers have an advantage over textbook writers in that they generally know those for whom they write and can activate their existing knowledge and focus attention where it will be needed. With the right reason for reading, even the driest manual can seem attractive. 'The Rose Detective' provides an example of a strategy that makes a task relevant and meaningful for younger students. In this article, the learning task was to do with plant propagation, so an introductory story was used to catch interest. The story, however, was also used to introduce the vocabulary that would be used later. Students wanted to know what happened in the story and they quickly absorbed the meaning of the technical terms (Blum 1982). Similarly, if there is a stimulating problem to solve, students will readily consult and master quite complex materials because it serves a purpose and they want to know the answer.

Teachers can also show students how to work and think with textual materials and how to be flexible in their strategies (Bouman 1987). When understanding falters, less able students often give up (Myers 1991). Remedial actions can be taught and practised so that students learn that there is value in persistence and that reading means thought, quest and strategy (Donaldson 1989).

There are a number of such strategies that teachers might practise with their students. For instance, they might *activate prior knowledge* by asking what the students think the text will be about. An alternative is to present three key words from the topic and ask the students to list as many words associated with them as they can. Older students might structure their responses into a concept map, a diagram which links related ideas together with labelled arrows, rather like a tree diagram. Key words have the effect of focusing attention on related information so that, chosen wisely, they can support the comprehension of the main idea. This is linked to *determining the purpose of reading*. It must be clear what the reader is to acquire from the text if thoughts are to be focused on what matters. The structure of the text has to be identified by the reader before becoming immersed in it. Here, tree diagrams help but readers can practise constructing their own from headings and emphasized words. Older students can turn *headings into questions* and answer them as they read. Another self-help technique is to *think of headings* for each paragraph or unit of text. This can be quite effective after the student has had some practice at extracting the main idea in a paragraph. However, it is important to illustrate the technique and practise it. It may also help to let the class see that the teacher values the strategy by expecting its use in examinations.

Some topics lend themselves to *prediction*. The reader stops and predicts what will be next, then verifies it. Even locating the 'most important sentence' in each paragraph and underlining it can be effective. An extension of this is to number or *tag* the pieces of information that support that main idea. Both strategies are enhanced if they are used to produce a *summary* after reading. Even the age-old practice of *note-taking,* one of the most common of the self-initiated study activities, is not to be despised.

Most teachers are familiar with memory aids like: 'Richard of York Gave Battle In Vain' (for the sequence of colours in the spectrum). Making mnemonics has a long history and was popular with Roman orators for helping them recall the elements of their speeches. They converted each important idea into a visual representation and imagined each item to be in a room of a familiar house. When giving the speech, they pictured each room in turn, 'saw' the item placed there and recovered the idea. Considering its effectiveness, it is surprising that *picturing* it is not often taught as a strategy for recalling information from text. Students should practise drawing a picture or sequence of pictures that tie together the important concepts in what they read. When the process gives rise to bizarre pictures, all the better: they are often more memorable.

Often, reading activities that call for mental effort aid understanding and learning. The lesson the student has to learn is that science text is for *thinking* with and, if they do the right kind and amount of thinking, understanding and recalling what the text has to say is not beyond them.

Scientific literacy, literally

The general point being made is that there is lot more to understanding textual materials than just words. On the one hand, anyone who writes science text needs to consider such aspects as structure, illustrations and mathematics. On the other, the reader must work at constructing meaning and they may need help.

This leaves a final but important matter. How far should we simplify text? After all, 'learning science means learning to control the discourse features which construct scientific knowledge' and there is the need to initiate students into the language of systematic thought. We must not forget that one aim of science education is for students to grasp at least some scientific English on their own (Unsworth 1991) – scientific literacy in the literal sense of the phrase. In at least the short term, the kind of scientific English that most students have to come to terms with is that of the textbook, worksheet and examination paper, so efforts will be directed to reading those materials. But progress cannot rely on happy accident. It has a starting point and it has a goal. This goal is more likely to be reached by thoughtful preparation and selection of scientific text and by making sure that students know what is expected of them when they read it.

References

Beck, I. L., McKeown, M. G., Sinatra, G. M. and Loxterman, J. A. (1991) 'Revising Social Studies text from a text processing perspective', *Reading Research Quarterly* 26: 251–76.

Beck, I. L., McKeown, M. G., and Worthy, J. (1995) 'Giving a text voice can improve students' understanding', *Reading Research Quarterly* 30: 220–38.

Blum, A. (1982) 'The Rose Detective – a strategy to train pupils to read biotechnical texts', *Journal of Biological Education,* 16: 201–4.

Bouman, L. (1987) 'A quest for clues', *Modern English Teacher* 15: 14–18.

Carrick, T. (1978) 'Problems of assessing the readability of biology textbooks for first examinations', *Biological Education* 12: 113–22.

Chambliss, M. J. and Calfee, R. G. (1989) 'Designing science textbooks to enhance student understanding', *Educational Psychologist* 24: 307–22.

Donaldson, M. (1989) *Sense and Sensibility: Some Thoughts on the Teaching of Literacy,* The University of Reading.

Duffy, T. M., Higgins, L., Mehlenbacher, B., Cochran, C., Wallace, D., Hill, C., Haugen, D., McAffrey, M., Vurentt, R., Sloane, S. and Smith, S. (1989) 'Models for the design of instructional text', *Reading Research Quarterly* 24: 434–56.

Fatt, J. P. T. (1991) 'Text-related variables in textbook readability', *Research Papers in Education* 6: 225–45.

Fleming, M. L. and Levie, W. H. (1978) *Instructional Message Design: Principles from the Behavioural Science,* Englewood Cliffs: Educational Technology Publications.

Gropper, G. I. (1988) 'How text displays add value to text content', *Educational Technology* 28: 15–21.

Guri-Rozenblit, S. (1989) 'Effect of a tree diagram on students' comprehension of main ideas in a expository text with multiple themes', *Reading Research Quarterly* 24: 236–47.

Hare, V. C., Rabinowitz, M. and Schieble, K. M. (1989) 'Text effects on main idea comprehension', *Reading Research Quarterly* 24: 72–88.

Holiday, W. G. (1975) 'What's in a picture?', *The Science Teacher* 42: 21–2.

Holiday, W. G. (1976) 'Teaching verbal chains using flow diagrams and text', *AV Communication Review* 24: 63–78.

Long, R. R. (1991) 'Readability for science', *School Science Review* 73: 21–33.

Myers, S. S. (1991) 'Performance in reading comprehension – product or process?', *Education Review* 41: 257–70.

Newton, D. P. (1984) 'Showing movement in children's pictures', *Educational Studies* 10: 255–61.

Newton, D. P. (1990) *Teaching with Text,* London: Kogan Page.

Newton, D. P. (2000) *Teaching for Understanding,* London: Routledge/Falmer.

Newton, D. P. and Merrell, C. H. (1994) 'Words that count: communicating with mathematical text', *International Journal of Mathematical Education in Science and Technology* 25: 457–62.

Noonan, J. (1991) 'Readability problems presented by mathematics text', *Early Child Development and Care* 54: 57–81.

Shuard, H. and Rothery, A. (1984) *Children Reading Mathematics,* London: John Murray.

Stahl, S. A., Jacobson, M. G., Davis, C. E. and Davis, R. L. (1989) 'Prior knowledge and difficult vocabulary in the comprehension of unfamiliar text', *Reading Research Quarterly* 24: 27–43.

Sweller, J. (1989) 'Cognitive technology, some procedures for facilitating learning and problem solving in mathematics and science', *Journal of Educational Psychology* 81: 457–66.

Unsworth, L. (1991) 'Linguistic form and the construction of knowledge in factual texts for primary school children', *Education Review* 43: 201–12.

Wolpert, L. (1993) *The Unnatural Nature of Science,* London: Faber and Faber.

Winn, B. (1987) 'Charts, graphs, and diagrams in educational materials' in D. M. Willows and H. Houghton (eds) *The Psychology of Illustration*, Vol. 1, New York: Springer-Verlag.

20 ICT and communication
Richard Boohan

Introduction

Since computers were first introduced into schools, there has been much debate about what exactly to do with them. Initially, they were seen as 'things to be studied', and there was a rapid growth in 'computer studies' courses, in which pupils learned about computer programming, how information was stored and processed, and so on. An important shift in perception was to see computers as 'things to support learning', to be used in subjects across the curriculum. But, at first, there was a tendency to use computers for 'drill-and-practice' – electronic versions of the old mechanical teaching machines. Used in this way, the computer is in control of the learner. A second shift in emphasis has been to see the computer as a 'tool for the learner'. Now, it is the learner who has the control over the computer. What are the characteristics of computers that make them potentially such powerful learning tools?

- Computers are fast. They can, for example, carry out calculations that would take a long time to do by hand. This does not just mean that they can save time by doing the same things that we would normally do except quicker; they also open up new possibilities and allow us to do things that we could not have done before. And every year, computers get faster.
- Computers are interactive. Long gone are the days when data was fed into a computer on punched cards to be processed, followed by a delay while the results were printed out. Computers don't just do one-off calculations. We can interact with them in ways that allow us to explore and try out new ideas and see the results almost instantaneously.
- Computers can store a lot of data. As computers have developed, there has been an exponential growth both in processing speeds and in the amount of data they can store. This cannot go on forever, but (at the time of writing) they still have a long way to go before they reach the physical limits. The storage capacity of computers gives us fast access to huge amounts of information.
- Computers can be connected to other computers. For many years, computers have been fast, interactive and able to store large amounts of data. For much of this time, however, they remained a technology that was peripheral to most people's lives. What has transformed the potential of the technology is that computers have brought about a revolution in communication.

In summary then, computer technology is powerful. Whether ICT is a powerful *learning* tool, however, depends on how it is *used*. ICT should *not* be used, for example, as a 'reward' or because it may be 'motivating'. Motivation is a complex issue, and ICT is not a magic button that can be pressed to make pupils more interested. In any case, many pupils may have far more entertaining things they can do on their computers at home. ICT should *not* be used in science lessons *simply* as a way of teaching ICT skills. It may indeed help to develop skills, and science teachers need to be aware of how their subject contributes to and builds on pupils' ICT capability in the context of the whole school. Additionally, to enable pupils to use specialist hardware and software, some skills will certainly need to be taught explicitly in science lessons. But the central justification for using ICT in science lessons has to be that it can *make a positive contribution to pupils' learning in science*.

This chapter reviews how ICT can be used in science teaching, and in particular, how it can support the communication of scientific ideas.

Using ICT to support learning in science

It has sometimes been said that computers in schools are solutions looking for a problem. In thinking about how ICT can be used to support learning in science, a better place to start is not to look at the characteristics of ICT, but at the characteristics of learning science. A useful way of thinking about science is as three closely inter-related aspects. First, science is a practical subject, and involves engaging with the real world and testing out ideas. Second, it is a theoretical activity, in which explanations involving 'imagined entities' are proposed to account for what happens in the real world. Finally, scientific knowledge is socially constructed and ideas need to be communicated and shared. Individuals do not learn in isolation; they learn by understanding the ideas of others.

Science as a practical subject

Data-logging offers enormous potential to support practical work. For example, a temperature probe can be used to measure the way in which the temperature of hot water changes as it cools, with the graph plotted 'in real time'. It means that we can shift our focus from the mechanics of taking readings and plotting them, towards the interpretation of the shape of a graph and the development of scientific understanding. Of course, this is not to say that we should not develop pupils' skills of measurement and graph construction at all, but often the limitations of pupils' skills mean that it may be difficult ever to get beyond this.

Science as a theoretical subject

Theory work often has unfortunate associations with rather boring activities. This is a pity, since it is the creation and exploration of theories which is what makes science exciting. There are many interesting kinds of activities which can engage pupils in theoretical thinking. How can ICT help pupils to create and explore theories? This sounds a bit ambitious until we remember that exploring theories is what they are doing when they use a simulation on a computer. There is also a lot of interest in getting pupils to create their own computer models, or in other words, to try out their own theories. However, while there is much written about the uses of computer modelling, it is yet to become common in the classroom.

Scientific knowledge as socially constructed

When computers were first introduced into schools, they were known simply as 'computers'. Then the expression 'Information Technology' was introduced – computers after all did more than just computation. Then 'IT' became 'ICT'. 'Information and Communications Technology' is intended to emphasize that computers are powerful tools for communicating information. ICT can be used to support pupils' reading and writing in science and the communication of scientific ideas. It is on this third application that the later part of this chapter focuses.

When to use and when not to use ICT?

ICT should not be used simply for its own sake. It should only be used if it helps to achieve appropriate learning outcomes. But how do we decide what these are? A useful way of thinking about this is to make the distinction between *authentic* and *inauthentic* labour (Scaife and Wellington 1993). Taking dozens of temperature measurements, recording these in a table and plotting the graphs by hand might be seen as *inauthentic* labour, if pupils are not really learning much by doing this. By leaving these tasks to a computer, the learner can engage in the *authentic* labour of analysing and interpreting results. Computers can shift the emphasis from lower order to higher order skills.

This does not mean that computers should always take over these kinds of tasks. Watching the mercury rise in a thermometer, as a pupil measures the temperature of boiling water for the first time (and being surprised that the temperature does not continue to rise as the water is heated) is something that should be experienced directly. Plotting graphs with a pencil to 'get a feel' for how a graph is constructed is an important learning experience. What we do need to do is to consider carefully what we want pupils to learn from each activity, and how computers can help with the inauthentic labour, and leave the authentic labour to the learner. There is no point for pupils to carry on doing routine tasks that have long ceased to have any learning purpose.

What is available?

There are many different software and hardware tools that can be used to support learning in science. Here we will look briefly at those most commonly used, and the kinds of activities that they can support. Useful overviews and examples of the kinds of activities in which ICT can be used as support can be found in Frost (1994), Chapman and Lewis (1998) and Chapman *et al.* (1999).

Word-processors

A word-processor is much more than just an electronic version of an old-fashioned typewriter. Perhaps a word-processor would be more appropriately named a 'thought processor'. (That is the way that I am using my word-processor now to write this paragraph.) As well as its obvious use for creating new texts, it can be used for interacting with and making sense of other people's texts. We shall look at some examples later in the sections 'Working with existing text' and 'Creating texts'. Tebbutt (1997) gives a very useful overview of the possibilities for using word-processors in science lessons.

Spreadsheets

Spreadsheets are very versatile tools with a wide variety of uses. They are simple for pupils to use, and they can either create their own spreadsheets or can enter information into a previously prepared template. The most basic use of a spreadsheet is to record textual or numerical data in a tabular form. Moving on, they can be used for analysis, doing calculations on data and plotting graphs. Pupils may analyse data that they have collected themselves (primary data) as part of investigations or practical work, and data that has been collected by other people (secondary data). Secondary data includes data that can be found in textbooks and reference books, from ICT sources, such as CD-ROMs or the Web. Spreadsheets are also a very useful tool for *computer modelling*. Carson (1997) gives an excellent overview of the different kinds of uses of spreadsheets, and Tebbutt and Flavell (1995) provide a wide variety of examples of different spreadsheet activities.

Databases

Database programs, like word-processors and spreadsheets, are commonly available 'office' applications, though perhaps less useful in science that the first two. Databases can do some of the same things that spreadsheets can do, but where they can be particularly useful is in sorting and making selections from large sets of data. It may be argued that pupils' understanding of their investigations can be enhanced by constructing their own databases using data they have collected. However, databases are more difficult to use than spreadsheets, and so the danger is that much time will be spent in learning how to set up a database and too little on understanding the data. And the databases that pupils create themselves are usually too small to justify the effort in terms of what they can do with the finished product. Using databases that have already been constructed and which contain large amounts of data offer more opportunities for developing pupils' learning in *science*.

Presentation software

There is a range of tools that can be used by pupils to create their own multimedia presentations. Examples include Microsoft PowerPoint and Corel Presentations, which may be included in 'office' software packages, and Hyperstudio, which has been designed specifically for the educational market. The use of presentation software is considered later in the section 'Presenting information'.

Subject-specific software

Data-logging and simulation software have an important and particular role to play in learning science, as we saw earlier. As well as the hardware for data-logging, there is a range of software programs for collecting and analysing the data. The best of these have sophisticated data analysis facilities, which allow pupils to interact directly with the graphical output, for example, by reading off particular values or finding the slope of a line. Ideas about how to use data-loggers in the classroom can be found in Frost (1998a). A review of available simulations and other science-specific software can be found in Frost (1998b).

CD-ROMs for reference

There now exist a number of general encyclopeadias on CD-ROM, and these provide very useful sources of information about science. In addition, there are a large number of CD-ROMs containing reference materials specifically for science, though the quality of these is very variable. Some are genuine multimedia environments, while others are really not much more than paper-based information transferred to a screen. The use of reference CD-ROMs is considered later in the section 'Finding information'.

The Internet and the World Wide Web

The terms 'Internet' and 'World Wide Web' are often (incorrectly) used interchangeably. It is important to clarify these terms. The Internet is the collection of computers, phone lines, cables, satellites, and so on, by means of which electronic information can be exchanged. The World Wide Web is a collection of websites with information in the form of 'hypertext' pages, and the transmission of this information forms just part of the traffic on the Internet. Probably the most obvious and widespread use of the Internet in education is to access websites to research for information. However, this 'one-way communication' is not the only way to use the Internet, and increasingly it is being used for more participative forms of communication. Jackson and Bazley (1997) give an overview of the potential of the Internet in science education, illustrated with a wide range of websites. The use of the Internet is discussed later in the sections 'Finding information' and 'Virtual communities'.

How can ICT be used for communication?

In the following sections, we will look at how ICT can be used to enhance the traditional classroom activities of reading, writing, researching and presentation. These will be considered under the following headings:

- Working with existing text
- Creating texts
- Finding information
- Presenting information
- Virtual communities.

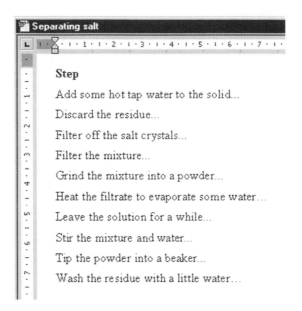

Figure 20.1 Using a word-processor for a sequencing activity

Source: Frost 1994: 58

In using the information on CD-ROMs and on the Internet, it is important to remember that electronic information is subject to copyright. There is a common misconception that information on the Internet is copyright-free. Just as with using material from textbooks, teachers need to be aware of these copyright restrictions and should pay attention to the school's policies and codes of conduct.

Another issue of which teachers need to be aware is plagiarism. Although there has always been the potential for pupils to copy work, the ease with which electronic information can be copied and modified can increase the opportunities for this. Pupils need to be taught how to acknowledge and reference the sources of their work.

Working with existing text

Reading is not a common activity in science lessons, and much of the reading that is done is *passive*, and without a specific purpose. DARTs activities (Directed Activities Related to Text) are designed to help pupils to become *active* readers (Davies and Greene, 1984). These techniques should be an important part of every science teacher's repertoire of teaching strategies. Traditionally, these have been paper-based activities, but ICT offers advantages, both to the teacher in preparing the activities and to the pupils in undertaking them. DARTs activities fall into two broad categories – *reconstruction* activities and *analysis* activities.

Reconstruction activities make use of text which has been modified specifically for the activity. An example of a reconstruction activity is shown in Figure 20.1, which is taken from Frost (1994: 58). This shows a set of instructions for a practical activity in which salt is separated from rock salt, but the steps are in the wrong order. Pupils

> **Reason**
> ... because it is just sand.
> ... because you will need to keep it in something suitable.
> ... so that the salt dissolves quickly.
> ... so that the salt dissolves quickly.
> ... so that the salt dissolves quickly.
> ... so that the solution becomes saturated.
> ... to let it cool and form crystals.
> ... to separate the crystals from the solution.
> ... to separate the sand from the salt solution.
> ... to wash through the last trace of salt.

Figure 20.2 *'Reasons' to add to the sequenced 'steps'*

Source: Frost 1994: 58

need to sort the statements on the word-processor (either by 'cutting and pasting' or 'clicking and dragging') into the correct order. Whether done using ICT or not, this physical re-ordering is important as it allows pupils to work in groups and to discuss the choices they make.

Sequencing activities can be helpful prior to practical work, as it helps pupils to engage actively in reading the instructions and to have a clearer idea of what they will be trying to do. Other kinds of texts are suitable for 'scrambling' in this way, for example, descriptions of the stages of a process or life cycle. The particular activity described here, in fact, has a second part to it which involves *matching* the statements. To each of the statements shown in Figure 20.1, pupils need to add one of the reasons shown in Figure 20.2.

Analysis activities use straight text without modification. They might involve, for example, identifying particular kinds of references in the text or choosing sentences which best express the key ideas of the text as a whole. In paper-based versions of analysis activities the original text would be marked by underlining or highlighting, with pupils working in small groups discussing their choices. Using a word-processor allows much more flexibility in marking the text. Pupils are able to try out ideas, discuss them with the group and change them much more easily than if they were using paper.

Creating texts

In the previous section, we saw how a word-processor can support pupils' reading; not surprisingly, a word-processor can also help pupils' writing. One possibility would be for pupils to type up their handwritten notes, though this is not a particularly productive use. It does give them the satisfaction of seeing their work presented well, and can improve their ICT skills, but it does not really add anything to the creative process of writing. A word-processor is much more than a tool for producing neat text. Writing directly onto a word-processor allows pupils to get

Question	Who	What	Where	Why	When	How
was ..... ?						
did .... ?						
could ... ?						
will ...... ?						
is .... ?						

Figure 20.3 A grid to support pupils' writing

Source: Tebbutt 1997: 96

started without the 'block' of having to get it right first time. Being able to draft and re-draft sentences allows them to try out different ideas before making a final decision. And being able to externalize ideas like this means that it becomes much more possible for writing to be a collaborative effort amongst pupils working in a group.

Being able to write something starting with a blank sheet of paper – or a blank screen – is an important ability to develop, but not all writing needs to be like this. Pupils can be provided with a template or a 'writing frame' within which they can write their text. This can be particularly valuable for lower-achieving pupils who would otherwise find it difficult to structure their ideas in a way that they are able to express in writing. For example, a writing frame for an investigation may include the prompts 'what I am trying to find out is …', 'what I predict will happen is …', and so on. There are many possibilities for different kinds of templates. The example shown in Figure 20.3 is taken from Tebbutt (1997), and is intended to help pupils to organize their work on the life of a great scientist such as Marie Curie. They can fill the cells with information, as appropriate, in responses to the questions generated by following the column label with the row label.

Concerns are sometimes raised that using ICT will diminish pupils' ability to write in traditional ways using pen and paper, though evidence does not support this. Indeed, quite the contrary. Feedback on pupils' work from teachers may be seen in a more positive light, since pupils have the opportunities to revise their work, which would be a very demotivating activity to undertake with handwritten work. Pupils' attitudes towards writing may be improved through the use of ICT since they can see the enhanced quality of the presentation.

Finding information

Two important sources of information for pupils to use in their research are CD-ROMs and the world wide web, and each has their advantages. CD-ROMs can contain huge stores of information, but in comparison to the web, what they offer is more limited. However, many CD-ROMs are of very high quality and are aimed at particular educational markets, and so it is easier to judge the suitability of the language and the level for the intended pupils. The web has the advantage of offering almost unlimited amounts of up-to-date information on any topic, but the quality of

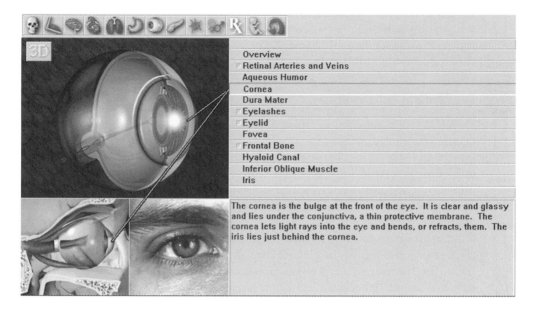

Figure 20.4 A screen from the BodyWorks CD-ROM

Source: BodyWork 5.0, Softkey Multmedia Inc.

sites is very variable and many of them are pitched at too high a level for use with younger pupils.

An example of a screen from a CD-ROM is shown in Figure 20.4. An important feature of multimedia on CD-ROM is the potential it offers for interactivity. For example text and diagrams may be hyperlinked so that information may be explored in a variety of ways, and specific pieces of information may be located using search facilities. This can make researching for information a much quicker and richer process than doing the equivalent using a textbook. In addition, multimedia offers possibilities that paper cannot – playing video and sound clips, for example, or interacting with a picture or diagram by enlarging or rotating it.

The World Wide Web is a big place, and pupils can easily get lost in it. It is possible to locate useful websites using search engines, but to find good sites on particular scientific topics is often not easy for teachers, let alone pupils. So, certainly for younger pupils, it is best to start from sites that have been identified for the lesson and to base activities on these. Finding good websites can take some time, so published sources of ideas for activities can be very useful. Examples of activities and accompanying websites can be found in Davis *et al.* (2000) and Sang (2000). A particular advantage of using the Web is that pupils can look at the sites of different interest groups and can consider the information they find in terms of its reliability and bias.

When pupils first come across a particular CD-ROM or a website, they will want to explore it, so it is probably a good chance to give them some opportunity to do this. They will do anyway! But it is important that they are given a focused activity to undertake, otherwise they will become distracted and their work will lack purpose. Younger pupils may need more directed activities, but older pupils can undertake more open-ended tasks. In using these multimedia environments, a key point to remember is that *interactivity* is something that happens when learners are intellectually engaged with the material, and is more than just clicking a mouse button!

Presenting information

Presenting information in the form of posters or leaflets aimed at a particular audience is a traditional and popular activity in the science classroom. ICT provides new possibilities for this. Word-processors (or for the more ambitious, desktop publishing programs) allow groups to work together to produce work which can be printed out and displayed. ICT also allows presentations to be made directly to a class, using a large monitor or an electronic whiteboard. Further involvement in the work can be provided through peer-assessment of each other's presentations. In whatever way the work is presented or assessed, it is important that the pupils understand that the important thing about the work is the content. By sharing the assessment criteria with them, this point can be emphasized. In using presentation software, pupils can quickly learn how to make quite sophisticated presentations, and can incorporate diagrams and pictures. They will also enjoy experimenting with different kinds of text displays, animations and sound effects, but it should be made clear to them that overuse of these will add nothing to the quality of the content (or of the presentation either).

Spreadsheets are very useful tools for exploring how to present data. Pupils can enter data quickly and explore different ways of drawing the graph before deciding on a final choice and then printing this out. This would simply not be possible by hand. Again, it is how well the message is communicated and not the use of fancy effects which is important. Figure 20.5 shows two graphs of the same data. The bar chart communicates a clear message; the three-dimensional chart is extremely difficult to read.

Thinking about how to present data, and being able to explore different ways of doing so, actually helps pupils to analyse and consider 'what is in the data'. This message applies to all presentation work – thinking about how to communicate an idea is a powerful way of understanding it.

Virtual communities

The linking of computers to the Internet opens up possibilities for the creation of 'virtual communities' of pupils and teachers, though this kind of work is at present in its early stages. Wardle (1999) describes the work of the Schools Online Science Project which aimed to involve pupils in interactive and participative learning using the Internet. An important finding of this project was the need to involve teachers too, and to encourage communication between them.

There are many possibilities for using the Internet as a way of interacting and communicating with others, for example:

- finding answers to questions from an 'ask an expert' website;
- exchanging experimental data by e-mail with pupils from another school, possibly in another country;

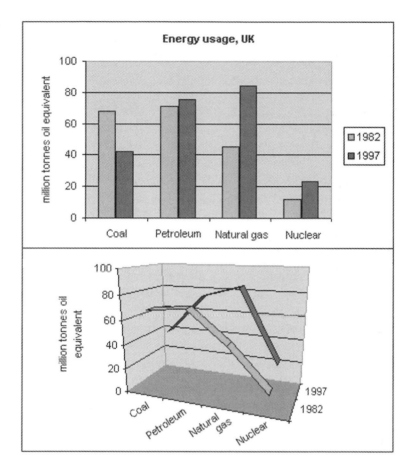

Figure 20.5 Communicating messages about data

Source: Data from Government Statistical Office website

- exchanging information and ideas through participation in electronic conferences;
- presenting individual pupils' work through their personal pages on the school's intranet (like the Internet, but accessible only within the school);
- communicating with other schools by creating a class's own website on the Internet.

One of the simplest ways of engaging with a 'virtual community' is to visit one of the many 'ask an expert' sites. Figure 20.6 shows an example of a page from the 'Dr Universe' site hosted by Washington State University. In response to a question posed by a pupil asking why the earth turns, the answers given by practising scientists give a clear insight into what is known about this, but just as importantly, go on to indicate where there are still questions to be solved. Such sites give pupils an insight that scientific knowledge is not a static thing to be found in textbooks, but is constantly developing.

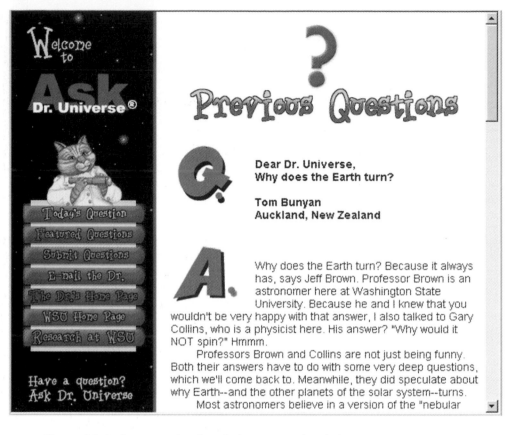

Figure 20.6 An example of an 'ask an expert' website

Source: 'Dr Universe' website, Washington State University

A website which allows pupils to communicate their work with others is Sci-Journal. Pupils can submit reports of their investigative work, and periodically a number of reports is published in an electronic journal, with the opportunity to contribute to a discussion about them. Another example of a way in which pupils can publish their work is the STEM project, run by the Science Museum. In this case, pupils publish their work directly on the school's website, and the STEM website provides links so that it can be made accessible to others.

A tool for the teacher

As well as enhancing pupils' learning, ICT can be a powerful tool for teachers to support their professional work. Using a word-processor to produce classroom resources is an obvious example. This not only helps in the development of the ideas and results in a high quality of presentation, but it allows materials to be updated and modified easily in the light of experience. In addition, it allows materials to be shared easily with colleagues, and departmental resources to be developed. Other applications, such as spreadsheets, may also be useful in developing resources for the classroom, and for some lessons the effort of producing an on-screen presentation may be worthwhile. Outside the classroom, spreadsheets offer very powerful and time-saving ways of managing pupil records.

The Web is playing an increasing role in supporting teachers' work. It can be used as a source of materials or information for use in the classroom, or to support teachers' professional development. The government plans that every school should be connected to the Internet by 2002; at the heart of this is the National Grid for Learning (NGfL) website. The Virtual Teacher Centre (VTC), which is part of the NGfL, contains collections of curriculum resources, guides for teachers, professional development materials, discussion areas, and so on. Some teachers are beginning to use the Internet directly in their teaching, by creating pages on the school's website to support pupils in classroom activities, projects and homework. Extending this further, pupils may even send their work by e-mail to teachers to be electronically marked and returned the same way.

Planning for ICT

In planning the use of ICT in science lessons, the most important question is 'how will ICT help pupils to learn science?' It may seem an obvious question, but its importance cannot be over-emphasized, and it relates to the issue discussed earlier about authentic and inauthentic labour. It is certainly *not* a good reason to say 'this topic is a bit dull, so I'll liven it up by getting the pupils to do some work on the Web'. Pupils who are busy are not necessarily learning, and pupils who are having fun are not necessarily motivated. Using ICT only has a purpose if it can help pupils to achieve learning objectives effectively.

How can you choose good software? In reviewing this question, Frost (1997) suggests a number of criteria which need to be met. To be useful in supporting learning, software needs to fit the hardware, the time available, the curriculum, the learners and the teachers. You can read about software and websites in the regular reviews which appear in the *School Science Review* and *The Times Education Supplement*, and the British Educational Communications and Technology Agency (BECTa) manages a web-based database of software reviews for NGfL.

There are practical issues to be addressed in thinking about how best to use the available hardware. There may only be a single computer in a classroom, so its use needs to be structured alongside the use of other resources in order that pupils can get access to it. If a computer suite is booked, this solves the problem of access but it creates others. It makes it more difficult, for example, to use computers as an integral part of work in the laboratory. Some activities on a computer may be done most appropriately in small groups, though group sizes may sometimes have to be determined by availability of hardware rather than on educational grounds.

ICT can change the role of the teacher in the classroom. Of course, if the technology goes wrong, then this role will be one of troubleshooting with little time left for teaching. But when things run smoothly, teachers have often noted that they feel 'less in the centre of things' and that pupils are able to work more independently. This does not mean though that teachers have nothing to do! It is important to plan the kinds of interventions to be made and the questions to be asked that can support and challenge pupils and keep them engaged in learning.

Good lessons have clear learning objectives which can be shared with the pupils and assessed by the teacher. This applies just as much to lessons that involve ICT as to any other. If the assessment criteria are clear and focused on the learning of science, then ICT can help to improve pupils' performance, rather than masking or disguising it.

ICT has the potential to change radically what pupils do in classrooms. But we should also remember that, fundamentally, it is just another tool that we can use alongside many others to enhance learning in science.

References

Carson, S. (1997) 'The use of spreadsheets in science – an overview', *School Science Review* 79(287): 69–80.

Chapman, C. and Lewis, J. (1998) *ICT Activities for Science 11–14,* Oxford: Heinemann Educational.

Chapman, C., Lewis, J., Musker, R. and Nicholson, D. (1999) *ICT Activities for Science 14–16,* Oxford: Heinemann Educational.

Davies, F. and Greene, T. (1984) *Reading for Learning in the Sciences,* Edinburgh: Oliver and Boyd.

Davis, H., Frost, R. and Hemsley, K. (2000) *Science On-line,* Coventry: BECTa.

Frost, R. (1994) *The IT in Secondary Science Book,* London: IT in Science.

Frost, R. (1997) 'Computer software for science teaching – choosing and using', *School Science Review* 79(287): 19–24.

Frost, R. (1998a) *Datalogging in Practice,* London: IT in Science.

Frost, R. (1998b) *Software for Teaching Science,* London: IT in Science.

Jackson, R. and Bazley, M. (1997) 'Science education and the Internet – cutting through the hype', *School Science Review* 79(287): 41–44.

Sang, D. (ed.) (2000) *Science@web/getting.started,* Hatfield: Association for Science Education.

Scaife, J. and Wellington, J. (1993) *Information Technology in Science and Technology Education,* Buckingham: Open University Press.

Tebbutt, M. (1997) 'Word-processors for science teaching – why?', *School Science Review* 79(287): 91–99.

Tebbutt, M. and Flavell, H. (1995) *Spreadsheets in Science,* London: John Murray.

Wardle, J. (1999) 'The Schools Online Science Experience', *School Science Review* 80(293): 65–70.

5 Science in a broader context

Introduction

Over the last two decades or so, there has been much concern that the science curriculum is too narrow. It presents an image of science that is too depersonalized and neutral, and it fails to emphasize that science is a human activity. Its focus has been on developing the kind of abstract conceptual understanding more appropriate for those pupils who later specialize in science, and fails to meet the needs of the majority of pupils who do not. Providing a foundation for future specialists is an essential aim for science education, but it should not be the only, or indeed the most important, one. We live in a society in which science plays a central role, and an education in science needs to do more than develop a narrow understanding of scientific concepts. Pupils should understand what science is, how it is carried out and how scientific knowledge is created. They should know about the contributions that science makes to society, both in practical ways and as a cultural achievement in itself. Science raises ethical and moral issues, and pupils need to consider these in order to prepare themselves for decision-making as citizens and as individuals. Science has too often been portrayed as a white, male, individualistic activity. Setting science in a broader context makes it more accessible as well as more appropriate for the needs of the majority. And understanding the broader context of science is just as important for future scientists, too.

There are a number of references to these broader aspects of science in the National Curriculum. For example, in the National Curriculum for England, pupils are expected to know something about the nature of science by being taught 'about the ways in which scientists work today and how they worked in the past, including the roles of experimentation, evidence and creative thought in the development of scientific ideas'. Pupils also need to 'consider the power and limitations of science in addressing industrial, social and environmental questions . . . and the ethical issues involved'. Broader cultural issues are addressed through the requirement to teach pupils about the 'ways in which scientific work may be affected by the contexts in which it takes place [for example, social, historical, moral and spiritual], and how these contexts may affect whether or not ideas are accepted'.

Despite the inclusion of these aspects of science into the National Curriculum, the fact remains that it is dominated by conceptual content and it is this that is emphasized in assessment. Although attention needs to be paid to these broader aspects, there is insufficient time in the present curriculum to do this properly. There needs to be a shift in the balance. In arguing that the content of the curriculum needs to be reduced, we are not trying to devalue the importance of conceptual understanding. Indeed, reducing the content may strengthen it. There is a huge body of international research evidence showing that much of the teaching of scientific concepts fails to develop a sound fundamental understanding. By doing less, we may do it better. If pupils leave school without an understanding of the key concepts of science, they can hardly be said to have had any kind of science education. But a science education that does not, in addition, teach pupils about how science has developed, its place in society and how it affects their lives is not much of a science education either.

- The first chapter of this section is concerned with the learning and teaching of the nature of science. Jonathan Osborne discusses some examples of classroom activities, based on historical and contemporary case studies of scientific research, which explore ideas about the way that science is done, and the role of evidence and argument. He argues that science education should aim to develop a critically informed public who are able to understand the discourse of science.

- Learning about socio-scientific issues involves a complex interplay between an understanding of the relevant science and an understanding of different value positions. Mary Ratcliffe reports on the outcomes of her research into the use of a framework for group discussion about science in social contexts. She also discusses some work into pupils' understanding of scientific research as presented in media reports.

- Some topics in the science curriculum lend themselves very clearly to multicultural and anti-racist approaches; others seem less obviously relevant. John Siraj-Blatchford discusses how he developed a sequence of lessons about particle theory as a response to a sceptical questioner who asked 'What is an anti-racist atom?'. He argues that an anti-racist perspective is relevant to all aspects of science teaching.

- Michael Reiss has written extensively about science in a pluralist society. Here, he gives some illustrations of the ways that science has developed in other cultures and the contributions that women have made to science. These stories represent only a tiny fraction of the many possibilities for using this kind of work to enrich science lessons and to move away from a narrow, male, Western view of science.

21 Learning and teaching about the nature of science

Jonathan Osborne

Why teach about the nature of science?

Today, all sciences are taught to all pupils from age 5 to 16. Yet, as we become increasingly dependent on the service sector of our economy, our society needs fewer and fewer individuals with a scientific knowledge or technical skills (DfEE 1996). Even in our daily lives, scientific knowledge becomes less and less useful with the ever increasing technological sophistication of our homes. We can no longer fix our domestic appliances without expert help. In such a context, what is the use and value of learning science?

Paradoxically, scientific issues are now increasingly permeating our daily lives. Whether it is the disposal of nuclear waste, the beef we eat, the warming of the climate, the effects of pollution or the cloning of humans, the relentless advance of science and technology has implications for the choices that confront us both personally and as a society. In this context, individuals do not require an extensive knowledge of science, nor even the ability to make practical use of it. Rather, what they need is an understanding of the nature of science – an ability to assess the level of certainty of scientists' claims; to appraise risks; to understand how scientists produce reliable knowledge; to distinguish correlations from causes; and an ability to translate and interpret common scientific reports presented by the media. In short, what science education should seek to develop is a public who will be able to 'read' and understand the discourse of science in a 'critical' way. Consequently, teaching about the nature of science is not an additional extra or an element to add variety, but a fundamental requirement of a science education for the next century.

Yet as science teachers we are often ill-prepared to address such issues. Ask yourself how we know any of the facts in Figure 21.1 and what evidence do we have to justify their assertion to children?

Moreover, how would you argue with someone who said that the correlation between smoking and cancer does not show any relationship as all the people who get cancer are genetically disposed to the disease developing? Hence, smoking is an irrelevancy.

Correlational studies, such as that which established the link between smoking and cancer, are a substantial part of the scientific enterprise. However, correlations are not causes and one of the most common fallacies in logical reasoning is inferring the existence of a causal connection from a known correlation. Hence the relationship between smoking and lung cancer has never been 'proved' – we have simply

> Day and night is caused by a spinning Earth
> All stable matter is made of combinations of 92 atoms.
> We live at the bottom of a 'sea' of air.
> Plants produce 'food' by using energy from sunlight.
> The Earth is over 4,500 million years old.

Figure 21.1 *Common ideas taught in school science*

eliminated all the alternative hypotheses that have ever been suggested. Science progresses by constructing new ways of seeing the world and eliminating those ideas which are false rather than 'proving' or deriving them from observations. The failure to establish any alternative hypothesis leads us to believe that there is a causal connection between smoking and lung cancer.

The National Curriculum specifically requires that the nature of science is addressed in science teaching. At KS3 pupils should be taught about the importance of evidence in supporting scientific knowledge. Moreover, examples should be related to the social and historical context by providing the opportunity to study how at least one idea has changed over time. At KS4, teachers are asked to take this further by exploring how scientific ideas are accepted or rejected on the basis of evidence; how scientific controversies can arise; and how scientific ideas are affected by the social and historical context in which they occur.

How, then, can such aspects be taught? The starting point has to be recognizing that scientific knowledge is an enormous intellectual achievement – the fruits of the work of some very creative, imaginative and determined individuals. After all, it is only 400 years since Giordano Bruno was burned alive in Rome for proclaiming that stars are suns – and that around them are other planets on which live other people. Galileo was only spared a similar fate because he recanted his assertions and, only in 1992, did the Pope finally pardon Galileo and admit that the church was wrong! When Charles Lyell and colleagues first began to argue in the 1830s that the fossils they were unearthing were evidence for an Earth much older than the version to be found in Genesis, it was very difficult for people to change a lifelong belief. In fact, Edmund Gosse, a reputable scientist of the time, went so far as to argue that the fossils had been placed there by God to deceive mankind! Similarly, Wegener's hypothesis, proposed in 1915, that the continents of Africa and South America were once joined seemed absurd, for what force could have separated two such massive and solid bodies?

What, then, is it about science that has made it so enormously successful at transforming our conception of the world we inhabit, despite such opposition? Valuable as the previous anecdotes are, teaching about the nature of science requires a more systematic approach and a good understanding of the nature of the subject we teach. Unfortunately, our own education has commonly ignored the nature of the subject and considered the philosophy of the subject simply extraneous. As a consequence, science teachers often hold naive views of the subject which would now be considered outmoded by most philosophers (Koulaidis and Ogborn 1995). An essential remedy is some further reading and Couvalis (1997) offers a useful contemporary interpretation of the nature of science.

When children are asked. 'What do scientists do?', they commonly answer that scientists 'do experiments and find out things'. Science education should aim to show the range and variety of methods of doing science and that there is no singular method. In simple terms, scientists collect evidence from observations that lead to conjecture about the real world and its nature. Such conjectures – the theories and ideas of scientists – are subjected to experimental test and either survive or fail. Initial ideas are always tentative and disputed but as they survive experimental tests, the model becomes more generally accepted. It is these processes – the commitment to evidence, the testing of the models and theories, and the significance of refutation that need to be highlighted to pupils.

Highlighting the nature of science requires good examples. Although contemporary science provides many exemplars of the tentative nature of scientific ideas and the contested nature of evidence, e.g. whether global warming is happening or not, such science is not a strong feature of the curriculum. Rather, much of the knowledge taught in schools is historical and the stories of its discovery are a rich vein that can be mined to illustrate the nature of the subject. A selection of examples is offered in what follows.

Example 1   Doing science

Historical case studies provide an invaluable means of focusing on what it means to *do* science. In a note to the secretary of the French academy on 1 November 1772, Lavoisier reported the findings of the experiment which led him to believe that the phlogiston theory was incorrect. Lavoisier used the Sun's rays focused by a magnifying glass to heat mercury in a floating tray in a bath of liquid covered by a glass dome. The phlogiston theory predicted that the mercury should weigh less afterwards and that the water level should drop because of the phlogiston gained by the air when the mercury was heated. Pupils can be given the account as a jumbled DART (Figure 21.2).

He covers the floating tin with a glass dome.
He heats the mercury using a magnifying glass and the Sun's rays.
He repeats the experiment using phosphorus.
He weighs the ash left behind and finds it weighs more.
Lavoisier now thinks that there is something in the air which combines with the burning substance to weigh more.
Lavoisier places mercury on a tin and floats it in a bath of water.
Lavoisier suspects that the phlogiston theory is wrong.
The phlogiston theory predicts that heated substances will lose their phlogiston and weigh less afterwards.
The residue left by phosphorus after burning also weighs more.

Figure 21.2 *Scrambled story of Lavoisier's work*

After that the pupils can then be asked to label each statement with one of the standard process words or phrases: *observing; making a hypothesis; doing an experiment; predicting; reaching a conclusion.*

This method can be applied to any story of a scientific discovery. Crucially, what it shows is that scientists do not just derive their ideas from their observations. Rather they speculate and dream up theories which they then test.

Example 2   What counts as evidence?

Here, the focus is on the evidence and its relationship to theory. This is a very important critical skill to develop because at the heart of science is a commitment to the value of evidence. Pupils will be increasingly confronted with reports in the media such as that shown in Figure 21.4.

Pupils need opportunities to examine evidence for and against theories as school science tends to reinforce the view that science is either unambiguously right or wrong. Contemporary science, in contrast, confronts us daily with findings that are *uncertain,* either lacking sufficient data, e.g. global warming, or alternatively, having poorly developed theoretical mechanisms, e.g. AIDS and BSE.

Therefore, it is important to introduce exercises into the class that require pupils to evaluate theories against evidence. For instance, when Darwin put forward his theory of evolution it was based on evidence he gathered from his trip to the Galapagos. There he discovered an enormous number of unique species of animals and plants. However, there was other evidence that contradicted his arguments and supported the biblical account. Pupils can be asked to examine the evidence (Figure 21.3) and sort them into those which:

a   support Darwin's theory
b   oppose Darwin's theory
c   support the biblical account
d   oppose the biblical account
e   support neither theory.

---

1   Darwin finds an enormous number of new animal species on the Galapagos Islands.
2   The Galapagos Islands are very remote and cut off from other land masses.
3   Many fossils of extinct animal species were found on the Dorset coast and elsewhere in the early 1800s.
4   Kelvin estimates the age of the Earth from its rate of cooling to be 15,000 years.
5   Edmund Gosse suggests that the fossils were put there by God to deceive mankind.
6   Horses are selectively bred for racing or strength.
7   There are no fossils or animal remains that link mankind to its nearest similar looking species – the ape.
8   Evolution has never been observed actually happening.

Figure 21.3 *Some evidence in considering theories of evolution*

Scientists warn of danger from Antarctic ice melt

Sea levels are likely to rise faster and higher than previous predictions suggested, say scientists who have finished the first accurate satellite study of the Antarctic ice sheet.

A four-year research project to measure the Antarctic ice has found that it has contributed little to rising sea levels this century – but paradoxically this means that the loss of land to the sea in the next century is likely to be far greater than forecast so far.

The results of the study indicate that for the past 100 years when sea levels have risen by a global average of 18 cm (7 in), factors such as thermal expansion of the oceans and melting mountain glaciers have played a far greater role than the melting of the Antarctic ice sheets.

Professor Duncan Wingham, of University College London and leader of the international project team, said: 'As a consequence of our research we should be able to produce more accurate predictions of future sea level rises. Indeed, it is possible that the consequences of global warming on sea level rise has been underestimated.'

Professor Wingham said it is reasonable to speculate that the rise in sea level next century is likely to be nearer to the higher predictions of 80 cm (31 in) rather than the lower predictions of 50 cm (20 in). The researchers who publish their results in the journal Science, collected more than four million radar measurements of the Antarctic ice between 1992 and 1996, which showed that the ice sheet's thickness changed by an average of less than 1 cm.

'Many millions of people throughout the world live within one metre of sea level,' Professor Wingham said. 'They could all be under water in two centuries if models of the thermal expansion of the ocean due to global warming are correct.'

'These findings make the Antarctic ice sheet look an unlikely source for the sea level rise we have observed this century. If this is the case we now have a problem explaining the rise,' he said. 'Other sources of rise must be underestimated. In particular, it is possible that the effect of global warming on thermal expansion is larger than we thought.'

('Independent', 1998, 16 October: 14)

Questions for discussion

1 What are the two theories identified in the article to explain the rise in sea level?
2 What is the evidence for preferring one theory to another?
3 How confident are the researchers of their findings and why?
4 What additional reasons might there be for believing this report?

Figure 21.4 Media report

Another good example can be found in Solomon *et al.* (1992) where pupils are asked to examine the evidence that confronted Alfred Wegener who proposed that the continents were floating on the rocks beneath.

Too often the science we teach in schools is what has been termed a 'rhetoric of conclusions' and pupils are never exposed to the idea that new scientific knowledge is tentative and that scientists are often *equivocal* about their claims using words like 'may' and talking in terms of probabilities. Such examples help to illustrate this vital point.

Example 3   Conjecture and refutation

New scientific ideas are often disputed and there may be legitimate theoretical objections. For instance, the thesis that global warming is caused by human activities is contradicted by the argument that the effect is caused by the natural warming between ice ages. Moreover, the period for which we have been collecting data is just too short to use to make any sensible prediction. When the idea was first put forward that day and night were caused by a spinning Earth that moved around the Sun, many arguments were put forward against the idea – many of which are again theoretical objections rather than evidence-based arguments. A valuable approach for illustrating the role of argument in science is role play. Pupils can be asked to act out an imaginary dispute between Galileo and his opponents. Each character has a role card with questions at the end. A typical example is shown in Figure 21.5.

Such 'dramas' highlight the importance of attempts to refute ideas as a means of establishing them and can be used with any controversial idea in the past such as Darwin's theory of evolution or Torricelli's idea that we live at the bottom of a sea of air. Many attempts, are made to refute new ideas – when they have all failed we believe ideas to be 'true' – by that we mean we think it is very unlikely that they will be found to be fallible.

Example 4   The social construction of science

Scientists do not do their work in isolation. They are normal human beings and their thoughts and ideas are influenced by the culture they inhabit and events happening in the world around them. Therefore, when talking about scientists it is useful to give an impression of what was happening in the society at the time. What wars were being fought? What great books were being written? What major historical events had just happened? Reading about science offers an opportunity to explore the influence of the culture on science, and also, of science on our culture.

Two examples picked from everyday science texts illustrate the potential of such resources. First, a portrayal of reproduction in sticklebacks in a biology textbook for 16-year-old students.

> In the mating season, the male stickleback develops a red breast and builds an underwater nest out of pieces of weed which he glues together with a substance made by his kidneys. He then lures a ripe female to his nest by showing her his red breast. The female enters the nest and lays her eggs. She leaves the nest

A defender of Ptolemy

You are an intelligent man and enjoy a good debate. You are a priest and are rising up in your career very rapidly and are now quite senior at the Vatican. You have read about the young Galileo's ideas and think they are absurd.

You believe that the Earth is clearly the centre of God's Universe. Rather than the Earth moving, there is a perfectly good theory that Ptolemy, a Greek, devised to explain the movement of the heavens. This has worked well for 1,500 years. Moreover, you have a number of points to make that you think Galileo's ideas cannot explain:

- The Earth is large and immovable whereas the Sun is small and appears to move.
- A spinning Earth would throw objects off into space.
- Birds and clouds above a spinning Earth would drift steadily westwards.
- If the Earth moved through space at the speed necessary to travel around the Sun in a year, the resulting wind would blow people off the Earth.

Discussion questions:

- How do you explain the movement of stars near Jupiter, which Galileo has shown appear to go round Jupiter rather than the Earth?
- Some stars (the planets) wander backwards once a year. Ptolemy's explanation is very complicated. Galileo's would be a lot simpler as all the movements of the stars could be explained by only one object moving. Doesn't this make it a better theory?

Figure 21.5 Role play character card

through the other side. The male may persuade several other females to lay eggs in the same nest.

(Roberts 1986: 323)

Surely, innocuous enough? However, a closer, critical reading raises several questions. The picture here is of the male seducer, 'persuading' and 'luring' the female almost against her will to engage in the process of reproduction. The possibility that the female may contribute as much to this process, that she may entice the male remains totally unconsidered. Moreover, the anthropomorphic notion that the male 'persuades' the female demonstrates the social and cultural notions which are being used to construct the 'scientific' version of events. This version of stickleback courtship is developed from the classic account of Tinbergen (1951) which shows females as the passive recipients of males' attention. However, more recently his account has been challenged by the work of scientists who found exactly the opposite of what Tinbergen had reported – adding colour made the male stickleback less likely to be attacked by another territorial male. Moreover, the work of other scientists, who chose to study the behaviour of *female* sticklebacks found that females defended their territories and their encounters were more aggressive than those in the all-male groups of sticklebacks. Commenting on this research, Reiss (1984) points to the fact that it demonstrates that 'the way scientists see the world depends very much on the way previous scientists have seen it' and 'that even the most famous piece of research is not necessarily correct' – surely both understandings that science education should aspire to communicate?

Second, contrast Richard Dawkins' version of the function of genes and DNA in his book *The Selfish Gene* (1976) with the standard view that the function of the genes is to transmit the characteristics from one generation to the next (Mendel's First Law).

> It is raining DNA outside. On the bank of the Oxford canal at the bottom of my garden is a large willow tree, and it is pumping downy seeds into the air. There is no consistent air movement, and the seeds are drifting outwards in all directions from the tree. Up and down the canal, as far as my binoculars can reach, the water is white with floating cottony flecks, and we can be sure that they have carpeted the ground to much the same radius in other directions too. The cotton wool is mostly made of cellulose, and it dwarfs the tiny capsule that contains the DNA, the genetic information. The DNA content must be a small proportion of the total, so why did I say that it was raining DNA rather than cellulose? The answer is that it is the DNA that matters. The cellulose fluff, although more bulky, is just a parachute, to be discarded. The whole performance, cotton wool, catkins, tree and all, is in aid of one thing and one thing only, the spreading of DNA around the countryside.
>
> (Dawkins 1976)

The distinction may be subtle but it is important. From Dawkins' point of view, the organism is merely the means by which the gene replicates itself – put simply, the chicken is the egg's means of reproducing itself. Second, together with others, Dawkins' thesis has given rise to a controversial body of thought known as evolutionary biology. This sees human behaviour as genetically determined and that which significantly reduces the role of free will in the account of human behaviour. The classical position limits the role of genes to the acquisition of the physiological characteristics of the organism, One might ask – which of these interpretations is more appropriate or even correct? But that would be to miss the essential point of such an approach which is to expose that, even in science, there exist multiple interpretations of similar data and that interpretations are made in the social and cultural context in which the scientists are situated.

Conclusion

Just as understanding the game of football requires a knowledge of the procedures and rules by which it is played, understanding the incessant stream of scientific claims prominent in the media requires some knowledge of what the 'game' of science is all about. If developing a scientifically literate populace, who will have the critical faculties to begin to assess the significance of scientific evidence and ideas, is to be an aim of science education, then teaching about the nature of science is not an indulgence but an essential act fundamental to a contemporary science education.

References

Couvalis, G. (1997) *The Philosophy of Science: Science and Objectivity,* London: Sage.

Dawkins, R. (1976) *The Selfish Gene,* Oxford: Oxford University Press.

DfEE (1996) *Labour Market and Skill Trends,* London: Department for Education and Employment.

Koulaidis, V. and Ogborn, J. (1995) 'Science teachers' philosophical assumptions: how well do we understand them?' *International Journal of Science Education* 17(3): 273–82.

Reiss, M. J. (1984) 'Courtship and reproduction in the three-spined stickleback', *Journal of Biological Education* 18(3): 197–200.

Tinbergen, N. (1951) *The Study of Instinct,* Oxford: Oxford University Press.

Further reading

Carey, J. (ed.) (1995) *The Faber Book of Science,* London: Faber. This book contains the selected writings of scientists from Galileo to Richard Dawkins and is a mine of information and stories for science teachers.

Matthews, M. R. (1994) *Science Teaching: The Role of History and Philosophy of Science,* New York: Routledge.

Roberts, M. B. V. (1986) *Biology for Life,* Walton-on-Thames: Nelson.

Solomon, J. (1991) *Exploring the Nature of Science: Key Stage 3,* Glasgow: Blackie.

Solomon, J., Duveen, J. and Scott, L. (1992) *Exploring the Nature of Science: Key Stage 4,* Hatfield: ASE.

22 Teaching for understanding in scientific enquiry

Mary Ratcliffe

Introduction

The 'scientific enquiry' strand of the science National Curriculum encourages pupils to relate their study of science to real world problems, particularly in social and environmental contexts (socio-scientific issues). Pupils are also expected to consider the way in which scientists work in generating evidence, using creative thought and sharing ideas. There are many opportunities for bringing contemporary science research into the secondary science classroom.

However, these are not easy areas to teach. The complexity of the issues, the demands on generating and evaluating evidence and coping with different value positions can make great demands on the teacher in providing and managing suitable learning activities. A socio-scientific issue is complex because of the interplay between values and understanding of the concepts involved. Scientific research can seem just as complex to pupils because of the interplay between evidence, explanatory theories and creative thought.

This chapter seeks to describe pupils' and teachers' actions in dealing with 'scientific enquiry' and to give some practical advice in handling learning activities. The first section examines the use of a decision-making framework for pupils' discussion of socio-scientific issues. The second section considers the use of media reports for examining the nature and outcomes of scientific research.

Using analytical frameworks in dealing with socio-scientific issues

The scenario

Four classes of 14-year-olds in a boys' comprehensive school followed the Salters' Science GCSE course. During lessons, besides being introduced to scientific concepts and relevant skills, they may have formed opinions about the applications of science and use of science in social contexts. In class they were faced with such questions as:

- What are you prepared to do to reduce energy consumption?
- What can we do about the world food problem?
- How should we transport potentially dangerous chemicals?
- What materials should we use to make domestic fixtures and fittings?
- Should land development take precedence over habitat conservation?

Options

Make a list of all the things you could do/think of relevant to the problem

This is phrased appropriately for each different problem

Criteria

How are you going to choose between these options?

Make a list of the important things to think about when you look at each option0

Information

Do you have useful information about each option?

What do you know about each alternative in relation to your criteria?

What information do you have about the science involved?

Survey

What are the good things about each option?
- think about your criteria

What are the bad things about each option?
- think about your criteria

Choice

Which option do you choose?

Review

What do you think of the decision you have made?

How could you improve the way you made the decision?

Figure 22.1 Framework for pupil discussions

In order to help teacher and pupils structure their deliberations, I provided a framework for small-group discussion (Figure 22.1). This was based on models of how we 'should'(*normative*) go about making decisions (Beyth-Marom *et al.* 1991) and how 'in practice' (*descriptive*) we make decisions (Hirokawa and Johnston 1989). Pupils also had relevant information about the problem. Small-group discussions were audio-taped; all written work was collected and teacher contributions in whole-class and small-group discussions were examined.

Pupil actions

From analysing the wealth of detailed data collected, a number of key points emerged concerning pupils' actions (Ratcliffe 1996; 1997). Some aspects of decision-making were not problematic: identifying options; identifying a basis for the decision. Other important features were lacking: the search for and evaluation of information; systematic consideration of options against criteria; critical review of the decision made.

In particular:

1   Pupils were able to analyse the advantages and disadvantages of an issue, but not in a systematic way against criteria they identified.
2   Few pupils were information vigilant. Those that were, sought and used information across all tasks and interviews. Pupils used little information about the underlying science.
3   Pupils used a few dominant criteria as the basis for the decision. These included economics and perceived effectiveness of the proposed solution. Ethical and environmental considerations, although appropriate to the contexts, did not feature frequently.
4   Adolescents can have decision-making strategies which are persistent over time. Some pupils, when interviewed individually, had a constant underlying rationale for views on a particular issue. However, group discussion could moderate their opinion.

Teachers' behaviour

Discussions of socio-scientific issues are value-laden. As teachers, we have our own viewpoint on an issue. The extent to which we expose this may depend on how we view the teacher's role:

- as a 'neutral' chair (Cowie and Rudduck 1990);
- in inculcating particular values;
- in assisting moral development;
- in helping pupils clarify their value positions (Layton 1986).

Our influences on pupils' views may be deliberate or unintentional. In this study, there was evidence that teachers have strong influence over *procedures* in class but far less influence over pupil *attitudes* and decisions.

Teaching and learning implications

Whatever method is used to enable pupils to understand the complexity of socio-scientific issues, with their interaction between value judgements and understanding of scientific knowledge, it is important to be clear of the purpose of the learning activity.

Purposes can include:

1 Relevance – encouraging pupils to relate their experience of school science to real problems and developing social responsibility (Ramsey 1993);
2 Motivation – for exploring the issue further (Gayford 1992);
3 Communication – assisting pupils in verbalizing, listening and argument (Solomon 1992);
4 Analysis – assisting pupils in skills of systematic and thoughtful reasoning (Kortland 1992);
5 Understanding – learning science concepts (Solomon 1984).

The outcomes of using a decision-making framework suggest there was potential for achievement of the first four purposes, but also some limitations. Socio-scientific issues have *relevance* to a real problem. Pupils were prepared to spend considerable time discussing the issues, but sometimes appeared to view the problem as distant from their personal involvement. Pupils were highly *motivated* by discussion, but this may stem not from the issue itself but from encouraging and valuing peer group discussion in its own right. However, this valuing of pupil discussion seems an important element in assisting pupils' development of responsible attitudes.

The discussion framework helped pupils in *communication* skills of verbalizing, listening and arguing coherently. The extent to which the framework was able to assist pupils in *analysis* is indicated by the pupil actions above. Pupils need a good understanding of the expectations and purpose of the task, helped by the teacher clarifying the uses of different parts of the framework. This is important if pupils are to spend more time discussing and analysing the issue than in clarifying procedures.

The fifth purpose of trying to use the tasks to teach 'new' science concepts was not an expected aim of the decision-making discussions. It was clear that pupils did not learn 'new' science by carrying out the tasks, but did clarify their understanding of some relevant science on a few occasions. Modification of the decision-making framework, in particular examining the reasons why the issue is raised, may provide a vehicle for learning science.

Providing a framework for discussion can prevent some common problems of peer group discussion (Cowie and Ruddock 1990):

- discussions allowed value to be placed on pupil contributions;
- there was little evidence of dominance by particular pupils;
- combative factions were rarely seen;
- group members all contributed in some way;
- pupils regarded group discussion as an aid to learning.

One problem which Cowie and Rudduck (1990) identify was observed in some discussions: the acceptance of an over-easy consensus in the face of complex issues. Despite the framework given, some individuals were willing to concede easily to the views of others without evaluation.

Other frameworks besides this decision-making framework can act as useful tools for providing structure. Possible frameworks include (Fullick and Ratcliffe 1996; Lock and Ratcliffe 1998) *consequence mapping* and *goals, rights and duties*.

Consequence mapping

This is brainstorming on paper but with some key differences. Pupils are set a 'what if?' question – e.g. 'What if the Government sets a target of 10 per cent of electricity to be generated from renewable energy sources by 2010?' (This is not a what if – this target has been set!)

They are then asked to consider the consequences of this question by placing the question in the middle of a sheet of A3 paper and generating the outcomes of this question. There are likely to be primary and secondary consequences, matters of opinion and matters of fact. From the pupil-generated consequence maps, the science, value positions and complexity of the issue can be teased out. To prevent any discussion from becoming one-sided, it can be useful to split the class so contrasting consequence maps are completed e.g. 'What if all 16-year-old pupils are encouraged to smoke?', 'What if all smoking for 16–18-year-olds is banned?'.

Goals, rights and duties

This structure is particularly useful for examining ethical issues where there is an impact on people. The problem or scenario is presented to pupils in the form of a case study involving a number of people. For example, consider the case of a woman and her 14-year-old daughter who know that the woman's mother died of breast cancer. Should they be genetically screened? The pupils can then consider the goals, rights and duties of particular people this might affect – in this case, the woman, her daughter, her husband, other offspring, the genetic tester, etc. If each group of pupils concentrates on identifying the goals, rights and duties of one person, the teacher can collect the outcomes in a table. This summary normally shows that the goals of one person may be in conflict with their duties and the goals of another person. The activity should allow pupils to see how different viewpoints on an issue, such as imposition of genetic screening, may *justifiably* be reached.

Interpretation of scientific research

A different approach to the 'scientific enquiry' strand is to illuminate the complexity of science research. Reports of scientific research which appeal to pupils and relate to National Curriculum content can be found fairly easily in newspapers, journals and on websites. As a team, science teachers and I have tried a number of approaches in order to help pupils understand the practices of scientific enquiry.

Science and certainty

In a pilot study (Ratcliffe 1999), pupils of different ages were presented with journalistic accounts of science research in order to examine their ability to understand a chain of evidence. Short articles from *New Scientist* tend to have a common format which incorporates major elements of scientific research and its evaluation.

The following set of questions encourages pupils to examine the chain of evidence in the article and appreciate the tentative nature of scientific knowledge. In each article, the research outcome is presented *with caveats*:

1   Underline any words or phrases which you do not understand.
2   Write down one or two things in the article which are known for certain.
3   Write down one or two things in the article about which there is some uncertainty.
4   Chris has read this article and says, 'This proves that … … … … … … (major claim in the article)'.

Do you agree or disagree with Chris? Explain why you think this.

In the study using these questions, three classes of pupils in the 11–14 age range of a mixed comprehensive school used the *New Scientist* articles as part of a 'normal' science lesson. Alex, their experienced science teacher, used the same structure for each lesson. She introduced the report as real research presented for an adult audience, indicating that the language level may be high. The article was then read as a class, volunteers each reading a paragraph or so, with Alex assisting with difficult words. Alex asked the class to complete the first question by themselves, requiring the article to be re-read. She then identified the words they had difficulty with and their meaning was explained, using other pupils as a first resource. The problematic vocabulary was mainly technical. Once these words had been explained there appeared few barriers to understanding the sense of individual sentences. Alex then asked pupils to complete the remainder of the questions, with a clear emphasis on giving their own opinions. She finished the lesson by collecting in a few reactions from pupils to Chris's statement.

Over half the pupils (61 per cent) disagreed with Chris's statement, with 40 per cent reasoning logically. Most pupils can identify established facts and areas of uncertainty within the articles. These results, combined with the more detailed analysis of responses (Ratcliffe 1999) suggest that many pupils can identify the chain of evidence in a report of scientific research. This pilot study provided the basis for work with a science department in using media reports to assist pupils' abilities to evaluate evidence.

Evaluating evidence

The science department was developing a new scheme of work for its modular GCSE course. It incorporated an evaluation of a report of scientific research into each Year 10 GCSE science module.

To help pupils appreciate the steps in scientific procedures, the following questions were posed:

1   What do the researchers claim? (i.e. what is the conclusion?)
2   What evidence is there to support this conclusion?
3   Is this evidence sufficient to support their claims? Explain your answer.
4   What further work, if any, would you suggest?
5   What scientific knowledge has been used by the researchers in *explaining* their results and claims?

Although the teachers had different teaching styles and priorities, the format of the lesson involving the report was similar. Each teacher:

- presented the report in the context of the module's science content;
- made general, but not specific, links to evidence evaluation in investigations;
- explained ideas but did not provide answers to questions;
- summarized pupil responses after completion of the questions.

The pupils recorded their responses to the questions and had the opportunity for discussion with their immediate neighbours.

Responses to questions 1 and 2 were categorized according to whether pupils reflected the key research outcome and a summary of the evidence.

Summarizing across all responses (n=188):

What do the researchers claim? Full response 63 per cent, partial response 32 per cent, 'wrong' response 5 per cent.

What evidence is there to support this conclusion? Full response 51 per cent, partial response 28 per cent, 'wrong' 13 per cent, no response 7 per cent.

Is this evidence sufficient to support their claims? Explain your answer No 47 per cent, Yes 23 per cent, Ambiguous 7 per cent, not answered 23 per cent.

What further work, if any, would you suggest? Suggestions for further work varied from a general exhortation for more testing to consideration of a range of different variables to alter. Many pupils made more than one suggestion. Of the 191 suggestions made, the largest proportion (53 per cent) was to repeat the research for different named variables. Other suggestions, which were report dependent, included suggesting a larger sample size (17 per cent) or a larger scale or longer time (17 per cent). Only 3 per cent suggested repeating the research as given, while 6 per cent were vague in suggesting 'further tests'. Only 4 per cent referred to any underlying scientific model, which was explicitly discussed in two reports.

What scientific knowledge has been used by the researchers in explaining *their results and claims?*
On only five out of the fourteen occasions was this question attempted to any degree. Responses fell into four categories (total responses=78).

1 Citations of terminology and vocabulary used in the report (69 per cent).
2 Comments on the properties of the research subject (24 per cent). These responses seemed to show a more general understanding of the content area.
3 Comments reflecting scientists' use of experimental procedures (15 per cent).
4 Comments indicating no scientific knowledge was used (4 per cent).

There was an expectation that pupils showing mature reasoning would consider that additional evidence was needed to validate the main research outcome presented in the media report. Across the whole year, 47 per cent of pupils completed the first four questions, regarded the evidence as insufficient and argued for extensions or variations of the research. A larger number (66 per cent) could indicate possible refinements, regardless of the extent to which they fully evaluated the evidence presented.

These two approaches are obviously not the only way in which media reports can be used in science lessons. The two sets of questions above were posed as part of a research agenda to examine the extent to which secondary pupils can engage with scientific reports intended for an adult audience. The results are optimistic – pupils enjoyed the activity and were able to follow the chain of evidence to some extent. The teachers who used *New Scientist* articles for the research study all plan to incorporate media reports of contemporary science research into science lessons in some way.

Recommendations for practice

If we want pupils to examine the nature of complex socio-scientific issues and to understand the nature of scientific enquiry, then there are a number of issues we need to address to allow for informed debate.

Purpose

Clarifying the specific purpose of the activity and sharing it with pupils is essential. The important goal may not be to get to a final decision or learn some 'new' science but to understand the complexity of the issue and to support analytical skills. Learning outcomes for these activities are best expressed as understanding processes rather than understanding concepts.

Context

It is helpful for pupils to understand the context of the activity. For socio-scientific issues, we can make the science base of the issue overt, indicating what principles or ideas may be important. In examining reports of scientific research, the emphasis is on the nature of scientific enquiry, including the creativity needed to go beyond empirical data to develop explanatory theories and models.

Pupil contributions – using evidence

Pupils enjoy sharing their views, but without opening them to scrutiny, the activity can lack focus and clear outcomes – the personality and prior 'prejudices' of individuals may come through more strongly than evidence. It can help to clarify the basis on which pupil comments are made – is this a 'top-of-the-head' opinion or one based on a particular piece of evidence? We may need to spend some time with pupils in sorting out the nature and accessibility of the information they think they need to come to a clear judgement. Pupils may say that we can be certain of conclusions and claims when further evidence has been collected – yet, in practice, we have to make decisions for action on the basis of incomplete or conflicting evidence.

Pupil grouping

It can help to group pupils so that there is a mixture of skills and good peer relationships. Some pupils seek information and evidence more naturally than others. These pupils seem better able to handle a systematic framework and can be useful group members.

Outcomes

Finally, we should carefully review with pupils the outcomes of the activity, in relation to the processes of scientific enquiry. This is an important process which is often overlooked. It may be at the heart of the development of analytical skills for pupils to see the quality of analysis and that different opinions on a complex issue may be legitimate.

References

Beyth-Marom, R., Fischoff, B., Jacobs Quadrel, M., and Furby, L. (1991) 'Teaching decision-making to adolescents: a critical review', in J. Baron and R. Brown (eds) *Teaching Decision-Making to Adolescents,* New Jersey: Lawrence Erlbaum Associates Inc., pp. 19–59.

Cowie, H. and Rudduck, J. (1990) 'Learning through discussion', in N. Entwistle (ed.) *Handbook of Educational Ideas and Practices,* London: Routledge.

Fullick, P. L. and Ratcliffe, M. (1996) *Teaching Ethical Aspects of Science,* Totton: Bassett Press.

Gayford, C. (1992) 'Patterns of group behaviour in open-ended problem solving in science classes of 15-year-old students in England', *International Journal of Science Education* 14(1): 41–9.

Hirokawa, R. Y. and Johnston, D. D. (1989) 'Toward a theory of group decision-making', *Small Group Behaviour* 20(4): 500–23.

Kortland, K. (1992) 'Environmental education: sustainable development and decision-making', in R. E. Yager (ed.) *The Status of STS Reform Efforts around the World,* ICASE Yearbook 1992.

Layton, D. (1986) 'Revaluing science education', in P. Tomlinson and M. Quinton (eds) *Values Across the Curriculum,* London: Falmer Press.

Lock, R. and Ratcliffe, M. (1998) 'Learning about social and ethical applications of science', in M. Ratcliffe (ed.) *The ASE Guide to Secondary Science Education,* Cheltenham: Stanley Thornes.

Ramsey, J. (1993) 'The Science Education Reform Movement: implications for social responsibility', *Science Education* 77(2): 235–58.

Ratcliffe, M. (1996) 'Adolescent decision-making, by individuals and groups, about science-related societal issues', in G. Welford, J. Osborne and P. Scott (eds) *Research in Science Education in Europe,* London: Falmer Press, pp. 126–40.

Ratcliffe, M. (1997) 'Pupil decision-making about socio-scientific issues, within the science curriculum', *International Journal of Science Education* 19(2): 167–82.

Ratcliffe, M. (1999) 'Evaluation of abilities in interpreting media reports of scientific research', *International Journal of Science Education* 21(10): 1085–99.

Solomon, J. (1984) 'Prompts, cues and discrimination: the utilization of two separate knowledge systems', *European Journal of Science Education* 6(3): 277–84.

Solomon, J. (1992) 'The classroom discussion of science-based social issues presented on television: knowledge, attitudes and values', *International Journal of Science Education* 14(4): 431–44.

23 What is an anti-racist atom?
John Siraj-Blatchford

Science topics such as genetics and nutrition are increasingly seen as relevant to the pursuance of anti-racism in education. The need to include scientific applications and implications from a world perspective is even more generally recognized. This chapter goes beyond these concerns to argue that an anti-racism perspective is relevant to all of our science teaching and that it has pedagogical implications that have a wider significance of great value to science education.

Education for all

The title of this chapter comes from a remark made by a sceptical colleague on considering the relevance of science to the Berkshire LEA policy: 'Education for Racial Equality'. So what is an anti-racist atom? I want to argue that an anti-racist atom is an atom equally accessible to all students, black as well as white, girls as well as boys, working-class as well as middle-class. This chapter is not, however, restricted to a consideration of access. Anti-racism in science is as relevant to an all-white school as to a school where some of the pupils are black. In adopting the title *Education for All*, the Swann Report of 1985 made this point clearly, and the underlying principle has now been incorporated in a limited fashion throughout the National Curriculum. But, while most educators will be aware of both the general and subject-specific National Curriculum statements concerned with providing a curriculum responsive to the needs of a multi-cultural society, perhaps less well known are the recommendations, or the relevance, of the Stephen Lawrence Inquiry (Macpherson 1999). Section 67 of that document suggested that consideration be given to *further* amendment of the National Curriculum in the interest of valuing cultural diversity and preventing racism. Changes to the curriculum are necessary if we are to provide students with an anti-racist education, but such changes shouldn't be considered sufficient: teaching approaches must also be improved.

Science and anti-racism

An anti-racist atom must, therefore, be a well taught atom. Its teaching must be firmly grounded in our knowledge of the history and philosophy of science, and racism, and in our understanding of cognitive and language development. Science is not, and has never been, a body of value-free knowledge to be passed uncritically down to subsequent generations. For evidence of this, one need look no further than the publications of the British Movement or the National Front which include the work of Lorenz, Tinbergen, Eysenck, Skinner and Morris as part of their reading lists. Right-wing political organizations regularly justify themselves by citing the 'findings' of socio-biologists. When challenged, it is clear that most popular cultural, chauvinist and racist beliefs are ultimately justified by reference to scientific or 'pseudo-scientific' ideas. Whether these ideas are concerned with genetics, or if they relate to some supposed inherent cultural superiority in 'our' modern science and technology, science educators must accept the central responsibility for addressing the issues and for dispelling the myths of race as well as for questioning 'blind' technological advance.

Of course, despite the great advances made historically in the Middle East, China, the Indian sub-continent and Africa, modern science did develop and become established significantly in Europe from the sixteenth century onwards and, given the prevailing scientific prejudices, this needs to be taken into account. The greatest progress in the past was made, not at all surprisingly, in those countries that experienced periods of greatest economic surplus. These were times when a number of privileged individuals were released from the daily need to provide for their own basic needs and were therefore able to pursue their interests in understanding the nature of the universe. European pre-eminence has thus been founded upon imperialism, colonialism and the slave trade. Historically, empires have come and gone and modern science could easily have developed in Africa or Asia instead. If one agrees that Western Europeans are not 'innately' more capable scientists, then every effort must be made to ensure that pupils are not left with this misconception. The contributions of black scientists must be included in the curriculum. Texts which portray images of only white, male scientists are clearly inadequate.

Implications for teaching and learning

Typically, school science has involved us in the selection of certain specific observations that it was hoped would lead students to some predetermined, desired conclusions. Unfortunately, this has served to hide the historically- and culturally-specific nature of the syllabus selection and it has also tended to reify just one account of the subject. The use of this 'discovery' approach has caused students who didn't discover 'correctly' to look to their own perceived inadequacies for the cause of this failure. When this has been combined with an alienating white, eurocentric, sexist and middle-class treatment of the history and the applications of science, we have a situation where black, female and working-class students have related their perceived failure to their 'blackness', 'gender', or 'social class'. The effect upon all pupils has also been to suggest that we are capable of 'discovering' major scientific ideas in a modern school laboratory or classroom within just a few hours (or even minutes). This has important consequences for the attitudes of these students towards those cultures and countries that have apparently 'failed' to make the discoveries our texts and materials value.

Anti-racist science must involve the students in practical activity but it must also provide firm anchoring points for the elaboration of their cognitive understandings. It must be 'child-centred', beginning where the individual student is 'at', and it must not be just 'white'-, 'male'- or 'middle-class'-centred. We must make our science teaching more 'relevant' not just in terms of events and experience, but starting where the student is – in their world of *ideas*. As Rosalind Driver (1985) and the CLISP team argued, by making the students' ideas more explicit they are empowered to make comparisons between one theoretical 'framework' and another.

Teaching about particle theory: an example of the approach

I will now describe how I used the approach outlined above to develop a sequence of lessons about particle theory. To support my teaching of this topic, I produced two 'factsheets' (see Figures 23.1 and 23.2) drawing on a range of different resources. These sheets contain information about various 'theories of matter' and how these have developed in different cultures.

There are a number of different ways in which these sheets could be used with a class of students. Some suggestions for small-group work are:

- Each group identifies and underlines one 'key sentence' from each of the sections on the factsheets which they think makes the most important point. Class discussion of what has been underlined helps to clarify students' understanding of the information.
- Students draw up a table with two columns headed 'people' and 'ideas'. Using the information in the text they find all those people (individuals or cultures) who have thought about the idea of matter as particles, and write a sentence summarizing what the idea was.
- On selected sections of the factsheets, students could underline in one colour those statements about matter that agree with their own theory and in another colour those with which they disagree.

However, the use of the sheets needs to be seen in the context of the sequence of lessons on particle theory, in order to illustrate the educational principles that I am suggesting. It should be noted that it is not only the reference to black Egyptian science that makes this scheme a more accurate portrayal of science and the scientific enterprise. The development of the ideas of the 'anti-racist atom' over these three lessons is intended to reflect the way in which scientific ideas are socially constructed and do not arise in an inevitable and pre-determined way from observations.

Lesson 1   Developing a particulate theory of matter

In the first lesson, different theoretical ideas are explored (students' own theories and historical theories), before arriving at the current 'scientific' model.

- The lesson begins with a whole-class discussion of 'air'. What is air? Is it anything? Is air a fluid? Can you pour it? Discussion is stimulated with demonstrations of a vacuum pump and of the pouring of air between two inverted beakers in a tank of water.

Aristotle

According to Aristotle, empty space was meaningless – matter must be continuous and reach out to the edge of the material world.

Aristotle believed that our Earth was a sphere and around that were spheres of pure elemental nature, Water, then Air, and finally Fire.

Aristotle's theory

In the third century BC, Aristotle suggested that everything was made up of four elemental qualities, Earth; Air; Water and Fire.

According to this theory, gases are mostly made up of 'air'; liquids are mostly made up of 'water' and solids of 'earth'. Aristotle got this idea from the 'four qualities' of Empedoles (500–430 BC). The qualities work with, or against each other, in alliance or in opposition. Water, for example, is opposed to Fire but allied to Earth. Each of these pure 'qualities' is made up of a pair of primary 'qualities'. Water has the primary qualities 'cold' and 'wet'. For Aristotle these were 'pure' elements and not simply water, earth, air and fire as we known them on Earth. Our Earthly water is a combination of all four elements, only mostly water. When we say we are putting our coats on to protect ourselves from the elements or talk about someone's 'fiery nature' we are using phrases that date from Aristotle's time.

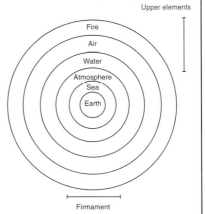

Theories of matter

Our earliest records of scientific enquiry into the subject date from the seventh century BC. At that time an aristocratic class in Greece became interested in the mysteries of life. Many people say that Thales was a Greek who studied for many years in Egypt at this time. Pythagoras was a pupil of Thales. Pythagoras was a teacher of Egyptian language and culture. This 'scientific' tradition was carried on by others such as Socrates, Euclid and Plato but it was a very long time before this knowledge came to Europe. The Arabs conquered the Greek Empire in the seventh century AD and Arab academics translated the Greek writing into Arabic and brought it to Europe. These writings were eventually translated from the Arabic into Latin in the Middle Ages.

Figure 23.1 Aristotle and the influence of Greek ideas

- Students are invited to imagine that they have a 'magic pair of spectacles'. They draw and they describe what air *might* look like. Each student produces 'My theory of gases'.
- Students share each other's ideas. How can they test their theories? How can we 'hold' the air to experiment with it? This leads to two practical activities – comparing the 'squashiness' of air and water in a syringe and the inspection of a range of materials (e.g. foam, fabric, wood, polystyrene) using a range of equipment (including binocular microscopes) to determine what makes some materials squash.
- Groups of three or four students then discuss their theoretical models in the light of the experiments, and negotiate a collective response. The collaborative group work ensures increased comprehension and concept development, and their drawings tend to move from representations of a 'continuous' substance to ones that emphasize discontinuity with matter broken up or separated.
- The groups report back to the whole class, and the teacher summarizes the ideas put forward stimulating a discussion: 'Why is it that air can be squashed?'.
- The groups then study the two factsheets on 'Aristotle' and 'Theories of Matter' and they adapt their theories as they find necessary or useful in the light of the evidence and discussions so far. On reporting back, the principles of the atomic-kinetic theory are clarified by the teacher, including the states of matter, presented as: 'the model most used by professional scientists now'.

Lesson 2   Applying the theory to further phenomena

In this lesson, the theoretical ideas that were developed in the first lesson are tested out, by using them to explain or predict a range of phenomena.

- The lesson begins with some demonstrations of some phenomena intended to stimulate thinking and discussion. Taking the syringe example further: 'What would happen if we kept on compressing the gas?'. A disposable lighter and carbon dioxide bottle are used to illustrate this. The demonstrated production of 'dry ice' is extended by putting some into a sealed balloon and leaving it on the overhead projector to warm up: 'What will happen?'.
- Students write their own notes and before/after diagrams. This leads to a more elaborate statement by the teacher of kinetic theory and a summary table of the 'states of matter' including structure, forces, and compressibility.
- A circus of activities is provided, with worksheets to reinforce the model. The phenomena explored include heating a block of ice, a simple steam engine, the expansion of a range of solids, the expansion of liquids and the expansion of air.
- Students report back, and there is an open-class discussion where the model is consolidated using the traditional 'springy' atom, and 3D kinetic models. The predictive value of the model is finally tested by heating a tin can with the lid on!

Theories of matter

Scientists invent theories. Good theories last a long time before something is discovered which they cannot explain. When this happens new theories are invented.

Particle theory from Africa

Hindu and Egyptian philosophers were the first to write about atoms hundreds of years BC. Their speculations may have first arisen in the context of blowing glass. The Greeks studied these writings and argued that all matter was made of tiny particles. Heron, a black scientist who worked in Alexandria in the first century described air as particles separated and in motion in empty space. These ideas were not popular until revived in the writings of Boyle in the seventeenth and eighteenth centuries.

Two paintings representing glass blowers at work from the reign of the first Osirtasen (Beni Hassan).

'Atoms', 'molecules' and 'particles'

Often the term 'particle' is used in physics to mean either an atom or a molecule. In this book we shall use the proper terms 'atom' or 'molecule' when referring to particular substances. For example, we shall speak of molecules of oxygen and atoms of iron. Sometimes, however, we shall want to refer simply to the fact that all solids, liquids and gases are made of individual specks of matter. It will not be important whether these are atoms or molecules. Then we shall use the term 'particle' to refer to them.

(Geoffrey Dorling 1992, p.11)

Atoms and molecules

The smallest piece of matter that can exist on its own under normal conditions is a **molecule**. Molecules are so small that they can't be seen, even with the most powerful microscope. A large glass of water contains around 10^{25} molecules! Molecules themselves are made up of **atoms** – sometimes just one, but more frequently several which have been bound together by a chemical reaction. Atoms are the building blocks from which the molecules of a substance are constructed.

(Graham Dolan, Mike Duffy and Adrian Percival 1996, p.56)

Figure 23.2 Theories of matter

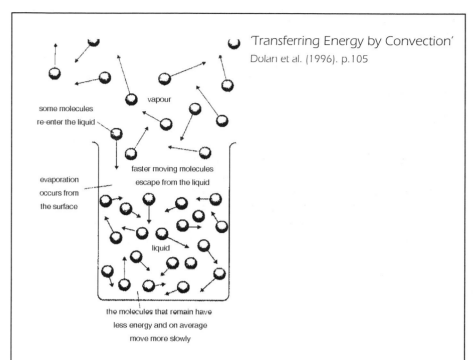

'Transferring Energy by Convection'
Dolan et al. (1996). p.105

some molecules re-enter the liquid

vapour

evaporation occurs from the surface

faster moving molecules escape from the liquid

liquid

the molecules that remain have less energy and on average move more slowly

Theories of matter: from Thompson to de Broglie

In the nineteenth century, scientists thought that atoms were the smallest particles that could exist and that they could not be split. However, in 1899 Thompson discovered a very small negatively-charged particle and this was named the 'electron'. Scientists then believed that atoms were made of electrons spread out in a positively charged sphere. But Rutherford's experiments on radioactivity in 1911 helped him to put forward a new model of the atom. In the 'nuclear atom' model, the atom consists of a very tiny positively-charged nucleus in the centre, with negatively-charged electrons in orbit around it. Most of the atom consists of just empty space! In 1923, de Broglie proposed an even stranger model of the atom – that matter had wave properties just like light and other radiation.

Scientific models

It is now appreciated that a scientific model is an aid to understanding and not necessarily a true description. In the same way a map showing only towns and roads is no more a complete representation of a country than is one showing only physical features; each describes one aspect and neither is wrong. Both models are necessary for an adequate description of the behaviour of matter and radiation: they are complementary not contradictory. The sensible thing to do is to use one or other model when it is appropriate and helpful.

(Tom Duncan 1994, p.447)

Lesson 3   Brownian motion

In the final lesson, the example of Brownian motion is used as a starting point for a consideration of the nature of scientific theory.

- Brownian motion is introduced as 'a phenomenon' to be accounted for.
- An historical account of its discovery and the theories used to explain it are given. (Brown was a botanist who noticed pollen grains moving about in water. He thought that the pollen was alive until he checked his theory by boiling the water). The 3D model is used in the clarification of the phenomenon.
- The idea that one theoretical model is only better than another, in as far as it is useful and appropriate to social purposes, can be developed from this starting point. Looked at from first and 'third world' contexts, scientific theory can be seen as a social product created in specific socio/historical time and space.

Conclusion

In this chapter I have argued that an anti-racist approach has relevance to *all* aspects of science teaching and to *all* students. I have illustrated this through an approach to the teaching of particulate theory, which illustrates how a sequence of lessons can be planned, taking account of the contribution of other cultures to scientific thought and reflecting the ways in which science has historically developed.

References

Dolan, G., Duffy, M. and Percival, A. (1996) *Heinemann Co-ordinated Science – Higher Physics,* Heinemann.

Dorling. G. (1992) *Nuffield Co-ordinated Sciences: Physics,* Longman.

Driver, R. (1985*) The Pupil as Scientist?,* Open University Press.

Duncan, T. (1994) *Advanced Physics,* fourth edition*,* John Murray.

Macpherson, Sir W. (1999) *The Stephen Lawrence Inquiry*, Stationery Office.

Further reading

Bernal, M. (1985) *The Afroasiatic Roots of Classical Civilisation: Vol. 1, The Fabrication of Ancient Greece 1785–1985*, Free Association Books.

Siraj-Blatchford, J. (1996) *Learning Technology, Science and Social Justice*, Education Now.

Toulmin, S. (1982) 'The construal of reality: criticism in modern and postmodern science', *Critical Inquiry,* 9 September.

24 Science education for all
Michael Reiss

By now it is increasingly being accepted that the model of science held, the way science is taught and the specific content matter learned are all too often restricted in outlook. Much school science is 'male' and 'Western' in focus, teaching style, content and assessment.

The consequences of a narrow, male, Western view of school science are far reaching and of two main sorts. First, many pupils quite correctly feel alienated from school science and drop out of it as soon as they can. Second, pupils continue to learn an impoverished form of science.

The aim of this chapter is to provide a range of examples to help enrich science lessons. Most of the examples are therefore of contributions to science made by non-Westerners and/or women.

Surgery

Every culture practises surgery. Trepanation of the skull, an operation to remove a portion of the cranium, may have been performed as long ago as 10,000 BCE. Examples of prehistoric trepanation have been found all over the world. They represent the oldest evidence of surgery. Several techniques are known (e.g. scrapping and cutting) but all involve removing pieces of bone. The rate of survival is indicated by healing processes at the edges of the bone. In the *majority* of cases significant bone regrowth is evident. This contrasts with the success rate in the 1800s in Western Europe when recovery was so unusual that one authority wrote that the first require-ment for the operation was 'dass de Wundarzt selbst auf den Kopf gefallen sein müsse' ['that the wound surgeon must himself have fallen on his head'].

By the time of the Fifth Dynasty in Egypt (around 2450 BCE) the use of splints and bandages to set fractured limbs was in practice. The world's oldest medical text is a Sumerian tablet whose style of writing dates it to the Third Dynasty of Ur, *c*.2158–2008 BCE or a little earlier. On it are mentioned washing, making plasters and bandaging.

By about 2000 BCE, wound surgery had reached the point in Egypt where there were separate doctors for the eye, the teeth, the belly and the 'hidden diseases'; there was even a 'shepherd of the anus'. By about 1600 BCE medical sutures and tapes are recorded in papyri. Cauterization (use of a red-hot implement to stop bleeding) followed about 100 years later.

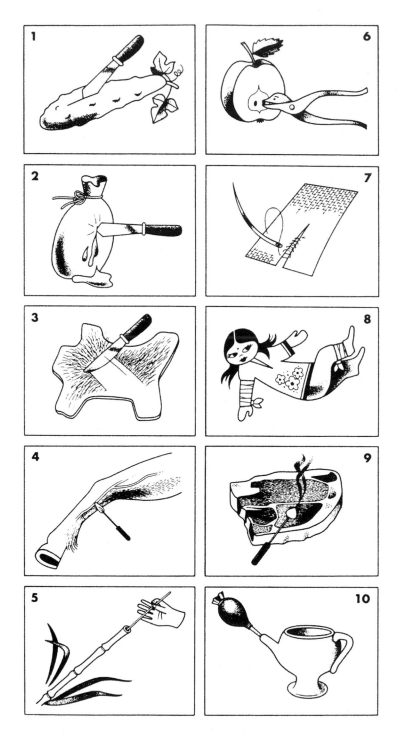

Figure 24.1 Experimental procedures that apprentice Hindu surgeons were required to practise in approximately 400 BCE

The Egyptians of this time were aware of the problems of infection. Malachite or honey was applied to certain wounds, just as myrrh was used in embalming. Recent experiments have shown that ground-up malachite (no doubt because it contains copper), honey and myrrh all prevent the growth of certain bacteria including bacteria of the typhoid-colon group (honey) and *Staphylococcus aureus* (malachite and myrrh). Similar experiments could safely be carried out under school laboratory conditions.

By approximately 400 BCE, apprentice Hindu surgeons were required to undertake a number of experimental procedures for practice (Figure 24.1). Among the many Indian procedures established at this time was the use of the tourniquet. To India, too, we owe the earliest treatment of cataracts. For this, a needle is used to push the opaque lens out of the way via an insertion behind the iris. Also first performed in India, as far as we know, were plastic and reconstructive surgery.

Plastic surgery in India probably originated with treatments to ear lobes infected or damaged through the widespread practice of piercing and stretching them. Subsequently, the techniques were used to reconstruct ears and noses lost in war. For example, a new nose could be built from a flap of skin folded down from the forehead (but, remaining, of course, still partly attached). The flap was of the appropriate shape and the nostrils were moulded over two little tubes.

In the tenth century CE, Abu 'Ali al-Husayn bin 'Abdallah bin Sina (generally known in the West as Avicenna) was a physician and a prolific writer. One of his books – the *Canon of Medicine* – runs to over a million words. This book points out the importance of diet in health, the influence of climate and the environment on health, the surgical use of oral anaesthetics, the contagious nature of some diseases, and the dangers of diseases spreading via soil and water. Ibn Sina recommended the testing of new drugs by experimentation on animals and humans. He advised surgeons to treat cancer in its earliest stages, making sure to remove surgically all the diseased tissue.

Personal health

There is a real danger when teaching aspects of health education, whether or not in the context of biology/science lessons, that hidden assumptions appropriate for one culture may be inappropriately, even if unintentionally, transferred to another culture. A classic example when discussing digestion is to ask pupils to write an essay on 'What happens when I eat a ham sandwich'. (Ham is not permitted as a valid food to Jews, Muslims, vegetarians and vegans.)

Munday *et al.* (1989) studied the perceptions of 11–14-year-olds in an ethnically diverse comprehensive school as to what constituted good gum health. A set of six colour photographs was shown to the pupils. These demonstrated pairs of healthy and unhealthy gums with pink, brown and black pigmentation. The pictures were selected to represent a range of ethnic types and to present differences between healthy and unhealthy gums that were apparent to a lay person. Each pupil was individually shown the pictures and was asked by a dental health educator to choose from amongst them those showing gums which were: (a) healthy and (b) unhealthy.

What Munday and her colleagues found was that, almost irrespective of their skin colour, 80 per cent of the pupils selected the healthy, pink gums as healthy, whereas fewer than 10 per cent of the pupils selected the healthy, brown or healthy, black gums as healthy. Indeed, the *unhealthy*, pink gums were far more likely to be described as healthy than the healthy, brown or healthy, black ones were. Only one child (a brown-skinned girl) made all the choices correctly. (She expressed a wish to train as a dentist.) All pupils were subsequently seen in tutor groups and told the 'correct answers'. This information was almost always met with alarm, surprise, disbelief and rejection.

It is clear that pupils would benefit from having teachers who could effectively help them to affirm a view of good health appropriate to their culture and ethnicity. In the same way, despite the fact that food is perhaps the most obvious manifestation of cultural diversity and therefore lends itself to a multicultural approach, teaching about food can all too often give the impression that the diets favoured by certain groups are unbalanced, or, at best, odd. This latter problem can occur when pupils are asked to keep food diaries or to log their diets into software which uses the language of the teacher or software writer.

Blood transfusions

Charles Drew was an Afro-American doctor who invented blood banks. He was born in 1904 in a ghetto in Washington, DC. In 1933 he received his Master of Surgery and Doctor of Medicine degrees. During the Second World War, Drew was approached by the British government and asked to start a blood bank programme for use on the battlefield. This he did. It was so successful that he was asked to organize an international blood bank project and to become the first Director of the American Red Cross Blood Bank.

Although he received many awards and honours, Drew experienced racism all his life. In 1941, he resigned his position with the American Red Cross Blood Bank after it was decided that blood from black donors should not be mixed with blood from white donors. In 1950, Drew was seriously injured in a car accident in North Carolina. He needed a blood transfusion but the hospital he was rushed to refused to treat him because he was black. Drew died before reaching a hospital that would treat him.

Selective breeding

Genetics may be a much older science than is generally realized. Figure 24.2 shows a sketch of a clay tablet dating from about 3000 BCE. The tablet is from Elam (now in south-western Iran) and appears to show a breeding record of what may have been domesticated donkeys. Notice the various types of mane. The script is known as proto-Elamite and has not yet been deciphered.

Pupils often hear about the possible problems of genetic uniformity among crops – a consequence of the current domination of the world's agricultural markets by a few very large multinational companies. It may help pupils to realize the consequences that too much genetic uniformity among crops may have if they know that this is not a modern phenomenon. There is good evidence that genetic uniformity was one of the major contributing factors to the devastating Irish potato famine of 1845–9. The famine resulted in the starvation of over a million people and the

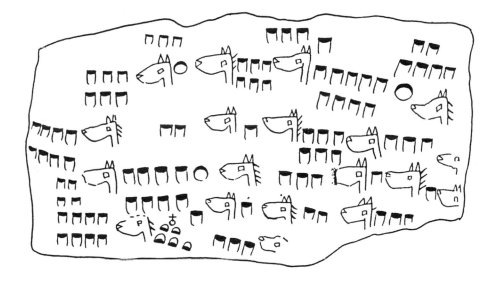

Figure 24.2 Tablet from Elam dating from around 3000 BCE and showing breeding records

emigration to the USA of about one-and-a-half million – and that from a population of only nine million people.

Unlike their counterparts in the Andes, where the potato was domesticated over 8,000 years ago and where numerous varieties of potato are grown, the Irish grew potatoes descended from only a few clones introduced from England and mainland Europe. These, in turn, were the result of just two samples of potatoes brought from South America to Spain in 1570 and to England around 1590. In the Irish potato famine, potato blight, caused by the a fungus-like organism named *Phytophthera infestans*, spread like wildfire. In the Andes, the mixture of different natural varieties – known as land races – provided some protection against the disease.

Throughout the years of the Irish potato famine, Irish farmers continued successfully to produce cereals, cattle, pigs, eggs and butter. Enough food was produced to ensure that no one in Ireland need have starved. However, farmers had to export these crops to England to get the money they needed to pay the rents they owed their English landlords. Farmers who failed to export their produce were evicted from their farms and had their cottages razed to the ground.

Decay and the preservation of foods

The topic of food preservation lends itself to a multi-cultural approach. Pupils should be able to suggest a variety of ways in which foods have traditionally been preserved. This list will probably be extended if members of their families are asked to name others. The most likely to be suggested are: drying, salting, curing/smoking, pickling, making into jams, freezing, canning and cooking. From such a list, it is then easy to teach that decay requires the presence of decay organisms, water and oxygen. Multi-cultural science needs to value all forms of indigenous science. So, if, for example, the lesson is taking place in a mainly white school, it is important that such traditional native methods as jam making are considered as well as other apparently more exotic solutions.

Most of these approaches to food preservation lend themselves to experimental investigation. Making edible jam that won't go mouldy for months or longer is not trivial!

Essentially the same tactics used in food preservation are used in embalming, which has been practised for thousands of years. The differences are due partly to the fact that the embalmer's work, unlike that of the cook's, does not have to remain edible. On the other hand, an embalmer has to ensure that the deceased looks as much as possible as they did before death, whereas no one expects a kipper to look like a herring.

Iron and steel

The lower half of the reactivity series – iron, lead, tin, copper, silver, gold – is the reverse of the order in which people isolated these metals before and during the Copper, Bronze and Iron Ages. At first all metals were obtained, not by smelting, but from relatively pure veins or nuggets. Iron was exceptionally valuable as it was obtained from meteorites.

The Iron Age probably started in Asia Minor around 1500 BCE. Pure iron has a melting point of 1540 °C, a temperature that could not be obtained that early. Early wrought iron was produced in the solid state by the chemical reduction of iron ore to iron at about 1200 °C with the aid of charcoal. If the ratio of fuel to ore is large, and the bellows are effective, the iron can be made to absorb so much carbon that it forms the alloy of iron and carbon known as 'cast iron'. This melts at 1150 °C.

It is more difficult to obtain iron from iron ore than it is to make bronze from copper and tin and the earliest bronze objects date from 3000–2500 BCE. However, iron has various advantages over bronze. It is harder and can be made to give a sharper edge. Iron ore is also very abundant, so that once the technology had been developed, iron became relatively cheap.

Africa became a major centre for the iron industry during the early Iron Age. The Bantu, in what we now call Malawi, produced large amounts of iron. 'Malawi' means 'land of flames' – the flames coming from the blast furnaces.

The first steel may have been made 2,000 years ago in what is now Tanzania. Steel is iron that contains between 0.1 and 0.5 per cent carbon in the form of iron carbide (Fe_3C). In 1976, the anthropologist Peter Schmidt persuaded some elderly smelters from the Haya tribe in Tanzania to construct a traditional furnace (Figure 24.3). A bowl, some 50 cm deep, is dug and lined with mud from a termite mound. The chimney is made of old, refractory slag and termite mud, and stands 150 cm high. Eight blowpipes are inserted to varying depths at the base of the furnace, and eight bellows are used to force air into the blowpipes. Swamp grass is burned in the bowl to provide a bed for carefully sifted charcoal. The charcoal and iron ore are then added through the top of the furnace and air blown continuously through the blow-pipes for 7–8 hours.

Measurements showed that temperatures in the blast zone of the furnace exceeded 1800 °C. Subsequent excavations have revealed over a dozen early Iron Age

Figure 24.3 Traditional furnace constructed by smelters from the Haya tribe in Tanzania. The temperature in such a furnace can reach 1800 °C. Furnaces extremely similar to this one are known from early Iron Age sites by Lake Victoria

furnaces at Kemondo Bay on the coast of Lake Victoria, one of the most heavily-used early Iron Age industrial sites in Africa. These furnaces had physical properties very similar to the reconstructed pit, including evidence of the insertion of blowpipes.

Radioactivity

Manya Sklodowska was born in 1867 in Poland. After working as a governess, she entered the Sorbonne in Paris as a student in 1891. She lived a most spartan existence, partly because of shortage of money and partly through personal choice, but graduated in physics with a First Class degree in 1893. In 1895 she married Pierre Curie and changed her name from the Polish, Manya, to the French, Marie.

Marie and Pierre Curie jointly carried out research into radioactivity (itself a term coined by Marie Curie). In 1896, Henri Becquerel discovered the radiation-emitting properties of uranium salts. Marie Curie postulated that the capacity to emit radiation was an *atomic* property and showed that the element thorium also emitted radioactivity. With her husband, she then started to look for further radioactive substances. The Curies used their savings to purchase pitchblende from which uranium had already been extracted and in 1898 announced the discovery of two new elements – polonium and radium.

In 1903, Marie and Pierre Curie were awarded the Nobel prize for physics, jointly with Henri Becquerel. Despite the fame attached to this, Marie still had to continue

Figure 24.4 Marie Curie at work in her laboratory

teaching physics at a girls' high school, in order to help support the family, until 1906. In this year Pierre, who was in poor health, was killed, knocked down by a horse-drawn wagon. Marie was appointed to fill his vacant chair at the Sorbonne – the first woman professor in France.

In 1911, opposition by some of her colleagues led to her being refused election to the French Academy of Sciences, but soon afterwards, in the same year, she was awarded the Nobel Prize for chemistry, thus becoming the first person to be awarded two Nobel Prizes.

Marie Curie was the epitome of a dedicated scientist (Figure 24.4). The four years it took to purify polonium and radium from pitchblende consisted of four years of continuous, hard, physical work, often spending day after day stirring the great quantities of material. She and Pierre refused to take advantage of the lucrative industry that grew up around their discovery and isolation of radium, believing that investigators should not profit from the results of their research. During the First World War, she and her daughter, Irene, worked in what became known as 'Little Curies', mobile X-ray cars set up by Marie Curie to take X-rays of soldiers injured by lodged bullets. In 1934, she died of leukaemia, presumably the consequences of repeated exposure to radiation.

Magnetism

Europe acquired the compass from the Chinese. In the book *Dream Pool Essays*, published in about 1086, the Chinese scientist Shen Kua wrote:

> Magicians rub the point of a needle with the lodestone; then it is able to point to the south . . . It is best to suspend it by a single cocoon fibre of new silk attached to the centre of the needle by a piece of wax the size of a mustard seed – then, hanging in a windless place, it will always point to the south.
>
> (cited in Temple 1991: 149)

Exactly when the compass was invented in China is uncertain: it was certainly hundreds of years before Shen Kua lived. A stone relief from the Han Dynasty, dated to 114 CE, shows a compass in use. What may have been a compass dating from 1000 BCE was excavated in Olmerc ruins in 1967 in southern Veracruz, Mexico.

The angle between the geographical North Pole and a compass needle pointing at the magnetic North Pole is known as the angle of declination. By the ninth century CE, this was known to the Chinese. Europeans do not seem to have known about it until the fifteenth century.

Astronomy

The list of women known to have made significant astronomical contributions is huge. Aglaonike, an astronomer of classical Greek times, was subsequently reported by Plutarch as being able precisely to predict the times of future lunar eclipses. Most classical writers considered such ability magic, and Aglaonike is reported to have encouraged such beliefs, being regarded by her contemporaries as a sorceress.

Caroline Herschel (1750–1848) was a German astronomer who came to England with her brother, William, in 1772. William's hobby was astronomy and, together, they embarked on a systematic survey of the entire night sky, making their own telescope for the project. At first Caroline had little enthusiasm for the survey, but in 1781 William discovered the planet we now know as Uranus and the two of them moved to a new home. Here, Caroline became increasingly involved in astronomy. In 1783, she discovered three new nebulae, but it was only when William was away from home that she had the chance to work on her own. It was during such times over the period 1786 to 1797 that she discovered a total of eight comets. In 1787 she was granted an official salary by the King. As Caroline wrote, 'the first money I ever in all my lifetime thought myself to be at liberty to spend to my own liking' (cited in Alic 1986: 129). Caroline continued to work throughout her long life, dying at the age of 97. She was buried with a lock of William's hair. She received many international awards and accolades and, with Mary Somerville, a Scottish writer on science, became the first woman to be made an honorary member of The Royal Society.

Margaret Burbidge (born in 1922) is a British astronomer who has worked on the creation of elements in space (nucleosynthesis), on quasars and on galaxies. In 1957 she published a paper with Geoffrey, her husband, William Fowler and Fred Hoyle. They produced a model showing precisely how a star that initially consisted mostly of hydrogen could give rise first to helium, then to carbon and oxygen, then to magnesium, silicon, sulphur, argon and calcium, then to elements such as iron, nickel, chromium and cobalt, and finally to heavier elements such as selenium, bromine, krypton, tellurium, gold and uranium. Margaret Burbidge has been a Professor at the University of California since 1964, and has been Director of the Royal Greenwich Observatory.

Jocelyn Bell (born in 1943) was a 24-year-old PhD student working with Tony Hewish at Cambridge University when they discovered pulsars. In the 1930s, three scientists had all predicted the existence of neutron stars. Such stars would be extraordinarily dense. They might be only a few kilometres in diameter, but have a mass comparable to that of our Sun. They would spin on their axes in seconds or even milliseconds, and have a gravitational force so strong that electrons could only escape at the magnetic poles, giving rise in the process to radio waves. It was these pulses that Bell and Hewish discovered. By now, over five hundred pulsars are known and Bell is a Professor of physics at the Open University.

Conclusion

This chapter can only hint at the wealth of material to help diversify science lessons. For further examples, together with more detailed suggestions as to how these may be used in teaching, see Ogilvie (1986), Millar *et al.* (1989), Temple (1991), Peacock (1991), Solomon (1991), Reiss (1993), Ronan (1983), van Sertima (1983) and Thorp, Deshpande and Edwards (1994).

References

Alic, M. (1986) *Hypatia's Heritage: A History of Women in Science from Antiquity to the Late Nineteenth Century*, London: The Women's Press.

Millar, D., Millar, I., Millar, J. and Millar, M. (1989) *Chambers' Concise Dictionary of Scientists,* Cambridge: Chambers.

Munday, P., Gelbier, S. and Nornoo, D. (1989) 'Gum – teenagers' perceptions of health', *Health Education Journal* 48: 85–8.

Ogilvie, M. B. (1986) *Women in Science: Antiquity through the Nineteenth Century – A Biographical Dictionary with Annotated Bibliography*, Cambridge, MA: Massachusetts Institute of Technology Press.

Peacock, A. (ed.) (1991) *Science in Primary Schools: The Multicultural Dimension*. Basingstoke: Macmillan Education.

Reiss, M. J. (1993) *Science Education for a Pluralist Society,* Buckingham: Open University Press.

Ronan, C. A. (1983) *The Cambridge Illustrated History of the World's Science*, Cambridge: Cambridge University Press.

Sertima, van, I. (ed.) (1983) *Blacks in Science: Ancient and Modern,* New Brunswick: Transaction Books.

Solomon, J. (1991) *Exploring the Nature of Science*, Glasgow: Blackie.

Temple, R. (1991) *The Genius of China: 3000 Years of Science, Discovery, and Invention*, London: Prion/Multimedia.

Thorp, S., Deshpande, P. and Edwards, C. (eds) (1994) *Race, Equality and Science Teaching,* Hatfield: ASE.

6 Putting it all together

Introduction

Teaching is inextricably bound together with learning. They are two sides of the same coin. If the pupil has not learned, has teaching taken place? A naive interpretation of the title of this section 'Putting it all together' might imply that teaching can be seen as the simplistic assembly of different identifiable elements. But teaching is a multifaceted and complex activity. There is no unique way of teaching. The actions that teachers take depend on their values, confidence and knowledge, and on the context in which they are working. A teacher makes a huge number of decisions before and during the lesson. Those who are learning to teach find that they spend hours planning their teaching, and they are less expert at thinking and making decisions during the lesson. They tend to stick to their plans, come what may! With experience, teachers develop a great deal of embedded knowledge on which they can draw. Planning becomes easier and reacting to what happens in the lesson becomes almost instinctive. The danger, though, of routine practices is that they are not thought about critically, because 'it's always done like that'.

In any one year, a typical science teacher may be responsible for the learning of three hundred individuals. That is a daunting task, yet teachers orchestrate it with apparent ease. Inexperienced teachers complain that the expert teacher makes this complex activity look so easy. A teacher has to consider the needs of each individual, to manage pupils and resources, anticipate what is coming next and prepare pupils for it. Pupils recognize good teachers and are remarkably consistent in their views about what makes a good teacher. An important part of teaching is establishing conditions where pupils can be self-motivated.

Motivation is a crucial aspect of learning, and something to which teachers have to pay attention, because of its impact on learning, behaviour and attitudes. Motivation is not directly measurable; it has many dimensions and it is not static. Moreover, motivation is not something that teachers can control directly. It belongs to the individual. Teachers cannot take actions that will inevitably lead to motivated learners, but there are certain actions that are likely to promote pupil motivation or diminish it. Many factors affect motivation including the confidence level of the individual, the difficulty with which they perceive the task, and their views of science. Learners are individuals with individual interests and different preferred ways of learning. The degree of personal responsibility and autonomy pupils are given can greatly improve motivation, and this need not be difficult to incorporate into lessons. Simple actions, such as allowing pupils a choice of writing style or project topic, give pupils more ownership of the work and provide opportunities for creativity. If learners own a task, and make it theirs rather than the teacher's, they are more likely to be motivated.

Pupils need to have sufficient self-confidence before they can begin to tackle a piece of work. A teacher needs to be aware of this and tackle lack of confidence with sensitivity. Learners with high self-esteem are more likely to be curious, creative and confident. Conversely, those with low self-esteem are more likely to be anxious and feel unable to attempt more open and creative tasks. The teacher plays a significant role in developing the self-esteem of learners. Positive relationships, good communication, clear boundaries and routines all help to establish a safe environment in which learners can take risks and struggle with difficult ideas. Inappropriate expectations (too high or too low), indiscriminate praise and harsh criticism will only do harm to how pupils see themselves as learners. An important role of any teacher is to inspire, challenge and excite pupils - to switch them on to science. To achieve this, the teacher has to know what ideas and understanding the pupils have, what interests them and what they would see as relevant, and to share with them what is being achieved and why. Teachers do make a difference.

- The word 'differentiation' can strike terror into the hearts of teachers, both experienced and inexperienced. At first glance it seems to be an impossible task for a teacher to cater for the needs of the thirty or so individuals that they are teaching at any one time. In their chapter, Stuart Naylor and Brenda Keogh explode some of the myths surrounding differentiation. They examine the elements involved in differentiation, and look at how differentiation can be realistically addressed using a range of strategies.
- Nick Daws and Birendra Singh base their chapter on trials of different formative assessment strategies carried out in some Essex comprehensive schools. They examine the effectiveness and practicability of different formative assessment strategies and argue strongly for greater use of such strategies in schools to improve pupils' learning in science.
- Pupils' progress in science depends on a variety of factors, but informed, effective teaching, within a structure of curricular continuity is one of the most important. Hilary Asoko and Ann Squires explore the nature of continuity and progression, the links between them, and ways in which both can be fostered.

25 Dealing with differentiation
Brenda Keogh and Stuart Naylor

Differentiation is a familiar word for teachers. Although it is commonly expected that teachers will include reference to differentiation in their planning, it is generally viewed as one of the most difficult things with which teachers have to deal. If differentiation were easy or straightforward then teachers would not be so concerned about it. The lack of confidence which many teachers feel about how they differentiate is evidence of what a complex challenge it represents. So what precisely is differentiation?

What differentiation isn't

This seems like an odd place to begin, but there is a lack of clarity about differentiation and no agreed definition, so it may be helpful to dispel some of the common myths about it.

1   Differentiation isn't something teachers do on special occasions or with 'special' pupils. If you look at it that way, differentiation becomes an added burden that is only necessary when you are teaching certain atypical pupils, such as those with Special Educational Needs. Research evidence suggests that differentiation is a concern when teaching all the pupils, not just some (Simpson 1997), and that aiming to provide a suitable curriculum for all the pupils is a more valuable approach. Russell *et al.* (1994) are quite explicit about this:

> differentiated practice represents a view of what 'good science teaching' might be – the provision of appropriate teaching/learning experiences for all pupils, not just those at the extremes.
>
> (Russell *et al.* 1994: 8)

2   Differentiation isn't just about choosing different curriculum content. Although careful choice of curriculum content can make it more likely that pupils will be offered suitable learning experiences, there is no guarantee that this will happen. Perhaps this is a particular concern in science, where much of the curriculum may be based on specified practical activities, and differentiation is viewed as providing different practical work related to different content. The purpose of differentiation should be to make a

difference to pupils' learning, and this does not necessarily require a separate curriculum.

3   Differentiation isn't just about what teachers do. However much you plan to provide differentiated teaching, this may not result in differentiated learning. Learning depends on a range of other factors such as involvement and motivation, and these are difficult to prescribe in advance. Woolnough puts this very succinctly:

> If students are motivated, and if they are given the freedom and opportunity, they will find ways of learning. If they are not, they will not bother.
>
> (Woolnough 1994: 111)

4   Differentiation doesn't have to rely on formal assessment. Although in theory National Curriculum assessment is designed to help teachers to modify their teaching to make it more appropriate, in practice the level descriptors are too blunt an instrument to be useful much of the time. Although formal assessment can offer some useful information, it tends to be insufficiently detailed and purely summative. By contrast, formative assessment, in which pupils are involved in their own assessment and learning targets are negotiated with them, has been shown to be effective in promoting learning (Black 1998).

5   Differentiation isn't the same as matching. Matching the level of difficulty of an activity to the pupil's capability is something that many teachers aim for, but it is difficult. It is difficult always to get enough relevant information about each pupil's capabilities, and there are practical difficulties in managing the process of matching in a large class. In science, there are problems in identifying how progression in understanding of specific scientific concepts develops, and defining the level of difficulty of activities in advance may not be possible. The way that the pupils' existing ideas affect their learning in science is an added complication. So there are severe limitations on any approach that requires close matching of tasks and pupil capability. Simpson (1997) found that even teachers identified as being good at differentiation had difficulties in allocating tasks that were appropriate to the pupils' attainment levels.

6   Differentiation isn't necessarily by task or by outcome. Although these two approaches to differentiation are valuable, on their own they are inadequate. Differentiation doesn't only go on at the planning stage (differentiation by task) or by the end of an activity (differentiation by outcome). It also goes on while pupils are working, when their responses provide useful feedback about the suitability of the task and the learning environment so that either or both of these can be modified at that time.

So what is differentiation?

There is no single agreed definition. James and Brown (1998: 5) describe it as teachers 'recognizing that children in their class differ in many ways, and then planning and teaching lessons so that, despite these differences, all children make the best progress possible'. Dickinson and Wright (1993) describe differentiation as 'intervening to make a difference'. They recognize that differences between pupils – such as in their prior experience, their learning capabilities, their preferred learning style and their motivation – make it inevitable that there will be differences in their learning. They suggest that the aim of differentiation is to maximize the potential of each pupil by intervening in the most suitable way.

What most of the frequently-used definitions seem to have in common is:

- a focus on learning
- a recognition of individual pupil differences
- an expectation that teachers will make conscious decisions to maximize learning.

However, any definition needs to be tempered with a good dose of realism. In most classrooms it will never be possible for teachers to plan to meet the learning needs of every individual pupil. A more realistic goal is to ensure that you are attempting to use some differentiation strategy (or strategies), that you review how successful it was in practice and that you try to improve the effectiveness of your attempts. The consequence of being over-ambitious is that failure is guaranteed!

How do we do it?

There are many useful summaries of the range of strategies that teachers can use in promoting differentiated learning in addition to differentiation by task and differentiation by outcome. Some useful references for differentiation strategies are James and Brown (1998), Lewis (1992), Naylor and Keogh (1997), NIAS (1995), Qualter (1996) and Stradling and Saunders (1993). The kinds of strategies suggested include the following:

Use a range of learning styles

Sometimes it may be possible for different pupils to cover the same content in different ways, such as using a structured workcard, designing a practical investigation, using a computer simulation or using a textbook for research. Each learning style may be more suited to some pupils than to others. Using a range of learning styles will ensure that no pupils are continually disadvantaged by the continuous use of teaching approaches that do not suit them. Although teachers may not be able to plan to meet individual preferences, offering a broad range of learning styles will be helpful to all the pupils. Fisher (1990) and Sheffield City Polytechnic (1992) offer useful examples of active learning approaches that can help to extend the range of learning styles used.

Take the pupils' ideas into account

This does not mean planning a different investigation or activity for every pupil! Teachers do need to follow a scheme of work and to plan their lessons in advance of finding out the pupils' ideas. However, it is often possible to provide an opportunity for pupils to contribute their ideas in advance so that the purpose of an enquiry or investigation is to test out their ideas. In this way, the pupils will all be working in the same general area and may well be carrying out similar investigations but with different purposes in mind.

Adjust the level of scientific skills required

The level of demand can be influenced by the scientific skills involved in an activity as well as by the scientific concepts involved. Even if the pupils are working on exactly the same content, the nature of any enquiry that they carry out can vary. Investigations and enquiries can be made more demanding by involving more factors, building on more extensive background knowledge, using more sophisticated techniques, requiring more careful observation or handling more data. By enabling pupils to design their own enquiries the teacher can provide opportunities for differentiated learning.

Adjust the level of linguistic skills required

Adjusting the level of linguistic demand in an activity can provide an effective means of differentiation. This can apply to the oral and written language used. The complexity of the text structure, the use of scientific vocabulary, the level of support offered, the use of pictorial representation and the use of everyday illustrations will make a difference to how accessible the activity is. Sometimes the scientific activity may be identical but the written recording may vary.

Adjust the level of mathematical skills required

Adjusting the level of mathematical demand in an activity can also provide an effective means of differentiation. The degree of precision in measurement, the level of quantification in observation or analysis of observations, the use of units or symbols and the scale of any numbers involved can make a difference to how accessible or challenging pupils will find the activity.

Vary the amount and nature of teacher intervention

Pupils vary in the amount and type of support, guidance, challenge and monitoring that they need to be successful. Sensitive teachers will take this into account. They will try to offer early support to the pupils who are slow starters, provide extra guidance to those who lack confidence, offer additional challenges to those who will rise to them and carefully monitor those who are easily distracted. Teacher intervention is more likely to be productive when the teacher knows the pupils well.

Use suitable questions

Questioning is probably the most useful form of teacher intervention. Questions can help to identify pupils' existing ideas, map out possibilities for scientific enquiry, identify individual learning needs and offer additional challenges. Many teachers differentiate by targeting particular questions to individual pupils, attempting to match the level of difficulty of the question with the pupil's likely ability to answer successfully. Preparing a range of possible questions in advance can help teachers be more confident in their questioning and to intervene more effectively. Feasey (1998) provides useful guidance on questioning styles and on how pupils can be encouraged to ask their own questions.

Vary the distribution of teacher time

The teacher's time is the most important learning resource available to the pupils. Targeting individuals or groups for extra attention at certain times can have a marked effect on their ability to carry out a particular activity. Other adults such as parents and classroom assistants can be involved in providing additional attention. Although resource distribution is usually carefully planned, teachers may not always plan the distribution of their time. Differentiation can be more effective where there is some degree of planning about how time is likely to be distributed.

Vary the degree of independence expected

In general, the greater the responsibility the pupils are expected to take, the more demanding the activity will be. Some degree of differentiation can be achieved through offering greater independence in learning, with responsibility for more significant decisions. Scientific enquiry provides many opportunities for pupils to act independently as learners, such as defining the problem, using a range of information sources and evaluating the procedure. Further suggestions for providing opportunities for independence in learning can be found in Jarman *et al.* (1994).

Vary the response expected

Some pupils can be expected to produce more detailed, more complex or more thoughtful responses than others. When teachers know pupils reasonably well, they are able to differentiate in their expectations of how pupils might respond to a challenge. This can include the answer to a question, a plan for an enquiry, the length and quality of a written report, the detail in a set of observations, and so on. It is important to ensure that every pupil's contribution is valued, and many teachers are highly skilled at managing discussion to facilitate this.

Vary the pace or sequence of learning

Pupils can undertake the same set of activities but complete them at different speeds. Some may be given a more demanding schedule than others; some may need additional support to complete the activities. Alternatively, they may follow a different sequence of activities through a topic. NIAS (1995) provides some excellent examples of differentiated pathways through a scheme of work.

Vary the method of presentation

Sometimes, the same activities may be presented in different ways to the pupils – for example, as a problem to solve, as a question, or as a procedure to follow. It may be possible to offer a choice of how the pupils engage in an activity so that their preferences can be taken into account. Using a range of approaches to presentation is part of using a broad range of learning styles.

Vary the method of recording

Different pupils may record, analyse and present data in different ways. The amount of detail, the degree of accuracy, the level of quantification and the complexity of the concepts involved will influence the level of demand. Pupils may carry out the same activity but then record, analyse and present their data differently as a means of differentiation.

Provide suitable resources

A range of resources can provide additional support or challenge for some pupils. Sometimes they may be offered a choice of whether or not they want additional support or challenge. Suitable resources can include reference texts, workcards, charts and pictures, audio tapes, and so on. Increasingly, computer-based resources will be available to provide additional support or challenge and alternative ways of presenting material. A systematic long-term approach to generating, obtaining, trading and sharing suitable resources will help to support differentiation.

Use activities that allow pupils to interact at their own level

Suitable activities include collaborative concept mapping, discussion of true/false statements, sorting and classifying, predict-observe-explain sequences and concept cartoons (Figure 25.1). For example, the level of demand in a single concept cartoon can vary as pupils bring different ideas and levels of understanding to bear on the situation. This is because pupils usually interpret a concept cartoon in ways that they find meaningful and relevant. Those with a basic level of understanding may interpret it on one level while those with greater understanding may consider more factors and underlying explanations. In Figure 25.1, there is a basic question of whether shadows add together to make a darker area. Additional factors that may be considered include how big the spaces are between the leaves, how much the leaves overlap in each tree, whether there are any other light sources and whether a single leaf blocks all or part of the light. Concept cartoons actively involve pupils and enable them to contribute their ideas, ensuring that there is a close connection between their ideas and any follow-up enquiry. Further examples of concept cartoons can be found in Keogh and Naylor (1997) and Naylor and Keogh (2000).

Many teachers find it very helpful to have lists of strategies such as these. Not only do they increase the range of approaches that they feel able to use, they can also help with planning, increase teachers' confidence and provide evidence to inspectors that individual learning needs are being recognized. It is unlikely that you would choose

Figure 25.1 A concept cartoon

to use all of them at the same time! It is necessary to use your professional judgement at the planning stage to consider which approach(es) is most likely to have a positive impact for differentiated learning.

What else can we do to help?

There are factors that influence whether or not differentiation is likely to be successful in addition to the strategies outlined above. These more general factors are concerned with the nature of the learning environment and the classroom climate which teachers and pupils create between them. They do not require any additional resources or unusual facilities, but they may require changes in the way that classrooms are organized. These additional factors include the following:

Actively involve pupils in their own learning

We believe that differentiation is most effective when it is viewed as a shared responsibility, with the teacher responsible for planning and organizing activities and the pupils responsible for taking an active role in maximizing their own learning. This kind of active involvement is achieved through using active learning methods, sharing learning intentions with the pupils, enabling them to make significant decisions about their learning and encouraging them to reflect on their learning. The intention is to help pupils to view differentiation as a process in which they play a useful part, rather than as something done to them by teachers.

Actively involve pupils in their own assessment

Formative assessment helps to make learning more successful. One of the important features of formative assessment is the involvement of pupils in self- or peer-assessment. Black (1998) notes that research evidence shows that this can be successful with very young children as well as with older pupils. Self-assessment helps pupils to understand the main purposes of their learning and to understand what they need to do to be successful in it.

Create a climate of enquiry in the classroom

Questions are the starting point for learning, especially, but not only, in science. A questioning climate in the classroom will enable pupils to understand the value of questions, to experience the relationship between questions and enquiry, and to make use of opportunities to ask their own questions. A questioning climate also helps them to see the curriculum as something which is negotiated and developed in response to their interests and learning needs, rather than always being fixed in advance by the teacher.

Create a flexible learning environment

Any lesson requires numerous decisions to be taken. There are decisions about grouping, timing, sequencing activities, resourcing, learning style, and so on. Normally these are decisions made by teachers, but there is nothing to prevent pupils being involved in making those decisions. A flexible learning environment is one in which some of those decisions are shared or negotiated with the pupils, providing opportunities for them to select the most suitable approach and to become more involved in their learning.

Create a supportive classroom climate

A supportive classroom climate will enable pupils to feel that they are valued as individuals and that differentiation is a person-centred rather than a curriculum-centred process. Classroom climate influences relationships, communication, interaction, involvement and motivation. Pupils who are willing partners in learning are more effective learners. Motivated pupils will be more willing to share the responsibility for their learning with the teacher, ensuring that the level of demand in an activity is reasonably well matched to their capabilities.

Establish routines that encourage the pupils to work as independent learners

Classroom management is also important in creating circumstances in which differentiation can be most effective. Establishing classroom routines that encourage pupils to act as independent learners enables the teacher to spend more time on monitoring, supporting, challenging and extending their learning rather than simply organizing them. This does not mean that pupils will be working individually, nor does it mean that they can do exactly what they want! It does mean that they are encouraged to take responsibility for some decisions about their learning and that they have access to resources and information wherever possible.

Work towards a whole-school approach

The kinds of roles, relationships and classroom climate described above rely on individual teachers and their pupils. However, the impact of individual teachers is greatest where there is continuity in the approach used from one class to the next, so that pupils build up a consistent set of expectations about their roles and responsibilities as learners. Decisions about whether to adopt a whole-school approach cannot be made by one individual teacher, but individual teachers do influence these decisions.

Being realistic

Being realistic involves recognizing that a teacher's influence on pupils' learning is limited. However, as much as we like to think that we are completely in charge in the classroom, this is rarely the case. Teachers are responsible for creating the circumstances in which differentiated learning might occur; pupils share the responsibility for differentiated learning with teachers.

The circumstances in which teachers work also make differentiation hard to achieve. Changes to the National Curriculum, large class sizes, Ofsted inspections, league tables and the reduction in LEA support are just some of the pressures that make the teacher's job very demanding. Differentiation is just one demand amongst many. It is also a complex task, as is evident from the lack of confidence that many teachers feel about their ability to provide for differentiated learning. But even though differentiation is an ideal which may not be fully attainable it is still necessary to work towards it in whatever way we can.

References

Black, P. (1998) 'Formative assessment: raising standards inside the classroom', *School Science Review* 80(291): 39–46.

Dickinson, C. and Wright, J. (1993) *Differentiation: a Practical Handbook of Classroom Strategies,* Coventry: National Council for Educational Technology.

Feasey, R. (1998) 'Effective questioning in science', in R. Sherrington (ed.) *ASE Guide to Primary Science Education,* Hatfield: ASE.

Fisher, R. (1990) *Teaching Children to Think,* Hemel Hempstead: Simon and Schuster.

James, F. and Brown, K. (1998) *Effective Differentiation,* London: Harper Collins.

Jarman, R., Keogh, B. and Naylor, S. (1994) *I've Done this Before: Continuity and Progression in School Science*. Hatfield: ASE.

Keogh, B. and Naylor, S. (1997) *Starting Points for Science,* Sandbach: Millgate House.

Lewis, A. (1992) 'From planning to practice', *British Journal of Special Education* 19: 24–7.

Naylor, S. and Keogh, B. (1997) 'Differentiation in teaching science', in A. Cross and G. Peet (eds) *Teaching Science in the Primary School. Book 1: A Practical Source Book of Teaching Strategies,* Plymouth: Northcote House.

Naylor, S. and Keogh, B. (2000) *Concept Cartoons in Science Education,* Sandbach: Millgate House.

NIAS (1995) *The Differentiation Book*, Northamptonshire: Northamptonshire Inspection and Advisory Service.

Qualter, A. (1996) *Differentiated Primary Science,* Buckinghamshire: Open University.

Russell, T., Qualter, A., McGuigan, L. and Hughes, A. (1994) *Evaluation of the Implementation of Science in the National Curriculum at Key Stages 1, 2 and 3. Volume 3: Differentiation,* London: Schools Curriculum and Assessment Authority.

Sheffield City Polytechnic (1992) *Active Teaching and Learning Approaches in Science,* London: Collins.

Simpson, M. (1997) 'Developing differentiation practices: meeting the needs of pupils and teachers', *The Curriculum Journal* 1(8): 85–104.

Stradling, R. and Saunders, L. (1993) 'Differentiation in practice: responding to the needs of all pupils', *Educational Research* 35: 127–37.

Woolnough, B. (1994) *Effective Science Teaching,* Buckingham: Open University.

26 Formative assessment in secondary Science

Nick Daws and Birendra Singh

Introduction

Formative assessment practice lies at the heart of effective teaching and learning. Formative assessment fuels pupils' motivation and confidence by enhancing the control and power that they have over their learning. It supports learning strategies that encourage the active participation of pupils. In our view, informed by social constructivist theory, the key elements are as follows:

1 Pupils should be provided with learning objectives, or 'criteria', expressed in language that they readily understand, which describe the intended learning outcomes of each module of course work.

2 To facilitate active involvement of pupils in assessing their achievements, mark schemes for classwork, homework, end of topic tests, etc. need to be disclosed to pupils and discussed with them. Pupils should be supported in marking and correcting their classwork, homework and test papers. It is desirable to involve pupils in varied forms of assessment that mesh with a wide range of learning styles; thus they may evaluate evidence provided by role play, pupil diaries, posters, audio and video-taped material, etc.

3 Pupils should review their progress continuously by identifying evidence of their achievement. Pro formas may be provided to support pupils in self-assessment of their work. A system for collating pro formas may support students' maintenance of a portfolio of their best work.

4 Teachers should discuss with pupils the evidence that they present of their understanding and skills. The discussion should identify pupils' strengths and weaknesses. Targets should be agreed with pupils to help guide their future work.

5 Pupils should participate in recording their achievements. Pupils' self-assessment pro formas may be incorporated into their records of achievement and evidence from them may be included in pupil reports.

Formative assessment therefore aims to further learning by encouraging pupils to:

- reflect on their learning in a structured and systematic fashion;
- engage in discourse with their teachers regarding their progress and what they need to do to improve;
- develop greater awareness of, and competence in, the processes of learning.

It is useful to contrast formative and summative approaches to assessment. The former acquire assessment data for the purpose of feeding back criterion-referenced information to pupils to provide a basis for diagnostic discussion relating to learning strengths and weaknesses and how these might set future learning priorities. Summative approaches on the other hand describe and compare pupils in a norm-referenced way – e.g. to rank order their performance on a set of end-of-topic tests, for selection, setting or reporting purposes. 'Diagnostic discourse versus dead data' is a phrase that vividly expresses the opinion of Professor Patricia Broadfoot, a leading researcher in the field of assessment, regarding the relative power of formative and summative approaches to advance learning (Broadfoot 1986).

Research studies (Daws and Singh 1996; Fairbrother *et al.* 1995; Ferriman *et al.* 1994) indicate that some science departments in secondary schools are attempting to implement some elements, but formative assessment is not generally practised. However, there is evidence that many science teachers believe formative assessment to be desirable. We speculate that teachers:

- find it hard to develop formative strategies in the face of pressures to prepare pupils for success in summative examinations;
- are unsure of formative methods;
- would welcome support and encouragement in their attempts to develop formative assessment approaches.

Exploring real examples

Three pilot studies were conducted during the summer term of 1996 in secondary science departments in Essex comprehensive schools. Each department implemented a different formative assessment strategy involving:

- Year 10 (14–15-year-old) pupils marking their own work at Gable Hall School;
- Year 8 (12–13-year-old) pupils using self-assessment sheets at The Bromfords School;
- Years 7, 8 and 9 (11–14-year-old) pupils recording their homework and end-of-topic test marks at The Deanes School.

Case Study 1   Pupils marking their own Year 10 mock exam papers

David Gwynn, Head of Science at Gable Hall School, taught a lesson in which he supported Year 10 pupils (15-year-olds) in marking their end-of-year mock exam papers. A video was made of the lesson and watched with David and two of the pupils, Matthew and John.

David started the lesson by returning to pupils the exam papers that they had tackled in a previous lesson. The class, set 4 of 9, comprised twenty-eight pupils. David invited them to re-read the first exam question to themselves and highlight what they considered to be 'key' words and phrases – ones that reminded them of important topics and concepts they had met in their coursework. Making explicit reference to the exam mark scheme, he guided pupils through the answers to each section of the first question in an interactive way. Individual pupils interjected and questioned the reasoning behind obtaining the 'official' answers. David invited pupils to explain their alternative approaches to tackling the questions. Other pupils raised their hands to further question or agree with the direction in which the discussion was moving.

David reported that he involved pupils in this way in order to develop their understanding of the ways in which examiners pose questions and expect them to be answered. He believed that by doing so, the pupils' sense of control over the assessment process would be enhanced and hence their confidence in tackling exams.

David explained that he believed that encouraging pupils to articulate and share their views was central to increasing their sense of ownership of the assessment process and boosted their confidence in preparing for exams, which are for many pupils a daunting and stressful prospect.

David emphasized that a parallel aim was to raise pupils' awareness of, and facility with, the problem-solving and reasoning processes lying behind successful responses to exam questions. Discussions with the pupils indicated that David's strategies were successful in achieving these aims.

We noted that David stuck religiously to the exam board mark scheme when revealing, at the end of the work on each question, how many marks pupils could award themselves. He asked individual pupils about how they had performed and provided encouraging remarks to increase their sense of achievement. John commented: '[Mr. Gwynn] makes you feel good about yourself; the way he keeps saying "you can all get As".'

Both Matthew and John, the two pupils interviewed, said that they felt confident when explaining their reasoning or interpretation of the questions to the rest of the class, as they knew that they would neither be condemned nor ridiculed. Rather, a frank, supportive and diagnostic discussion would occur, because all pupils realized that this was in everyone's interest.

Pupils in the video are seen annotating their scripts to correct and augment their original answers. We wondered whether pupils were tempted to award themselves marks that they hadn't obtained legitimately. When discussing the issue, Matthew and John were clear as to why honesty was the best policy. David was confident that all the pupils in the class soon came to recognize the importance of obtaining a realistic portrayal of their achievement on this type of assessment. He believed they understood that the purpose of the exercise was to improve their understanding of topics and problem-solving strategies, and of working within marking conventions, to maximize their *future* exam performance. In reviewing a sample of scripts from the lesson, we could not find one example of wilful misrepresentation of performance.

Case Study 2　Year 8 pupils' self-assessment sheet

Brian Pratt, Head of Science at The Bromfords School, has trialled a self-assessment sheet, devised by his department, with a class of thirty Year 8 pupils. Pupils stuck the A5-sized sheet onto a left-hand page in their exercise books at the beginning of a module. On the sheet was a list of learning objectives (Figure 26.1). As pupils

---

Year 8 Revision Module

The following is a list of the major points covered in each lesson of the revision module.

1   Do you know how objects can be charged and the types of charge?
2   Can you draw out series and parallel circuits each with switches that control lamps?
3   Do you know how to construct an electromagnet? What can you do to increase the strength of such a magnet?
4   How do you explain the differences between solids, liquids and gases? What actually happens when solids dissolve?
5   What methods do we have for separating mixtures and how do they work?
6   How can you determine the conditions necessary for microbes to grow?
7   Can you use a key to identify an unknown plant or animal?
8   Do you know the stages in the reproduction of a mammal?
9   Can you identify the parts of a flower and explain what each part does?

The following key words can be searched on the Internet or the CD-ROMs:

- Static electricity
- Electrical circuits
- Electromagnets
- States of matter
- Distillation
- Filtration
- Bacteria
- Classification
- Life cycles
- Pollination

Figure 26.1 The Bromfords School self-assessment sheet

worked through the module they indicated on the facing right-hand page where they had evidence of achieving the learning objectives.

Brian invited a group of ten pupils from the class to discuss with him how useful, or otherwise, they found the sheets in helping them progress through science modules.

At the first meeting, pupils reported that it hadn't taken them very long to find where they had addressed the learning objectives implicit in the sheet's questions in previous work. They could fill in the sheet as they had done their science homework.

They had found the exercise worthwhile as it had alerted them to points that they did not understand very well. Some pupils expressed the view that, when discussing the partly completed sheet with their teacher, they were able to focus on areas they had already identified as ones in which they needed particular support. They felt that this increased the usefulness of their conversation.

The second meeting a week later was as well attended as the first. The pupils had not added a lot to their sheets, but some pupils said that they had begun using their sheets to help them decide what to revise for their end-of-topic test. They felt that the sheets would be particularly useful for pupils who had been absent. The sheet would show them what topics they had missed and where they needed to catch up.

The way three pupils, Daniel, Chris and Wendy, were using their self-assessment sheets represented distinctly different approaches.

Daniel

In the first meeting, Daniel seemed to notice that many of the other pupils' responses to the questions were much more detailed than his. In the second meeting, he had expanded his responses, but they still didn't match the level of detail of some others. Daniel seemed to want to get the job done with the minimum of effort, as though just 'filling in' the worksheet was the object of the exercise.

Chris

Chris's responses to the questions suggested that he was confident that he had a good understanding of the issues. He had located where the issues were addressed in his textbook, but it was not clear how he decided that his knowledge and understanding of them was sound. He had written some comments on his sheet indicating the level of his misunderstanding of some topics. In his answer to Question 1, he wrote, 'I know how objects are charged but not sure about type'.

Thus he admitted to possible gaps or bare patches in his knowledge, but seemed to feel that locating where the issue is addressed in his textbook was sufficient, for the time being at any rate, rather than exploring ways of attempting to advance his understanding. There is evidence that Chris had interpreted questions in idiosyncratic ways. For example, in response to Question 8, 'Do you know the stages in the reproduction of a mammal?', he wrote, 'Yes I know and the mammal I'm talking about is a human (Diagrams of womb)'.

This answer suggested that Chris might not be aware of the more general features of mammalian reproduction – a point that his teacher could pick up with him.

Wendy

In the first meeting, Wendy expressed the view that she was glad that she could pursue the self-assessment in a way that didn't require checking by her class teacher. She valued the more independent approach it offered to help her advance her learning. The direction and structure offered by the questions was reassuring, in that it provided a framework to guide her efforts in reviewing past work and identifying evidence of having covered it. She was also stimulated to research answers to some questions in greater depth.

In the second meeting, Wendy reported that during a lesson, when the opportunity arose, she and a friend took the initiative to ask their science teacher if they could dissect a buttercup to double-check that the parts shown in the book could be identified in an actual flower. Thus the sheet had prompted Wendy to explore an area of science in a proactive way and in some depth. It had given her the confidence to take control of her learning, and to co-opt the support of her friend, teacher, and the resources of the science class, in order to advance her science learning. A change in her attitude towards science could be detected. She stated that she hadn't really been positive about science, but felt that it was important to work at the subject to get good test marks. She implied that, typically in science, proceeding through a topic at the pace determined by the teacher for the whole class could drain motivation. She also indicated that she had limited opportunities and, for various reasons, she lacked a willingness to engage the teacher on particular aspects and pursue them further. The self-assessment sheet stimulated her to go in more depth into issues that she found particularly interesting. Responding to the sheet in this way offered the possibility of adopting a more satisfying and personally-directed approach.

Case Study 3   Year 7, 8 and 9 pupils recording their marks for homework and end-of-topic tests

We looked at a sample of pupils' record sheets and discussed how the sheets were used with three science teachers and a group of pupils from Years 7, 8 and 9 (11–14-year-olds). This sample indicated that the end-of-topic test record sheets (Figure 26.2) were more complete (90 per cent) than the homework record sheets (30 per cent). One teacher stated that, 'The end-of-topic test record sheet is used more regularly. The pupils are more interested in their results here, especially the level they have achieved.

The pupils agreed that this was a more important sheet for them than their homework record sheet. They said that they enjoyed looking up the levels they had attained in each test on the wall chart. Pupils expressed satisfaction at being able to monitor their progress over the year with respect to levels of achievement. One pupil had lost his record sheets but had drawn into his book the outline of an end-of-topic test record sheet, and filled it in. He had not copied his homework record sheet and was unconcerned that he did not have a similar homework record.

The teachers tended to leave completion of the end-of-topic test record sheets to the pupils and they found that the pupils differed in the extent to which they filled out their sheets.

However, the end-of-topic test marks, which may be used in setting pupils, and the 'official' National Curriculum levels, were considered important by pupils. Additionally, the active task of checking the mark obtained on a test against the wall chart of corresponding levels, was one that pupils enjoyed. Thus approaches that are active and involve important summative assessments motivate pupils to take the recording activity seriously.

The teachers interviewed agreed that pupils needed encouragement to use the homework record sheets profitably: 'Only a few pupils use the sheets themselves. I have to encourage most of them. [Then they] do enjoy filling their sheets.'

SCIENCE DEPARTMENT

YEAR 7 : PUPIL RECORD CARD

Name _Lisa_   Tutor Group _7GN_

*The following table lists your test results and the **approximate National Curriculum**
level that has been achieved for each test.
Different tests may cover different levels and no test is above level 6.*

TEST RESULTS AND LEVELS

TOPIC	TEST DATE	%	LEVEL
MEASURING	5th october	30	4
LIFE	12th Dec	34	4
WATER	18th Jan	63	5
ELECTRICITY	29th feb	43	3
MATERIALS	2nd may	58	4
ENVIRONMENT			

*Your homeworks will be marked out of 10. If you obtain a mark of 7 out of ten you
have achieved the set task.
You will not be given marks for classwork but comments will be made about your
work.*

Figure 26.2 An end-of-topic test record sheet completed by a pupil

This teacher felt that the homework sheets could catalyse a diagnostic discussion
with pupils about how they were progressing and what they could do to improve
further. Her colleague echoed the view that teacher encouragement was important.
'Pupils are not likely to use the sheets to come to teachers to discuss their
homeworks. But teachers can take the initiative and use the sheets to discuss individuals' progress with them.'

Some pupils stated that they felt that the extent to which they filled in their homework record sheets depended on how often their teacher reminded them to do so.
The pupils were in agreement that they tended not to discuss their homework marks
with their teachers. However, several mentioned using the sheets to compare their
performance with those of their friends. Pupils who obtained relatively high marks
for their homework tended to have a more complete record of homework performance. Two pupils mentioned that they reviewed the pattern of their homework
record to identify where to focus their revision for end-of-topic tests.

Discussion

Are formative assessment approaches practicable?

David Gwynn's lesson (Case Study 1) illustrates aspects underpinning the successful integration of formative assessment into teaching and learning. Both the teacher and the pupils understood the rationale of the approach, and both parties had developed the skills necessary to conduct a collaborative and problem-solving discourse. Their shared understanding and ways of working had developed over time and through regular practice at marking end-of-topic tests and homework.

The strategy of critical reflection on explicit learning objectives, and participative approaches that allow pupils to engage in collaborative and diagnostic discourse in a variety of ways, have gradually become embedded into the teaching and learning culture of the class. Formative assessment is given a prominent formal place in the curriculum in terms of time and activities specified in the department's scheme of work. This reflects the departmental view that such strategies promote quality learning.

The approach trialled in the other two schools also showed promise in terms of benefits to pupils' learning. Implications for capitalizing on the potential for involving pupils more in the direction and management of their own learning through formative assessment approaches suggest themselves. These include further exploration of:

- giving time to negotiating with pupils;
- target-setting;
- encouraging independent approaches to progress learning.

These may require modifications to teaching and curriculum practices that need to be considered carefully. A start has been made and small steps can be taken in directions that attempt to enlarge and integrate these approaches into teaching – rather than stress existing arrangements through attempting to bring about whole-sale curriculum changes.

What are the benefits of formative assessment?

Science learning

Pupils in all three case studies provided evidence that, by engaging in formative assessment practices, they exercise *'deep learning'* strategies (Gipps 1994), which promote long-term secure conceptual understanding. Pupils involved in class marking, reconstructing the exam questions in the light of course work, probing and questioning the reasoning behind answers and articulating their alternative approaches, were grappling with concepts and procedures in deeper ways than required for a superficial memorization of facts.

Similarly, some of the pupils at The Bromfords School were reflecting on their science understanding, identifying gaps and formulating their own approaches to addressing them. Some high-achieving pupils at The Deanes School were enhancing their revision strategy with reference to their record sheets.

All these ways of engaging with formative assessment suggest that pupils are learning in ways that exercise and extend their existing knowledge and skills, and that long-term understanding is being promoted.

Generic skills

Developing confidence and skills in learning is likely to be important in producing life-long learners. The process skills of articulating views, listening to others, and contributing in ways that build on others' points, were evident in the self-marking activity. Similarly, learning in self-directed ways, swapping attention to class discussion and then back to neighbours' conversation, annotating scripts, highlighting key words, identifying evidence of achievement and illustrative material of concepts, are skills that require practice. They also require a learning climate that gives pupils opportunity to rehearse them if they are to progress. Devolving some responsibility, again in supported and incremental ways, is required. So, too, is a learning environment that is non-judgmental, values all pupils' contributions to a debate and looks to all to share insights and views in order to develop collectively both group and class understandings.

Motivation

Watts and Bentley (1987) have commented on the efficacy of such *'non-threatening learning environments'*, but they have recognized the difficulties of realizing them in practice. Formative assessment practices, we contend, provide practical ways of helping to sustain them; they are conducive to reducing stress and anxiety and develop positive teamwork skills. Encouraging pupils to appraise exam questions and mark schemes critically, and to reflect on their own science achievements through self- assessment and recording approaches, develops their awareness of processes of assessment and learning. The pupils we interviewed certainly seemed to gain confidence and a feeling of empowerment through developing a greater sense of ownership over their learning. Their attitudes towards science as a subject seemed to be more positive as a result.

Differentiation

All the formative assessment approaches discussed allow individuals to use them in ways that they feel are most appropriate. The self-assessment and recording sheets can provide windows on pupils' learning. They can reveal to teachers ways of intervening that channel support and help, through diagnostic discourse and target setting, individualized to pupils' learning needs and focused on clearly specified learning objectives.

How are formative assessment approaches successfully implemented?

The point and purpose of the self-marking exercise and the ways in which teacher and pupils interacted were well understood. A clear rationale for the formative assessment approach is required if pupils and teachers are to use it effectively. They need time and opportunities to practise the requisite skills to carry out successful formative assessment. This requires a supportive and collaborative context for both pupils and teachers.

Effective formative approaches develop step by step and require time and perseverance. Teachers working collaboratively with pupils are best placed to achieve them.

Final remarks

Certain teaching and learning strategies, such as fostering collaborative, democratic discussion that critically appraises the processes of learning and assessment, helping pupils to monitor their learning against clearly specified learning objectives, supporting pupils in taking some responsibility for managing their learning, and so on, are symbiotic with the practice of formative assessment; they feed off each other.

Implementation of formative assessment practices is likely to cause questioning of, and pressure for modifying, existing curriculum arrangements. If formative assessment is to be integrated into teaching and learning, then frank appraisal and preparedness to review and change are required. The prize is more satisfying teaching that fosters deeper learning, enhances pupils' confidence and their motivation for learning, and in so doing develops life-long learning skills.

References

Broadfoot, P. (1986) *Profiles and Records of Achievements*, Eastbourne: Holt, Rinehart and Winston, 1986.

Daws, N. P. and Singh, B. (1996) 'Formative assessment; to what extent is its potential to enhance pupils' science being realised?', *School Science Review* 77(281): 93–100.

Fairbrother, R. W., Black, P. and Gill, P. (1995) *Teachers Assessing Pupils*, London: Kings College, London/ASE.

Ferriman, B., Lock, R. and Soares, A. (1994) 'Influences of the National Curriculum assessment in Key Stage 3', *School Science Review*, 75(274): 116–20.

Gipps, C. (1994) *Beyond Testing,* London: Falmer Press.

Watts, M. and Bentley, D. (1987) 'Constructivism in the classroom: enabling conceptual change by words and deeds', *British Educational Research Journal,* 13(2): 121-35.

27 Progression and continuity
Hilary Asoko and Ann Squires

Introduction

The words progression and continuity are frequently used, often in the same breath and sometimes as if they were interchangeable. It is important, therefore, to clarify the meaning of these terms and to recognize that they are distinct, although interrelated.

Progression relates to the pupil's learning. It describes the personal journey an individual pupil makes in moving through the educational system.

Continuity, on the other hand, is a characteristic of the curriculum and its implementation by the teacher. It operates in the broadest sense and also at the level of the finest detail. It refers to design, both in long-term planning and in lesson planning and it refers to a teacher's informed and sensitive interactions with pupils as a lesson proceeds.

The term 'progression' is sometimes used to describe the ways in which a curriculum is structured and sequenced. Thus people talk about building progression into schemes of work or classroom practice. In essence, this relates to challenge rather than to learning. It means first giving pupils things they can easily achieve, to build confidence, and then increasing the demand of the task or reducing the support provided. This interpretation of 'progression' is an aspect of continuity. Here 'progression' is used exclusively in relation to pupils' learning.

The link between progression and continuity is strong, but not so strong that our best attempts at continuity can *guarantee* progression. Teachers often feel disappointed in themselves and in their pupils. However, planning and teaching with a commitment to continuity, both in structure and in detail, is the most effective way to support a pupil's progression and it provides the best chance of achieving successful and satisfying outcomes.

Imagine the start of the school year, with a new class. To the pupils this is another stage on their journey through education. The teacher may be different in many ways, both personal and professional, from the teacher they had last year. The work may make new demands. The pupils will have to adapt and some may find it difficult. The teacher is faced with the task of getting to know the pupils and translating long-term plans into work appropriate for them. Records may provide information about what they 'did' last year and some indication of the strengths and weaknesses of individuals. The teacher has past experience to draw on. When the pupils move on at the end of the year, they should have 'made progress' as a result of the teaching. This means there is a sense of direction to the work. To a large extent this direction is determined by National Curriculums and examination syllabuses, translated into whole school and departmental plans. However, plans are made in the ideal world. In reality, however good they are, they need to be adjusted and adapted to suit particular circumstances and requirements. Individual teachers, with their own ideas, values and opinions, adapt and implement plans in relation to individual pupils. If this is not done skilfully some pupils will feel disorientated and confused. They may become disillusioned with the subject. Learning will become a chore and teaching an uphill struggle. If it is done well, pupils will feel confident and interested and prepared to tackle new work. Continuity will be maintained and progression supported.

A pupil's progression in science

Progression in learning science describes the personal journey an individual pupil makes from first experiencing aspects of the physical world towards an understanding of it in scientific terms: an appreciation of the methods, ideas and significance of science. This journey may involve stops and starts, small steps and sudden leaps, wrong turnings and difficulties to overcome. For the pupil the journey is something of a mystery tour. It is the teacher, who knows where things are leading, who is able to plan an appropriate route and provide help of the right kind, at the right time.

Progression in learning science can take many forms. Within a given context it might involve shifts from being aware that something happens to being able to make it happen or from observation, description and comparison to explanation.

For example:

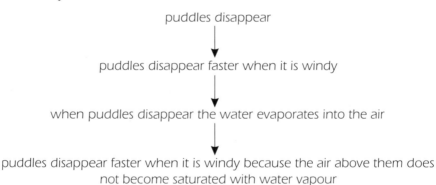

Pupils may progress from explanations couched in everyday language to the intelligent use of scientific language. They can come to expect explanations to be supported by evidence and to subject the evidence to rigorous scrutiny. Qualitative descriptions and comparisons may lead to quantitative measurements; explorations give way to investigations and experiments. Ideas used in single contexts become linked to other ideas or are used in wider contexts so that apparently different events are seen as explainable by a single set of ideas. Ideas about evaporation, for example, can be used to explain washing drying, hardening of nail varnish and parts of the water cycle as well as puddles disappearing.

Some steps on the journey are especially difficult. These are the ones which involve the learner in abandoning well-tried and trusted ideas. Whilst some of these ideas can be challenged by physical evidence, it is often the evidence, not the idea, which is disbelieved. Pupils who believe that heavy objects fall faster than lighter ones will not necessarily be convinced by a demonstration. They are likely to see what they expect – that the heaviest object lands first, or they will try hard to find fault with the test in order to hang on to the idea. Here the teacher must challenge the thinking and provide a new perspective from which to view the evidence.

The learner's progression is the cumulative effect of different kinds of learning event, large and small. Some will involve language learning or the development of practical know-how; some will involve extending ideas already held into new contexts or making connections between ideas; some will involve abandoning existing ideas and constructing new ways of accounting for familiar events and phenomena.

Just as a pupil's long-term progression is made up of particular learning steps, the teacher's long-term provision of curricular continuity is made up of particular elements of support for learning. The teacher's role is to recognize the many different kinds of learning step and identify and provide the necessary support.

Building background knowledge

Much of pupils' early development in science involves taking notice of and discussing an ever broader range of experiences. A pupil needs confidence to cope with new ideas and experiences. This confidence comes from having a background of familiar things to draw on and the language to talk about them. In a strange context where pupils lack knowledge and experience, they are not in a position to use capabilities which they could easily use elsewhere.

Teaching may therefore involve drawing attention to significant familiar experiences and stimulating discussion of them so that explanations have meaning. For example, learning about the rotation of the earth as an explanation for day and night is more meaningful to someone who is aware that the sun is not always in the same place in the sky and that darkness is an absence of light.

Some areas of science learning are long-term tasks which both require and develop a broad background knowledge. When studying materials, for example, pupils may be well aware of broad categories such as plastic, metal, fabric or wood. However, knowledge and recognition of specific metals or fabrics, or discussion of their properties or origins, demands background knowledge accumulated as a result of exposure to many experiences and pieces of information. The teacher's role is to seize opportunities to develop such knowledge whatever the topic in hand.

Modest steps in understanding

A pupil may recognize some examples of metals and know that metals conduct electricity and other materials do not. Here the teacher can open up new possibilities, perhaps that some metals may conduct better than others, or that the length of a wire may have an effect. An existing idea can thus be refined by small steps.

Major leaps in understanding

Major leaps in understanding often allow a shift from description of observed events to explanation in terms of abstract ideas and models. Beginning to think about materials in terms of their constituent particles is a leap in understanding. It is a new insight which, once available, can be tried out in a range of contexts. Pupils who have begun to think about particles in the context of sugar dissolving in water might be challenged to consider whether similar ideas might be used to think about puddles drying in the sun. Once such a major leap has been taken, the idea can be refined and developed by thinking about how particles move in relation to one another, or about the different particles in different materials. The teacher's role is to introduce the idea clearly, at the right time and in the right context. In the longer term opportunities must then be provided to use, reinforce and develop the idea. It is also important for the teacher to know when to stop and to ensure that pupils don't feel that they have lost contact with what they already know.

Constructing frameworks of understanding

Science ideas about the world form a coherent framework. Young pupils may not have developed the bigger ideas which apply across many contexts. As understanding develops and ideas become more sophisticated, they also become wider in their application and pupils come to recognize that the ideas used in one context may be equally well applied in another. Ideas about personal energy, for example, are the start of a progression towards a concept of energy which embraces physical, chemical and biological contexts. The teacher's role is in drawing attention to the wider application of ideas. Relating different contexts, either within science or between science and everyday life, may involve recognizing and resolving conflicting ideas.

Relating ideas to evidence

Just as pupils learn to distinguish between events and accounts of events, they need to distinguish between their experiences and the ideas they construct to describe and explain these. Progression in learning involves pupils becoming aware of the need to think explicitly about their experiences, to put ideas to the test and to recognize the value of evidence, both positive and negative.

Although pupils can find out what happens in a given situation, the teacher needs to appreciate that the ideas which explain what happens may need to be introduced explicitly. For example, pupils can discover that objects travel further on smooth surfaces than on rough ones. However, the ideas about frictional forces which explain this are not self-evident from the activity.

Awareness of learning

Satisfaction and confidence in learning depend upon an interest both in our own ideas and those of others. We sometimes only know what we think when we hear what we have to say about it. Ideas may only show themselves as inadequate when we start to spell them out to someone else. It is often a discussion of differing views which leads a pupil towards better understanding. Articulating and considering ideas is essential. It is the teacher's role to stimulate interest in the ideas of science as well as its practical experiences, so helping pupils to become aware both of what, and how, they learn.

Curricular continuity

A teacher may foster curricular continuity in different contexts:

- in terms of planning for and interacting with the pupils they teach
- in contributing to decision-making about planning and teaching within school
- in local and inter-school developments
- in formulating national policy.

All of these will eventually impact on individual pupils.

In curriculum planning we need to keep in focus the variety and complexity of the pupil's task. What will make learning easier and what are the barriers which make the task more difficult or even impossible?

The role of the teacher is vital, as guide and mediator between science and the learner. The teacher has made the journey already and guided others through it. The teacher has the professional knowledge and skills to plan experiences and to relate in appropriate ways to pupils as they work.

Planning and adapting

The logic of the subject may suggest a particular curricular sequence of concepts. Spirals may be built in to ensure revisiting and extending of ideas. In an ideal world we could plan activities which would result, reliably, in smooth progress and desired learning. But planning, particularly for the long term, tends to make assumptions that everyone will start from the same place, bring the same skills and experience, be subject to the same influences and, therefore, respond in the same way. Pupils, though, are individuals and the interactions and interventions of teaching must be responsive to them.

Nevertheless, planning can be informed by past experience and by research evidence. Plans can be adapted to take account of the ideas and experiences, both helpful and otherwise, which pupils are likely to bring to their science learning. National Curriculums provide guidance on what should be taught, but teachers need to decide how to structure teaching so that pupils' progression is supported. A knowledge of research into children's learning can be helpful here.

Expectations

Research shows the wide range of preconceptions which pupils can hold (e.g. Driver *et al*. 1994b). It is important to guard against low expectations which may arise from a misinterpretation of this research. Many of the studies have been concerned with thinking and behaviour *in the absence of instruction*. Effective teaching does make a difference. Research can say something about where to begin and the problems which may be encountered but it cannot say what the goals should be. Sometimes the teacher will meet constraints which are unlikely to respond to teaching at that time. It is essential to distinguish such cases from other constraints, such as lack of background knowledge, which can be addressed by appropriate provision.

A sense of direction and purpose

Science tries to understand the physical world through its 'big ideas'; its ways of investigating and seeking evidence and its commitment to developing ideas in relation to the evidence.

The big ideas of science are where a pupil's journey is leading; they provide a sense of direction even for the earliest work. A teacher who knows that a long-term aim for pupils is an understanding of motion in terms of outside forces acting on things will, even from an early stage, encourage pupils to notice the surfaces and surroundings of objects. This doesn't mean imposing explanations on the pupil who is not yet receptive, nor does it mean watering down the incomprehensible. It simply means knowing where things are leading and preparing the way.

However, the ideas and skills of science are not ends in themselves; science makes its contribution to society and the lives of individuals. A teacher who shows an enthusiasm for science and its role in society can help pupils to appreciate this.

Record-keeping, review and liaison

Successful review and liaison depend upon effective communication of information about pupils' progress, both between pupil and teacher and between teachers. Teachers have to find effective ways for pupils to make explicit their developing understandings and abilities so that their progression can be followed. This will involve discussions with individuals during learning as well as formal assessment procedures. It may include pupils' self-assessment, particularly as pupils develop an interest in their own learning.

Some of the most valuable communications are those informal discussions between colleagues, both within and between schools, about pupils or teaching. More formal written communications document pupils' progress or curriculum plans. Meetings at which curriculum planning and implementation are discussed provide opportunities for practicalities to be decided. They can also allow the sharing of views on issues such as science learning or the aims of science education and help to promote shared goals and a common approach.

What information is useful?

Preparing and referring to recorded information is very time-consuming. Providers and users of information should share views as to what is important. Communications need to be sharply focused, yet detailed enough to avoid misunderstandings.

Information communicated in an abbreviated form may have little use or be open to misinterpretation. References to having 'done air pressure' or to having 'reached level 4' give no indication of the experiences pupils have had or of the deep-seated ideas they may hold.

Joint initiatives

SCAA indicate that joint activities with a specific focus on curriculum and/or assessment can benefit pupils in the following ways (SCAA 1996: 13):

- developing a better sense of the continuous nature of learning from primary through secondary school;
- having their previous experiences and achievements recognized and valued;
- experiencing appropriately challenging work which builds on skills, knowledge and understanding acquired in previous key stages;
- having similarities and connections with prior learning made explicit.

Although this advice is given in relation to continuity between primary and secondary school, it applies equally to other transitions.

Transfer of records between schools

As pupils transfer from primary to secondary school, particular efforts are needed to maintain continuity of curriculum and to monitor pupils' progression. The ideal arrangement is when the staff of two schools view continuity as a shared enterprise. The statutory transfer of records will take place in the richness of direct collaboration. Even without the advantage of such a close relationship, primary and secondary schools find benefit in supplementing the statutory transfer of information and SCAA gives guidance on this and other aspects of transfer (SCAA 1996).

References

Driver, R., Squires, A., Rushworth, P. and Wood-Robinson, V. (1994b) *Making Sense of Secondary Science*, London: Routledge.

SCAA (1996) *Promoting Continuity between Key Stage 2 and Key Stage 3,* London: SCAA.

Further Reading

Driver, R., Leach, J., Scott, P. and Wood-Robinson, C. (1994a) 'Progression in students' understanding of science concepts: implications for curriculum planning', *Studies in Science Education* (24): 75–100.

Jarman, R., Keogh, B. and Naylor, S. (1995) 'I've done this before', *Continuity and Progression in School Science*, Hatfield: ASE.

Lee, B., Harris, S. and Dickson, P. (1995) *Continuity and Progression 5–16: Developments in Schools,* Slough: NFER.

Index